GRAYSLAKE AREA PUBLIC LIBRARY

3 6109 00351 0747   W9-BNL-884

88
Money-Making
Writing Jobs

Robert Bly

NO LONGER OWNED BY
GRAYSLAKE PUBLIC LIBRARY

SOURCEBOOKS, INC.®
NAPERVILLE, ILLINOIS

GRAYSLAKE AREA PUBLIC LIBRARY
100 Library Lane
Grayslake, IL 60030

Copyright © 2009 by Robert Bly
Cover and internal design © 2009 by Sourcebooks, Inc.
Cover photos © Veer, iStockPhoto.com/Emrah Turudu

Sourcebooks and the colophon are registered trademarks of Sourcebooks, Inc.

All rights reserved. No part of this book may be reproduced in any form or by any electronic or mechanical means including information storage and retrieval systems—except in the case of brief quotations embodied in critical articles or reviews—without permission in writing from its publisher, Sourcebooks, Inc.

This publication is designed to provide accurate and authoritative information in regard to the subject matter covered. It is sold with the understanding that the publisher is not engaged in rendering legal, accounting, or other professional service. If legal advice or other expert assistance is required, the services of a competent professional person should be sought.—From a Declaration of Principles Jointly Adopted by a Committee of the American Bar Association and a Committee of Publishers and Associations

All brand names and product names used in this book are trademarks, registered trademarks, or trade names of their respective holders. Sourcebooks, Inc., is not associated with any product or vendor in this book.

Published by Sourcebooks, Inc.
P.O. Box 4410, Naperville, Illinois 60567-4410
(630) 961-3900
Fax: (630) 961-2168
www.sourcebooks.com

Library of Congress Cataloging-in-Publication Data
Bly, Robert.
  88 money-making writing jobs / Robert Bly.
     p. cm.
  Includes bibliographical references and index.
  1. Authorship—Vocational guidance. I. Title.
PN153.B59 2009
808'.02023—dc22
                         2008037582

Printed and bound in the United States of America
BG 10 9 8 7 6 5 4 3 2

Dedication

For the Gelmans—David, Jacob, Jeff, and Lisa

A man who cannot phrase his thoughts cleanly on paper probably has no thoughts worth notice. The style is the man. If the prose is heavy-footed and sluggish, so too, in all likelihood, is the mind of its author.
—Robert Silverberg, *A Time of Changes*

Pen and paper. That's what I loved. You make little marks on paper, and if you make enough of them, you have a story, and isn't that pure magic? The small voice told me that's what I was put on Earth for, and that is what I should do. The other little voice said, "Yeah, but that won't buy bread."
—Frank McCourt, *Parade*, March 9, 2008

Some poor fools had to waste their lives writing in order for us to have sufficient reading material.
—John Irving, *A Prayer for Owen Meany*

I have never quite been able to imagine what might induce a person to become a professional writer. The public has no idea that writing is a disease, and that the writer who publishes is like a beggar who exhibits his sores.
—Michael Kruger, *The Executor*

Acknowledgments

I'd like to thank my agent, Bob Diforio, for finding a home for this book, and my editor, Peter Lynch, for making it much better than it was when the manuscript first crossed his desk—and his extraordinary patience in waiting for it to get there.

Special thanks to the folks at the American Writers & Artists Inc., American Medical Writers Association, Specialized Information Publishers Association, Business Marketing Association, and other associations and professional societies that helped me fill in the blanks about many of the writing opportunities they recommend.

Thanks also to Andrew Frothingham, Andy Helfer, Andy Neff, Linda Ketchum, Charles Flowers, David Kohn, Barry Sheinkopf, Craig Wolff, Dr. Andrew Linick, Gary Blake, Terry Whalin, Michael Masterson, John Forde, Clayton Makepeace, Steve Slaunwhite, Dianna Huff, Peter Bowerman, and many others too numerous to mention here who shared stories, tips, and expertise about their writing specialties with me over the years.

3 6109 00351 0747

808.02
BLY
1.10

Table of Contents

Introduction

"No man but a blockhead ever wrote, except for money," said Samuel Johnson.

But he was wrong. Thousands of bright, creative people have a burning desire to write. But most end up unpublished and unpaid for their work.

The reason is their narrow view of "writing," which to them generally means "books and magazine articles"—or for some, "novels and movies"—which closes them off to other markets in need of good writers. Most aspiring authors don't realize there are literally dozens of other venues, aside from books and magazines, where writers can get published—and get paid—for their work.

Many have found lucrative, little-known niches—far less competitive than Hollywood or the bestseller lists—and often just as profitable. For example:

- MM writes essays in a daily e-newsletter read by nearly half a million online subscribers. From this, he has built a publishing empire with annual revenues of $30 million. He has also written bestselling nonfiction books, short stories, poems, and a novel.

- BE, a successful freelance writer in the Midwest, makes an excellent living writing marketing materials to help dentists get more patients. TM, himself a dentist, became wealthy writing and publishing a business newsletter that told dentists how to build their practices.

- Since graduating college in 1979, AH has earned hundreds of thousands of dollars—first as a staff writer and now as a freelancer—writing superhero comic books.

- AN, who graduated from the same college as AH in the same year, makes a handsome six-figure income as a stock analyst for a major brokerage firm, where he spends most of his time writing research reports on the companies whose stock his firm's brokers sell.

- SW, a journalist and nonfiction book author, makes an additional $10,000–$20,000 a year writing book reviews in his spare time. He literally gets paid to read!

- GB, a former magazine writer and the author of ten books, also makes a six-figure income, teaching basic writing skills to corporate managers for $3,000 a day.

- PH, who a few years ago was stocking cans in the dog food aisle of a grocery store for $6.50 an hour, earns close to $400,000 a year writing sales letters for an investment club.

- JH writes simple letters to raise money for charities. Even though he only works a few hours a day, his income is more than $400,000 a year.

- LK, a freelance medical writer in Manhattan, specializes in writing about nuclear medicine for trade publications, health care ad agencies, and medical manufacturers.

- CM, perhaps the world's highest-paid freelance copywriter, makes more than a million dollars a year—primarily writing special reports on nutritional supplements and alternative medicine.

- PS has built a successful marketing business writing ads almost exclusively to sell hearing aids.

And the list goes on...and on...and on!

In this book, you'll discover dozens of outlets and markets for your writing that you either never knew existed, or just never thought much about before.

By exploring these special writing opportunities instead of writing for the file drawer, you can now write for publication, have others read your words, and get paid handsomely for your efforts—enabling you to make the transition from amateur to professional writer, or from a marginal writing income to a six-figure or even seven-figure income.

I've been a writer for three decades and a full-time freelance writer since February 1982. I am not the most successful writer in the world—far from it: I've never even come close to writing a bestseller, nor have I written for television or Hollywood.

Yet, I am not a slacker either. I've made millions of dollars from my writing, and my annual income from writing is well over $600,000. Freelance writing has allowed me to live the lifestyle I wanted to live, doing what I want to do, when I want to do it: no boss, no 9-to-5 office job, no more endless dull meetings and taking orders like I did when I was a corporate employee.

"The benefits of working for yourself are numerous, including the freedom to set your own schedule and choose your assignments," writes Leslie Kramer in *Positive Thinking*. This book can give you the same wonderful freedom, opportunity, and annual six-figure income that I've enjoyed all these years.

Most writers I know struggle financially for two reasons. First, the type of writing they do is low paying. Second, they only know how to do a single kind of writing, and are therefore dependent on one market for all their income.

In their song "I Am," the group Train sings: "I never had a day when money didn't get in my way." Poor pay stops many writers from pursuing their literary ambitions. With the smorgasbord of writing opportunities in this book, you can make enough money taking on commercial writing assignments to allow you to pursue your art at your leisure.

This book offers dozens of concise chapters, each presenting a different writing opportunity. For each writing task, you learn who the clients are, how to approach them, what they need written, tips for writing effectively in that genre or format, how to make sales, and what you can charge.

My recommendation is that you study the book and then pick at least two, and preferably three or four, writing opportunities to pursue. Having multiple streams of writing income can enable you to earn a freelance "salary" that even a doctor, dentist, or airline pilot might envy. And, it offers income protection should one or more of your markets dry up or taper off.

Take me, for example. I am active as a freelance copywriter specializing in direct marketing, earning hundreds of thousands of dollars a year writing sales letters for corporate clients. I earn another few hundred thousand dollars a year writing and selling simple information online. But I also write a blog, an online newsletter, a magazine column, articles, and nonfiction books, as well as give lectures and seminars. I tell you this not to brag, but to show you how vast and varied the opportunities are in today's world to make a handsome living doing what you love: writing.

There are countless books on writing, publishing, and marketing for writers. But none provides a broader spectrum of money-making opportunities for writers than this book. Whether you're an aspiring writer or an experienced pro, in these pages you'll find opportunities to expand your range, add thousands of dollars to your income, and handle interesting— even fascinating—writing assignments many of your fellow writers don't even know about.

I do have one favor to ask. If you have a positive or negative experience with any of these writing opportunities, or discover new ones, why not share them with me so I can include them in future editions of this book? You will receive full credit, of course. Just contact:

Bob Bly
22 E. Quackenbush Avenue
Dumont, NJ 07628
Phone: 201-385-1220
Fax: 201-385-1138
Email: rwbly@bly.com
Web: www.bly.com

CHAPTER 1

Abstracts

Overview

When science fiction author Arthur C. Clarke passed away in 2008, his obituaries noted that he was the author of *2001: A Space Odyssey* and the inventor of the communications satellite. But early in his career, Clarke earned money as a writer in a little-known, less glamorous niche: writing abstracts for scientific papers and articles.

If you read scientific and medical journals, or look up technical papers online, you'll notice that at the top of the article is an abstract. The abstract is a concise one-paragraph summary of the report or study, which are of great value to medical and scientific professionals. When these abstracts are clear and accurate, they can communicate important research findings and new ideas in a few well-chosen words.

The abstract helps readers decide whether the article is worth reading in its entirety, or in cases where there is a fee, worth downloading. In my own research for writing scientific and technical articles and books, I find that a good abstract often gives me all the information I need without downloading the full article, because a well-written abstract reveals the key finding and makes its importance clear. It's a real time-saver. And writing a good abstract is a small but valuable skill that you can parlay into staff or freelance writing profits.

As you can imagine, abstract writing is not the most lucrative writing niche in this book, nor is it one of the larger opportunities. Yet there is something both challenging and satisfying about the work: you read papers that are often lengthy and complex, and have to summarize their findings and make sense of them in just 100–250 words.

Abstracts are often written by technical editors working on staff for publishers of scientific and medical journals. Most of the articles and papers published in these journals are written by specialists in the field for other specialists in the field. But thanks to the Internet and online search, the abstracts of these papers are read by thousands of people who are not specialists in the field—often not even technically trained. Therefore, your objectives as an abstract writer are to be clear, concise, and accurate—that is, not alter the author's meaning or intended message—while describing his research to readers of all levels in a clear and engaging fashion.

What It Pays

The salary for an entry-level technical editor is $20,000–$30,000, while a more experienced technical editor can earn $40,000–$60,000 a year or more. According to www.indeed.com, the average annual salary for technical editors in the United States is $43,000. Should you land a job with a scientific, medical, or technical journal, writing abstracts could well be one of your responsibilities. You can also approach editors at these publications to see whether they hire freelancers to prepare abstracts from article manuscripts prior to publication.

Nuts and Bolts

Most scientific and technical journals have predetermined word-length requirements for abstracts, but they are usually 100–250 words, written as a single paragraph.

The writer is given a copy of the final, edited version of the article or paper. In rare instances, if the paper is not clear to you, you may ask the senior editor (your boss or client) or the author of the paper for clarification. But usually you are expected to understand and interpret the article on your own. If science and medicine bore you, or you do not have the patience to wade through dense, jargon-laden prose to figure out what an author is saying, abstract writing is not for you.

According to Daniel Kies of the College of DuPage Department of English, an abstract should give the reader the following information:

- *Purpose:* the author's main idea and his reason for writing the paper

- *Scope:* the focus of the paper

- *Method:* the procedures and equipment used to conduct the research

- *Results:* the consequences of the author's research findings

- *Recommendations:* actions to take based on the results

- *Conclusions:* what the results of the research mean

What You'll Write

Often medical and technical writers are employed to write just the abstract so that results of the study are accessible to more readers. The abstract might be more readable if someone other than the researcher writes it.

Can you understand an abstract? Could you improve upon the sentence structure and readability? If you needed to take that information and put it in plain folks writing, for a journal or newsletter, how would you word it?

In his book *Speechwriting: The Master Touch*, speechwriter Joseph J. Kelley Jr. notes, "Everything God created has a kernel of excitement in it, as has everything civilization invented or discovered." You need to find the kernel of excitement in a dull and dry scientific report and highlight it in an abstract that makes others want to read further.

Many scientific publishers make only the abstracts of their articles and papers available for free on the Internet. To download the entire article, you have to pay for it. Therefore, the quality of your abstract can directly generate revenues for publishers by increasing the number of paid downloads from their journals.

This last point is not insignificant. Specialized publishers do a brisk business selling article reprints, both to individuals as well as corporate clients. A scientist at a corporation may want to order a copy of an article relevant to his research; if his company doesn't subscribe to the journal, he may be willing to buy a single copy of just that article.

Meanwhile, if a favorable article about his company's new product is published in a magazine, the company's marketing director may want to order five thousand reprints to give the salesforce. According to a study published by the Ross School of Business at the University of Michigan, U.S. corporations spend $16.5 billion annually buying articles and other content—and often, the abstract is the primary "advertisement" for these articles.

Because the publisher wants the abstract to be easily found by search engines, the writer must use keywords related to the subject. Titles and abstracts for papers are filed electronically, so both should incorporate the keywords a reader would search to find the kind of information presented in the article.

Your responsibilities as a staff or freelance technical editor could also include editing the full article or paper. This might be limited to copyediting for style. Or if the text is unclear and disorganized, you may be asked to do more substantial editing.

What It Takes

Editing technical and scientific articles requires the ability to read lengthy, often complex material and boil it down to a few clear, tightly written sentences. A background in the topic of the article is helpful but not required. All technical editors should own a good dictionary in their field; for example, medical editors must own a recent edition of *Dorland's Medical Dictionary*.

Writing abstracts requires intense concentration and patience to get through dense technical material. Although the major ideas of a paper are often presented in short sections with subheads such as "overview," "introduction," "summary," and "conclusions," you must read the whole paper; otherwise, you risk missing a critical point that the author buried in the text and forgot to highlight elsewhere.

Don't repeat wording from the article in your abstract if there is a way to say it better. As the abstract writer, your job is not to cut and paste, but to summarize articles in a clear, attention-getting, and engaging manner, so that readers who need the information are motivated to read the article.

Getting Started

Job openings and freelance work for technical editors are listed on job sites such as monster.com and on freelance sites such as Elance (elance.com). In addition, when technical and scientific magazines want to hire editors, they advertise the positions in their own pages, usually in classified display ads in the back of the publication. So if you are interested in editing for an engineering magazine in the chemical industry, you should subscribe to the major publications in the industry, including *Chemical Engineering* and *Chemical Engineering Progress*.

There is no shortage of articles requiring abstracts. According to an article in *Current Science*, about 515,700 scientific and technical articles are published worldwide annually. The American Society of Magazine Editors reports that of 22,652 different magazines published in North America, 5,986 are consumer magazines and 16,666 are trade, technical, and scientific journals.

Additional Resources

The Elements of Technical Writing by Gary Blake and Robert Bly (Allyn & Bacon, 2000).

CHAPTER 2

Advertising

Overview

Thousands of organizations—from Madison Avenue ad agencies and *Fortune* 500 corporations, to small local businesses—need ads written to sell their product. American businesses spend more than $60 billion a year on newspaper and magazine advertising, plus billions more on radio, television, cable, and online ads.

Traditional advertising, as practiced on Madison Avenue, used to be a glamour field. In the 1960s, young people who wanted to write or have another creative career would work for advertising agencies as a way to make a good living until they published their novel or sold their screenplay. TV commercials and magazine ads were the major vehicles through which packaged goods and other national brands were marketed to American consumers.

As a result, the supply of eager young wannabes outweighed the demand, and jobs on Madison Avenue were highly competitive; often an aspiring copywriter or art director started as a receptionist, secretary, or even in the mailroom just as a way to break into the agency.

Today, the competition for copywriting, art director, account executive, and media positions in ad agencies remains fierce. However, Madison Avenue has lost some of its luster. Spending on electronic media, particularly email marketing and organic search, is increasing at a rate that far outpaces budgets for TV and print ads. Many pundits are proclaiming that social media, such as blogging, Facebook, and YouTube, are the primary influencers of today's consumers, making Madison Avenue and its ad campaigns obsolete.

What It Pays

The U.S. Bureau of Labor Statistics reports that advertising copywriters earn a median yearly income of $54,410. Copywriters who rise up the ranks—whether to become a senior copywriter or creative director at an ad agency, or a marketing communications manager or marketing director at a corporation—can earn more than $100,000 a year.

As for freelancers, a salary survey by copywriting coach Chris Marlowe shows that about one out of five freelance copywriters earns $100,000 a year or more. A really good freelance writer who proactively promotes her copywriting services and works long hours can earn $200,000 a year or more.

Nuts and Bolts

Ever since Volney Palmer opened the world's first advertising agency in 1843, advertising professionals have been arguing, debating, and searching for the answer to the question, "What makes a good advertisement?" That this debate has never been settled is obvious to anyone who has ever created an ad for a client's approval—or tried to get top management to approve a piece of copy.

Despite the billions of dollars spent by American business in creating, running, testing, and measuring advertising effectiveness, no one has discovered a magic secret that will ensure a winner every time. If such a secret existed, the person who knew it would be a multibillionaire.

However, most professionals in the advertising business agree, more or less, that a good ad:

- **Stresses a benefit.** The main selling proposition is not cleverly hidden but is made immediately clear. Example: "How to Win Friends and Influence People."

- **Arouses curiosity and invites readership.** The key here is not to be outrageous, but to address the strongest interests and concerns of your target audience. Example: "Do You Make These Mistakes in English?" appeals to the reader's desire to avoid embarrassment, and write and speak properly.

- **Provides useful information.** The headline "How to Stop Emission Problems—at Half the Cost of Conventional Air Pollution Control Devices" lures the reader because it promises useful information. Prospects today seek specific, usable information on highly specialized topics. Ads that provide information the reader wants get higher readership and better response.

- **Reflects a high level of knowledge and understanding of the product and the problem it solves.** An effective technique is to tell the readers something they already know, proving that you, the advertiser, are well-versed in the industry, application, or requirement.

- **Has a strong fee offer.** Good ads tell the reader the next step in the buying process and encourage him to take it NOW.

What You'll Write

The most common projects assigned by advertising agencies are print ads, radio commercials, and sales promotions. TV commercials are typically written by staff copywriters and produced by independent directors and production houses.

In ad agencies, the "plum" print assignment is writing full-color ads for national advertisers. Indeed, many agencies do not even create small black-and-white space ads for clients because there is no glamour or money in it. Many ad agency people will also tell you small ads don't get noticed; to make any impression, you need a full page at least and preferably a two-page spread.

Most copywriters will confess—in secret—that it's harder to write a small ad than a big one. In a big ad, there's plenty of room to include all the copy you want and experiment with creative visuals and layouts. In a small ad, your copy is limited. You must tell the complete selling story in the fewest possible words. Copywriters who succeed in this medium are masters in the art of compression.

Any advertising that sells products or services to business, industry, or professionals and not to consumers is business-to-business advertising. Products and services featured in these ads are bought by business people for their professional, not personal, use.

A business-to-business advertisement may offer products that business people use to run their firms. These include supplies such as light bulbs, pencils, copier paper, and equipment such as copiers and fax machines.

A business-to-business advertisement may also offer products that business people use in the manufacturing process, in the actual production of their products. These include pumps, turbines, conveyor belts, and factory robots.

A business-to-business ad may offer a product that is used as a raw material or is incorporated into another product. An example of a product incorporated into another product is semiconductors, which are used to make personal computers.

Finally, business-to-business advertising may be used to promote a wide range of business services: everything from data processing and management consulting, to messengers and coffee and snack services.

What It Takes

What facts should be included in your body copy? What should be left out? The decision is made by listing all the key points and then deciding which are strongest and will best convince the reader to respond to your advertisement.

Before you write your ad copy, make a list of all the features of your products and the benefits of each feature. For instance, a feature of an air conditioner is that its energy efficiency rating is 9.2; the benefit is a lower electric bill.

After making a complete list of features and benefits, list them in order of importance. Then begin your body copy with the most important benefit. Incorporate the rest of the benefits on your list until you have sufficient copy. Now you've written copy that highlights the most important reasons to buy the product, given the space limitations of your ad.

Your copy should be specific about the product's features and benefits. "Platitudes and generalities roll off the human understanding like water from a duck," wrote Claude C. Hopkins in his classic book, *Scientific Advertising.* "They leave no impression whatsoever. Good advertising is effective largely because it is specific."

Getting Started

An ad agency or local small business needs an ad written. Sit down with your new client and ask him the following questions; your thoroughness will both impress the client and give you the facts you need to write a persuasive ad:

1. What are all the product benefits?

2. What are all the features of the product?

3. How is the product different and, hopefully, better than the competition?

4. What does the buyer expect when he or she plunks down a few dollars for the product? And do we deliver?

5. What methods, approaches, and sales techniques is the competition using?

6. How is the audience for this product different than the general public?

7. How much can the buyer reasonably expect to pay?

8. Does the average buyer have a credit card or a checking account?

9. Will the product be purchased for business or personal use?

10. Can we expect to get multiple sales from a buyer?

11. What is the logical "backend" to sell someone after he has purchased this product? (*Backend* refers to other products in the product line offered to someone who has bought the primary product featured in the ad.)

12. Will we need to show the product in color?

13. What's the "universe," or what's the total number of potential customers?

14. Who will buy the product: teenagers or octogenarians, men or women, executives or blue-collar workers?

15. Is there a market for overseas sales?

16. Should we offer monthly installments or some other payment plan?

17. Will the product be a good gift item?

18. Should the copy be long or short?

19. What should the tone of the copy be?

20. Should we test the price?

21. Should we test copy approaches?

22. Is there a seasonal market for the product, and are we taking advantage of it?

23. Are testimonials available from satisfied customers?

24. Do we need photographs or illustrations?

25. Which appeals have worked in the past for this product?

26. What objections might arise from a prospective customer? How can we overcome these objections?

27. Should we use a premium?

28. Should we offer a money-back guarantee?

29. Is this item also sold by retail? Are there price advantages we can stress for buying direct from the ad?

30. Should we consider a celebrity testimonial?

31. Can we tie in the copy to some news event?

32. Can we tie the copy to some holiday or seasonal event?

33. Does the product sell better in a particular region or climate?

34. Should we consider using a sweepstakes?

35. Can this product be sold through a two-step advertising campaign? (In a two-step campaign, ads generate inquiries rather than direct sales.)

36. What must we do to give readers a sense of urgency so they will buy the product now?

37. Can we use scientific evidence in the sales approach?

38. Have we allowed enough time to write, design, and produce the ad, and place the insertion order?

39. Can the customer order by telephone?

40. What unsuccessful approaches have been used to sell this product?

41. Can we get powerful "before" and "after" pictures?

Additional Resources

The Advertising Manager's Handbook by Robert Bly (Prentice Hall, 1993).

The Copywriter's Handbook: Third Edition by Robert Bly (Henry Holt, 2006).

American Association of Advertising Agencies offers helpful news and resources for copywriters: www.aaaa.org.

CHAPTER 3

Annual Reports

Overview

Who publishes annual reports? Companies who sell stock on any exchange, are public, and are required to produce a comprehensive financial report every year. Although some privately held companies may do an abbreviated version of the standard annual report, 99 percent of annual reports are done by publicly owned companies, as required by the Securities and Exchange Commission (SEC).

Freelance corporate writer Maryclaire Collins writes in her book *How to Make Money Writing Corporate Communications*, "Companies that publish these reports for the public often produce them in a slick, colorful format that incorporates a significant amount of narrative about the company's products and performance. This calls for writing that seamlessly integrates discussion of financial matters with company braggadocio. While some companies staff individuals who specialize in writing the annual report, others might call on freelancers, or opt for a consulting agency that specializes in this type of writing."

The annual report summarizes a company's performance for the past year and promises great things for the year ahead. Annual reports are generally divided into two parts: the descriptive narrative of the company's year at the front, and the financial and accounting data at the back.

What It Pays

Writers don't produce annual reports for glory or fame, or to obtain literary and artistic fulfillment. They perceive, quite correctly, that annual reports are a lucrative writing assignment for which freelance writers are frequently hired—and they want to get their share of the loot.

Writing a large annual report for a major corporation is a lucrative assignment, paying $10,000–$20,000 or more per project. Even for a small annual report for a medium-size corporation, you can charge $5,000–$9,000 or more.

On a per-word rate, figure annual report copy at $1–$3 a word. That includes revisions, and there are normally lots of revisions on this type of assignment.

Pages can be light or heavy on text, but figure 200–300 words of text on average per page. On a per-page rate, annual report writers charge $500–$750 per page.

The advantage of large assignments such as annual reports is that if you get a few assignments, you are well on your way to making your income goal for the year. For example, if a corporate writer completes half a dozen annual reports per year, those six assignments alone could bring him $60,000 or more. By comparison, some corporate writers I know charge only $300 for press releases. To earn $60,000 at this rate, you'd have to write two hundred press releases! That's a lot of assignments to handle.

If you can get one, two, or three annual reports for clients and do them annually, that's a solid base from which to build a profitable freelance writing income. One writer I know wrote the annual reports of six companies every year. This brought him $60,000 a year in income. The assignments occupied him full time for about four to five months; the rest of the year he was free to vacation or pursue other projects.

Nuts and Bolts

According to an article in the newsletter *Creative Business*, more than $5 billion is spent each year on annual report production. About 20 percent of that, or $1 billion, is spent on creative services: writing, design, illustration, and photography.

There is a lot of opportunity for you in this market. According to the *Creative Business* article, about ten thousand publicly owned corporations must produce annual reports in accordance with SEC guidelines. The good news for you is these companies are open to trying new writers. Each year, three companies out of every ten choose a different vendor to create their annual reports.

The best way to become familiar with annual reports is to get your hands on a bunch of them and read them carefully. There are two ways to get copies of annual reports. If you buy stock in a company, even a single share, you'll automatically receive an annual report from that company once a year. Many shareholders throw them away without reading them. You should start a reference library of them.

If you don't own or don't want to buy stock, call a stockbroker. Tell him you are thinking of buying the stock of company X, and would like an analyst's report along with a company annual report. Or you can call the corporation directly. Ask the operator for the investor relations department. When you are connected, simply state that you want a copy of the company's latest annual report. It will be sent to you without charge. Another alternative: Pick up *Forbes* or *Fortune* magazine. In many issues, free annual reports from companies advertising in the issue can be obtained simply by completing and mailing a return postcard included with the magazine.

Read the annual reports as a writer, not a shareholder or consumer. Study them for tone, style, content, organization, length, and format. Make notes on the topics covered, the various sections, and the number of words and pages devoted to each. Write out a list of the contents of several reports in outline form. Note the similarities between reports. These are the same sections you will have to write when you are given an annual report assignment.

What You'll Write

The first section of the annual report tells the company's story in narrative form (for large firms, this narrative might consist of several separate sub-sections, each devoted to one of the firm's various operating companies, divisions, or subsidiaries). This is the portion of the report you are hired to write.

The second part, sometimes called the management discussion, consists mainly of numbers reported by the corporation's accounting firm. This copy is usually contributed by the accounting firm or corporate accounting department.

In an article in *Writer's Digest*, annual report writer Stephanie Ferm of SM Communications notes: "Today's typical report encompasses more than the obligatory chairman's letter, product reviews, and financial highlights. Many now include lively company histories, employee profiles, or features on corporate philanthropic commitments. Some major conglomerates have recently added proactive reports that reinforce corporate initiatives on such social issues as the environment, health care, and education. The most innovative of the lot are experimenting with videos, newsletters, newspaper formats, and computer disks to supplement or enhance their financial reports. For the past two years, Marvel's annual report has been in the form of a comic book."

Freelance writer Loriann Hoff Oberlin, in her book *Writing for Money*, describes the writer's role in annual report publishing as follows: "What they [employees and stockholders] demand [in an annual report] is an honest account of business. They want to know where and how the organization has helped others, what makes the company special, what makes it better than others in the industry. The public likes to learn this year's success stories, how major problems were tackled, and whether the company was a good steward of private and public money. Finally, people want to know what's in store for the future, and the organization's place in that larger picture."

For publicly owned *Fortune* 500 corporations, who do the biggest, most elaborate reports, length can be anywhere from thirty to forty pages or more. You write all descriptive narrative. The financial stuff in the back, usually printed in finer type, is prepared by the client's accountants. You have nothing to do with this; you don't even edit it. So don't worry about it.

What It Takes

Doing an annual report usually entails multiple meetings with the client, numerous telephone calls for fact-checking and follow-up questions, reading through and digesting a mound of printed material the client has provided, writing a detailed outline, and writing a first draft plus several revisions.

Writing an annual report takes many weeks of work. If your billing rate is $75 an hour, and you are charging the client $9,000, you should not be surprised if you spend well in excess of one hundred billable hours on the job. Annual reports pay well, but they are a labor-intensive assignment over which the client is likely to be fussy and demanding. You will earn every dollar you get.

Getting Started

The corporate communications managers have overall responsibility for producing the annual reports. Some hire writers directly to produce the copy, then hire designers separately to do the layout. Others give the entire job to their PR firms, ad agencies, or graphic design studios. The agencies or studios either have staff copywriters write the reports or hire freelancers, like you, to do them. I suspect the majority of annual reports are written by freelancers, whether hired directly by the corporation or indirectly through an agency.

Additional Resources

Annual Reports allows you to view annual reports of many different corporations online and is searchable by company name. It's a great resource for writers who need to familiarize themselves with annual report writing and design as well as potential clients: www.annualreports.com.

CHAPTER 4

Articles

Overview

Writing magazine articles is the bread and butter for thousands of free-lance writers. Pay can range from nothing and abysmal to decent and occasionally high.

Magazine writing has an aura of glamour that corporate writing does not. Many writers who freelance for commercial enterprises dream of seeing their bylines in more traditional journalistic media like newspapers and magazines.

For those writers, publishing in the local paper is a great goal while reporting for the *New York Times* or *Vanity Fair* is the gold standard. The great thing about editorial freelancing is that even when the specifics of pitching vary slightly, the rules of the game are standard. That means as long as you can learn what makes a great article and how to sell it to the right people, you can become an editorial freelancer.

Though each type of media and each publication will have its own requirements, all are looking for the same kinds of pieces. These might include hard news, feature stories, and editorials. Though there are plenty of media that concentrate on historical or stagnant stories, in which the information has not recently changed, we will concentrate here on the kinds of publications looking for newsworthy content.

What It Pays

Fees for freelance article writing are all over the lot. At the low end of the spectrum are local magazines that do not pay for articles. They are often a good place to get a few articles published with your byline and gain experience. At the high end are major consumer magazines from *Playboy* and *Esquire* to *Family Circle* and *Cosmopolitan*. They can pay up to a dollar a word, and are tough to break into because the competition is fierce.

In the broad middle are publications ranging from hobbyist and specialty magazines for consumers to business magazines and trade journals covering specific industries. The pay is $100–$1,000 per article, depending on topic, length, and complexity.

Nuts and Bolts

Query letters—letters to editors outlining articles you'd like to write for them on assignment—should follow in many ways the same form as the story you will write. All queries should include the basic idea for the story right up front, at least in the first paragraph, just as you would summarize or give the most important information in the lead of your article.

Then you want to tell the editor why this is an important story for his publication to tell. You want to explain its significance and why that will resonate with readers. You also want to include information about yourself, including your experience and other publications and media you've worked for. If you do have special expertise in the subject of your story, mention that as well.

What You'll Write

So, how do you figure out what makes a good story and who is most likely to pay you for reporting it? Remember that being a good observer is one of the key qualifications for the job, so let's start there.

Let's say it used to be very easy to find a parking spot in your neighborhood. Slowly, you begin to notice it's harder and harder to park late at night and on weekends. Soon, the city begins to erect signs limiting parking to several hours. In the local bars and coffee shops, neighbors are discussing an increased number of parking tickets and the possibility of meters being installed. Hey, you say to yourself, that's a change; it could be an article.

Begin by researching your story, finding the exact details, and locating sources. Then you take all the information—from hard facts to colorful scenes to quotes from your sources—and compile it into a cohesive whole that tells the story of this change and its impact.

But all you need for your query letter is the germ of that idea and some basic facts to back it up. You don't need to have exact quotes yet, but you do want to give the editor something to sink her teeth into. You might try calling the parking authority and including the number of tickets issued this year for that block versus the number of tickets issued last year for the same block.

What It Takes

In theory at least, almost anyone can write and report editorial content. You need not be an expert on the subject matter, though you may become one in the course of completing your article. You should be a good writer, researcher, and observer. Because interviewing sources is a huge part of the job, you must be an inquisitive person and able to think on your feet for follow-up questions. Most publications do not reach out to freelance writers to assign articles, so you have to come up with story ideas yourself. You do not need to have a degree in journalism to publish an article. The best type of credential a journalist can have is experience. Journalists display these through their clips, which are sample articles. These can be photocopies or links on a website.

There are some skills that must be learned for this kind of freelancing. Publications expect you to know certain terminology and to demonstrate competence in using those techniques. Newspaper editors will expect you to know AP or Chicago style and to report information in what is called an inverted triangle. That means the most important information goes at the beginning of the story, giving the editor the freedom to essentially lop off the bottom of the piece if it runs too long, leaving the story basically intact.

Other key terms include *nut graph*, essentially the thesis statement of a piece, and *lead*, the introduction, which can vary from "soft" (a colorful scene or description) to "hard" (a shocking fact or a sentence that summarizes the article). Radio news directors and producers expect you to know how to write for radio and how to record and edit audio. You also want to display good grammar and spelling.

Getting Started

Unless you are already a well-known writer or have a friend who is an editor, it's very unlikely you will get assignments simply by waiting for your inbox to fill up with requests. So how do you get work?

The most traditional avenue to assignments is through pitching. Pitching involves letting an editor know your idea for a story, usually through a query letter sent via snail mail or email. Knowing how to pitch, what to pitch to whom, and when and how is a skill almost as important as learning how to write or produce for the medium.

There are several sources for finding out about outlets that accept or seek work from freelance writers. I highly recommend investing in the latest edition of *Writer's Market,* an annual list of publications and contacts, much like a phone book. Other great sources for freelance work are online. These include websites like Mediabistro, Journalism Jobs, The Association for Independents in Radio (AIR), Journalism Net, Investigative Reporters and Editors (IRE), HotJobs, TV Jobs, and Craigslist. These sites list publications that accept freelance queries, plus offer freelance job postings alongside full- and part-time positions.

Every magazine and newspaper has its own rules and preferences, some of which are explicit and some of which are learned by reading between the lines. For instance, most publications outline their requirements somewhere on their websites, indicating which editor to email or if that editor prefers phone calls. The editor may want to see clips, a résumé, or the finished piece, or she may want nothing more than a short summary of what you plan to investigate. Often, a publication lists upcoming themes or a call for pitches on a specific subject. Some try to let freelancers know what kinds of stories they are looking for, but many expect that freelancers worth their salt will understand without asking what kinds of stories work best. If you have questions, it is usually possible to ask an editor for guidelines.

Additional Resources

The annually published *Writer's Market* (Writer's Digest Books) lists thousands of consumer and trade magazines and their requirements for freelance articles. You can also subscribe to the online version: www. writersmarket.com.

CHAPTER 5

Banner Ads

Overview

Banner ads are seeing a resurgence today. A banner ad may have only half a dozen words, but you can get paid $500 or more to write it.

Banner advertising was the first form of advertising on the Internet. A banner is a graphical and often animated ad, usually placed at the top of a web page. The advertiser's goal is to have viewers click on it to take them to more information about a product.

In the 1990s, Web users didn't think twice about clicking on a banner and being taken to another site. So banners were good at doing their job. But that was when the Internet was still in its infancy and banners were a novelty. Because users didn't know any better, ads that used trickery to get them to click were effective. One tactic that got people to click was a banner that posed as a game. The "Catch the Monkey" ad had an unheard of click-through rate of 8.2 percent (2.5 percent was considered to be a good click-through rate.) It didn't matter if you clicked on the monkey or missed, you were always directed to Treeloot.com, a gaming website.

Though these methods of trickery are still used today, after more than a decade of exposure to such banners that distract them from the task at hand, savvy Web users began to avoid them. By the end of the 1990s, "banner blindness" had set in and banner advertising began to fade.

But the last few years have seen a lot of change. Because of improved technologies and a marketplace full of strong competition, the quality of banner and display advertising has increased, and users' perception of online advertising has improved. Large companies and corporations have recognized the potential for creating brand recognition through banners.

To take advantage of this and to capitalize on bigger money, the leaders in Internet advertising are scrambling to take the lead to grow their networks. Recently Google beat out Microsoft in their war to purchase DoubleClick, thus adding the largest collection of sites to sell banner and display ads. Not to be outdone, Microsoft is currently in negotiation with aQuantive, the parent company of Atlas, another of the large banner networks. Yahoo, in the meantime, has taken a large share of ownership in Right Media, giving it some leverage in this arena.

What It Pays

No online writers specialize solely in banner ads. Rather, a copywriter or website might offer banner ad writing as one of many services in addition to email writing, content writing, web page optimization, and keyword research.

I started charging clients $500 for a single banner ad, which typically ran anywhere from six to twenty words in length. Then I realized to come up with the banner ad I submitted to the client, I created numerous variations before choosing the one I liked.

I figured, "Why not show a few of the best of these to the client as well?" Now for $500, I give clients a package of three banner ads to choose from. They perceive a lower cost per ad and greater value, yet it takes me no extra time, since I was creating at least that many anyway and showing just one.

Nuts and Bolts

Most small- and medium-sized businesses use Internet advertising as a direct response sales tool, meaning the web surfer sees the ad, clicks on it, sees the website or landing page, and buys the product. The problem with this sales model when it comes to banner advertising is that it relies on interruption. People who see a banner are presumably on a web page that they want to be on, and to click it interrupts them from what they are doing.

Therefore, banner advertising, though still viable as a direct response tool, may be better suited for image advertising or branding. Because of its broad reach and high frequency, a banner can be very effective for increasing brand awareness. Unfortunately, it is not easy to measure that effect. Branding is a long-term tactic that slowly builds results over time.

Like a TV commercial, viewers may not take immediate action when they see your banner, but they will remember your name when they are ready to buy. But unlike a TV commercial, users still have the ability to take immediate action. So because banner advertising has become less expensive *and* because it can both build awareness of your product and get an immediate response, it may well be a very cost-effective form of advertising, as long as you understand that building awareness is part of its purpose.

What You'll Write

Banner ads are written to fill standard-size ad units. These include:

- Large rectangle, 336 x 280 pixels
- Full banner, horizontal box, 486 x 60 pixels
- Leaderboard, larger horizontal box, 728 x 90 pixels
- Skyscraper, vertical box, 120 x 600 pixels
- Square button, 125 x 125 pixels

Leaderboards and skyscrapers are positioned outside the part of the screen containing the content, so even though they are large, many online advertisers shun them, preferring squares, large rectangles, and banners.

Too few impressions won't generate significant impact, while too many impressions delivered to a given user results in oversaturation and a waste of media dollars. A study found that the conversion rate on the first impression was the highest. Studies show that click-throughs and conversions are highest during the first three exposures and decline sharply after that. Because the effectiveness of banners decreases over time, it's a good idea to create new banners every month or so, or rotate different banners through the same locations. A study performed by DoubleClick determined that click-throughs on banners fall off drastically after the fourth viewing by an individual.

How long you run your banner on a given website depends on the stickiness of the site and how often a visitor returns to it. For example, on a site like MySpace where users return several times a week, or even multiple times in one day, you change your banner ad more frequently.

Cost is the final factor in determining whether banner advertising can work for a client. Generally, pricing is done in one of three ways: cost-per-click (CPC), cost-per-thousand (CPM), and free with exchange. The prices can range drastically from (practically) free to well over $100 per thousand.

What It Takes

According to a study performed by Atlas Institute Media, placement has a much greater influence on online ad performance than creative copy and design do. Being in the right places the right number of times can make a difference.

According to Wendy Montes de Oca, a marketing manager with Early to Rise, the best placement for banner ads is large rectangles at the top or middle of the page or within the content. An eye-tracking study by the Poynter Institute indicates that banner ads at the top left of the page or positioned close to the body of an article get the most attention. The keys to success in banner advertising, says Wendy, are a powerful headline and a strong graphic image that enhances the headline. Also effective is using notable personalities in banner ads or asking a controversial question in the headline.

Getting Started

Don't approach Internet marketers, corporations, and ad agencies offering to write banner ads only. Get your foot in the door by offering other copywriting services covered in this book: email marketing, websites, and advertising campaigns. Then let your client know you can handle banners, too. You won't get rich with these small assignments. But they're quick and easy to do, and pay well on a per-hour basis.

Here is a short list of additional banner and display advertising networks that can place your ads to be seen by thousands of viewers all across the world. You can also view numerous banner ads on these networks:

www.Advertising.com

www.Valueclick.com

www.Doubleclick.com

www.RightMedia.com

www.CasaleMedia.com

www.Cpxinteractive.com

www.AdBrite.com

www.BannerSpace.com

www.perfecttraffic.com

Additional Resources

The Online Copywriter's Handbook by Robert Bly (McGraw-Hill, 2002).

Ad Designer allows you to create your own banner ads online: www. addesigner.com.

CHAPTER 6

Billboards

Overview

Billboards. Some people call them the scourge of the highways. Yet if there is an involved, memorable, funny, or haunting message, then people remember what they see. Because it is usually something viewed in only a few seconds, the message is given in one to seven words with perhaps a picture or graphic to reinforce the impression. Then it is gone. If the message is powerful, then the reader remembers it later.

The message must be direct and easy to understand. Writing billboard copy is not the time for cute riddles and intriguing puzzles. The reader may see the puzzle or riddle and try to work on it while driving past the board. But without the opportunity to stop, turn around, and look at the board again, the reader will be frustrated in not having the opportunity to get the right answer from the board. The moment will be gone and the reader won't know if he found the message.

When on the highway, start looking at billboards and seeing what messages you get and which hit the strongest in the shortest amount of time. Then figure out why some really get your attention and others don't.

There are other types of billboard writing as well. Apart from using the side of a city building or a rooftop, you can also use the side of a moving van, public transportation vehicles such as buses, personal recreational vans (RVs), cars, and even airplanes. You can also write copy for an aerial billboard.

What It Pays

Your earnings are subject to the message being created, the client ordering the job, where the billboard is located, and the budget involved. Ask your prospective client what the budget is for the billboard project and get as much information as possible before considering your fee. Getting the client to confirm the budget amount is the best way to set a fee, or let the client put out the numbers first, then decide if you are comfortable or need an adjustment. Aspects to consider in determining your fee are: how big the target market is based on where the billboard is located, who the target market is (general public, only women, only men, teens, or older citizens), and the intended result of the message.

Nuts and Bolts

Billboard writing needs a direct, focused target and message. If you've not written any before, practice by looking at highway billboards and considering how you could write or create better ones. In fact, if you have a great idea for a billboard already, call the client, ask for an interview, and show the client your idea. You never know; you may not get the job, but the client may remember you later for a new project, especially if the usual writer is already busy on another project.

What You'll Write

You write the billboard message based on the methodology of delivery, the target market, and the product's message. The message will not likely be longer than seven words. You should have tons of notes about the product and from interviews that help you create the grab factor you need for the message. This type of writing is more than just writing several words and hoping for the best—you conduct quite a bit of research that helps create the message, because it does take knowledge and creativity to convey just the right message to a fast-moving market.

What It Takes

Tom Chandler, of www.copywriterunderground.com, has a great article on copywriting for billboards (see the link under Additional Resources). To create great copy, he suggests the following:

- Have lots and lots of ideas (keep a journal or writing pad handy).
- Know where your billboards are located.
- Remind yourself what you are doing or trying to accomplish.

He also advises you hit the reader with a benefit that is aligned with the creative theme of the message goal, and that the message last longer than a millisecond in the attention span.

Getting Started

Start building a portfolio with sample pieces you create by improving billboards already on the highway. In addition to any sample pieces you create, keep notes about where you saw the original and what the delivery methodology was.

Depending on what subjects you feel comfortable writing about, compile lists of local companies that could use your service, including companies you see advertising on the highway. Even better, suggest updated signage copy. But obtain a signed contract showing they have retained you to write copy for them before revealing the actual copy you want to present. At minimum it should state that they cannot use your ideas without payment.

Additional Resources

Great American Billboards: 100 Years of History by the Side of the Road by Fred Basten (Ten Speed Press, 2006).

Advertising Outdoors: Watch This Space! by David Bernstein (Phaidon Press, 2004).

Buyways: Billboards, Automobiles, and the American Landscape by Catherine Gudis (Rutledge, 2004).

At Tom Chandler's website, you can find an article on writing effective billboard copy: www.copywriterunderground.com/2007/11/07/how-to-write-a-billboard-or-copywriting-at-70-mph.

Indoor Billboard Advertising Association specializes in restroom advertising: www.indooradvertising.org.

Outdoor Advertising Association of America serves and protects the interests of outdoor advertising: www.oaaa.org.

Outdoor Billboard is a resource for people in the outdoor billboard industry: www.outdoorbillboard.com.

At WatchFire (a digital outdoor billboard company), you can request a copy of "Will Digital Outdoor Make or Break You: 10 Critical Facts You Need to Know Before Buying": www.watchfiredigitaloutdoor.com/request-literature.aspx.

CHAPTER 7

Biographies

Overview

Many people like to read about how others lived and succeeded or failed in parts of their lives. Often, as part of encouragement for life modeling, biographies of successful people are the most inspiring. There is much to be learned if the writer entertains as well as informs the reader. While historical facts can be memorized, they are usually remembered more effectively when learned as part of an overall story, with definitive points of interest and drama.

For example, an aspiring ballerina might find great inspiration in reading and studying books about her favorite ballerinas and what they went through to make it as stars of the stage. When pictures are included as well, then by studying how a ballerina uses her arms, legs, and feet, and what expression she has on her face, a young ballerina can try to emulate that picture and that success.

What It Pays

Biographies can be done in different ways, therefore the payment structure is largely based on whether the story is under contract with a publisher. In that case, a publishing house may give an advance to a writer to finish the manuscript. The writer may also receive royalties from book sales. Pay is based on the writer's name (famous or not so famous), popularity, timeliness of the biography's subject, and the ability to market the book and reap high returns.

You can get additional mileage from your work by publishing outtakes of one or two special events in your subject's life that interest certain magazines at certain times of the year. In the example of the ballerina, during the holidays a reader might like to know what it was like to perform the Sugar Plum Fairy or the Snow Queen in the Christmas production of *The Nutcracker*.

Of course, interesting tidbits of scandalous gossip about celebrities are very entertaining, too! *Writer's Market* is the best place to find out what publications pay for certain word-length stories and the publication's slant. Sometimes you can command a larger payout; always negotiate.

Nuts and Bolts

Research is your primary task when starting a biography. Gather as many facts and notes as possible about your subject, and begin outlining the person's life. Detail and accuracy is very important; dates and events are a matter of historical record, not made up on the spur of the moment. When inaccuracies slip into a declared true story, it is the beginning of falsehood that can pass into other people's writings should they use your work as research and verification. It can also damage your writing career and open you up to legal trouble.

What You'll Write

Start with an outline of the person's life, then continue to add offshoot moments of interest as you do more research. If you do your work well, you'll have tons of notes, along with recorded interviews with people who knew the subject, or even from the subject personally. (Transcribe recordings; it's easier and less time-consuming than going back and forth on your audio.) Be accurate when quoting. Always verify a quote if there is any question about what was said.

Other written pieces may include query letters or book proposals (to get your work published), request letters for further information from different sources, and sidebars of interesting information about the subject—maybe a world event that occurred and coincided with the subject's own events and how it might have affected the lifeline of the subject.

What It Takes

Organization, ability to tell an interesting story, and attention to details and facts are the primary skills needed to achieve success in writing biographies. Research is also very important. While gathering well-known or documented facts might be easy enough, there are many hidden details in a person's life that can be infinitely more interesting than anything written before. That's why you should find any writings the subject may have done during his or her lifetime that would shed light on what seems a very ordinary event on the surface. What happened behind the curtain can change your viewpoint of an event, or give you insight into why something happened the way it did.

Getting Started

Getting started in biography requires a nose for news, so to speak. Start by selecting people who interest you, and make a list. Then create files for each of them, and gather information from articles, books, and websites. When online, you should always check the source and double-check the information. Back up everything with sources when writing for publication.

Read as many other biographies as you can of your subject; it is interesting to see how different authors treat the same subject. You may find a writer whose style and method of writing is similar to what you would like to do.

Another option for getting started is taking journalism classes that teach you how to interview, write stories, present both sides, and provide proof of your sources. Also keep in mind that writing biographies is more like writing feature stories, where there is more color than in a straight news story.

Additional Resources

Writing Biography by Lloyd Ambrosius (University of Nebraska Press, 2004).

Works on Paper: The Craft of Biography and Autobiography by Michael Holroyd (Counterpoint, 2002).

A Pocket Guide to Writing in History, Fifth Edition, by Mary Lynn Rampolla (Bedford/St. Martin's, 2007).

Writing Life Stories, Second Edition by Bill Roorbach (Writer's Digest Books, 2008).

Writing Biographies & Getting Published (Teach Yourself) by Ina Taylor (NTC/Contemporary, 1999).

History Makers: A Questioning Approach to Reading & Writing Biographies by Myra Zarnowski (Heinemann, 2003).

CHAPTER 8

Blogs

Overview

Every second, two new blogs are launched on the Internet, and Americans are spending more and more time online. As a result, businesses are increasingly aware of the need to create and maintain blogs, which has created an exciting new opportunity for writers.

More and more companies now pay writers to ghostwrite or write blogs for them, with some freelance bloggers earning as much as $100,000 a year. Writers with popular blogs are also getting book and movie deals based on their blogs.

Despite the thousands of bloggers, only about 7 percent have any interest in blogging for money. Of that percentage, few actually understand the process. This leaves a world of possibilities (and paychecks) for the dedicated writer.

What It Pays

Bloggers can make money from both advertising space on their blogs, and by blogging for businesses. Top bloggers have reported as much as $2 million in annual income, but they are the exception, not the rule.

Most bloggers can expect to make $2–$10 per blog post when employed by a professional blogging company. Freelance bloggers average $1,000 a month from each company they blog for. However, because blogging is a new venture, everything is subjective. With the right situation, $5,000 a month from a single company is not out of the question.

Nuts and Bolts

There are three ways to make money blogging. The first is to create your own blog and sell ad space to advertisers. Blogs are inexpensive to create. The time required to set up and maintain one is minimal. But it could take years for your blog to gain popularity, and advertisers won't invest in blogs until they have proven themselves as high traffic areas.

Several professional blogging companies, such as 451 Press or Dot Ventures, hire writers directly. This is the second way to make money, and a great choice for inexperienced bloggers. Professional blogging companies represent hundreds of businesses looking for content. As an employee of a blogging company, you are required to submit a specific number of posts each month. The blogs vary in topic and length, and you are paid per post.

Your final option is to contact companies directly. Many companies don't have the time or resources to create and maintain their own blogs. That's why freelance bloggers are in high demand. Most companies are delighted to use part of their advertising budget to pay a blogger. You could easily be on the payroll of four, five, or even six companies.

What You'll Write

Blogs are generally short (250–500 words a post). They should be conversational and address topics of interest for their readers. If you are writing freelance, your blog posts might cover a wide variety of topics, from sports to furniture. But each idea should promote the products or services of the company you represent.

The best, most profitable company blogs draw customers not usually inclined to visit that company's website. So write something to attract such guests. Discuss benefits of new products or post a question. Asking readers to respond to your post encourages camaraderie, and readers will be more inclined to return. Whatever you write, make it creative and engaging.

What It Takes

Bloggers need some storytelling ability. When stories and experiences are included in posts, the reader feels a connection that entices them back to the site.

You must be able to relate information. Your goal is to drive the reader to the company's main web page. This is a key component of any blog. You need a combination of stories and informative content to entice your reader to move to the company homepage.

Blog posts must have clarity. You are writing to the masses. Writing should be engaging, but simple. If you write at an advanced level, you lose many potential readers.

You must know something about the industry you are blogging about. Don't contact an investment company if you don't have some knowledge of finance. Only pursue the companies whose products or services you're knowledgeable about.

Be Internet and search-engine savvy. Know what search engine optimization (SEO) is and how to use it to your advantage. The more potential customers you drive to a site, the more money you can request from the company you represent. Some companies require videos and images in your blog postings. Learn how to do this if you don't know already.

Getting Started

If you've never written a blog, browse popular blogs, then start your own. Practice before soliciting business. Join blogger forums and learn what others are writing and how they build readership.

If you're a novice blogger, and would like to start with a professional blogging company, most companies instantly allow you to sign up as a writer (no experience necessary). They lead you through a brief tutorial, then give you their support information. After that, it's up to you.

Once you have experience blogging and would like to work directly for a company, here are some steps to follow:

- **Browse web pages.** Find services or products that interest you, and target these companies. Check to see if the company already has a blog. If they do, move on. There are plenty of other companies who need bloggers.

- **Write a proposal.** Show your worth by writing a clear, professional email. Keep it simple and less than 200 words. If you're not sure who to contact, call the company and ask for the name and email address of the advertising manager. You might also find company contact information on social networking sites.

- **Be prepared to address concerns.** Some companies have yet to grasp the importance of blogs. If you have your own blog, show them the amount of traffic you receive. If not, refer them to popular blogs. Companies understand numbers and will probably give you a chance.

- **Write.** Coming up with fresh topics is always difficult. Find things that interest you. Read the blogs of competing companies to get more ideas. Try to think of what your readers might want to know about it.

Blogging is a fairly new industry, so take advantage of it. And make sure you have fun while writing those engaging posts!

Additional Resources

Blog Schmog by Robert Bly (Thomas Nelson, 2007).
You can find job postings (companies soliciting blog writers) at www.about.com and www.problogger.com.

An e-book by Angela Booth, *Blogging for Dollars: How to Become a Career Blogger*, is available at abmagic.com/Blog/blogging.html.

CHAPTER 9

Booklets

Overview

There are hundreds of thousands of businesses in the United States, and all of them need to market themselves by highlighting their expertise. To do so, they create a tremendous amount of e-books, reports, brochures, and white papers, as well as booklets.

Many companies that rely on booklets to spread the word about their services aren't writers, so they hire freelance writers like you to produce them. By marketing yourself as a booklet writer, you can become part of a very lucrative field. In addition, you can self-publish your own informational booklets and sell them directly to consumers. This can be done both online and offline.

What It Pays

Fees for booklet writing, as in most types of professional writing, can be all over the map, depending on your region, experience level, and company budgets. Beginners might want to start low, around $300–$400, while established freelancers can charge $3,000–$4,000.

Writers usually charge a flat fee per project or an hourly rate. If you quote an hourly rate (usually $35–$150 per hour for beginners), be sure to accurately assess how much time it will take you to complete, and carefully keep track of your time while working on the assignment. This includes research time before you start writing.

A skillful booklet writer can offer more value to her clients, and therefore increase her fees, by adding booklet consulting and helping clients with their booklet marketing strategy, or by teaching others how to write booklets. By developing relationships with printers and graphic designers, the writer can also offer to oversee the production of the booklet, removing this additional headache and adding a project management fee to the quote.

Nuts and Bolts

So what exactly is a booklet? It is a small book designed to educate a target audience with tips and strategies that help solve a problem. The most popular type of booklet is the tips booklet, which is usually sixteen to twenty-four pages and 3½ x 8½ inches (small enough to fit into a standard business envelope, perfect for mailing to potential clients). They usually have a plain color cover and minimal graphics or design. Many businesses, from large corporations to entrepreneurs, use them to grow mailing lists, generate leads, or sell for profit.

What You'll Write

Booklets cover a wide range of topics, from simple how-to tips to highly technical subject matter described in layman's terms. It all depends on your background and what you already enjoy writing about. As mentioned earlier, the most common type of booklet is the tips booklet, but you might also write longer booklets, including some that exist only as PDF documents.

Typically, each booklet consists of an intriguing headline that entices people to read the booklet, a table of contents, a brief introduction, the booklet content itself, and any sources cited in the booklet. Depending on the purpose of the booklet, it might also include back matter with additional offers, telling the prospect where to go for more information or to order products.

Learn as much as you can about the client's intentions for the booklet, so you can plan what to write, as well as suggest things to include that she might not have considered.

What It Takes

Since you may write booklets about industries you know nothing about, you should have excellent research skills. You also need to know how to interview experts on the subject, including how to weed out any superfluous information and get to the material your client deems important for the booklet to be successful.

You also need to be a good listener and take good notes, both from experts you interview, as well as your client. Good communication skills are also important, because you want to make sure you understand what the client needs the booklet to accomplish. You need good organizational skills to keep your booklet material and research together, and excellent time management skills to make sure you complete the booklet by the client's deadline and stay within budget.

Getting Started

To market yourself as a booklet writer, you need booklet samples for your portfolio to show potential clients. Start collecting these samples by offering your free services to associations and nonprofits in your area. You can also check sites such as Craigslist (craigslist.org), Elance (elance.com), or Guru (guru.com), and look for people who need booklets written.

You can also write your own booklets on subjects you know about, and sell them online. Almost every subject imaginable has a large potential audience of people who are willing to pay good money to learn about it.

Additional Resources

Booklet writer Paulette Ensign offers booklet resources, tips, and a free e-newsletter at www.tipsbooklets.com.

You can also find booklet opportunities at the Freelance Writing Jobs site: www.freelancewritingjobs.com.

CHAPTER 10

Books

Overview

More than 300,000 books are published annually, yet with rampant consolidations in the publishing industry, there are fewer mainstream publishers than ever to sell your book idea to.

For most writers, the notion of writing a book with their name on the cover is never far from their thoughts. They think of it as the ultimate step to fame and fortune. As a book author, you can acquire both, though normally, writing a book offers each in relatively small doses.

What It Pays

Unless your book becomes a bestseller, you probably won't make much money from it. Advances for nonfiction books are $3,000–$15,000; $7,000 is a typical figure. Half the advance is paid upon signing the publisher's contract, with the balance due upon acceptance of your manuscript. Remember, this is an advance against royalties. So if you receive a $10,000 advance, and you are paid a royalty of $1 per book, you won't start receiving royalty payments until book number 10,001 is sold.

Royalties are typically 10–15 percent on hardcovers and 6–8 percent on trade paperback editions. Books sold through mail order usually pay a 5–6 percent royalty. Some publishers base royalties on the cover price of the book. This is known as a *gross royalty*. Others base it on net revenue from the sale of each book, known as *net royalty*.

A friend told me that the late Rosser Reeves was earning $25,000 a year in royalties from *Reality in Advertising,* twenty-five years after the book's initial publication. Nice, but don't count on it. More than eight out of ten books published do not earn back their advance.

Nuts and Bolts

You have a great idea for a nonfiction book. Your spouse thinks it's a great idea. Your parents think it's a great idea. Even your neighbor who hates to read thinks it's a great idea. But will a publisher think it's a great idea—enough to pay you an advance, commission you to write it, and publish and sell it?

That depends largely on your book proposal. Here's where you demonstrate persuasively that your idea has merit. Of course, even a solid idea and a great book proposal can't guarantee success, but they can tip the odds in your favor. But if either the idea or the proposal is weak, your chances of a sale are slim to none.

It's no secret what book editors look for when reviewing book ideas and proposals. You'll improve your chances of winning a publisher's contract by testing your book idea against a few key questions. Principle among these questions is whether there is a large enough audience interested in the topic to justify publishing the book. The major New York publishing houses aren't interested in highly specialized books written for small, narrow audiences. If you want to write the definitive work on LAN/WAN internetworking, for example, seek out a publisher of technical books.

Big publishers are primarily interested in "bookstore books"—that is, books that appeal to a general audience or at least to a large segment of the general population. Examples of such audiences include parents, small business owners, corporate executives, fitness enthusiasts, movie buffs, users of personal computers, teenagers, and other large affinity groups.

A book aimed at a major publisher must appeal to an audience of hundreds of thousands of people, if not millions. To sell your idea to the editor, you must demonstrate that such an audience exists. In our proposal for *How to Promote Your Own Business* (accepted and published by New American Library), Gary Blake and I cited statistics showing there are more than ten million small businesses in the United States, and 250,000 new businesses started each year.

One excellent source of market data is *Standard Rate and Data Service* (SRDS), a book listing U.S. magazines that accept advertising and their circulation. SRDS is available at your local library or from the publisher (www. srds.com). If you're proposing a book on freelance writing, for example, you could look up writers magazines and find that the two largest publications in the field have a combined circulation of more than 300,000; this is the potential market for your book.

However, only a small percentage of the intended audience will actually buy your book. And a major publisher hopes to sell at least five thousand copies of your book. So, if you're writing a book that appeals only to the 44,171 branch managers working at banks nationwide (e.g., *How to Manage Your Branch More Efficiently*), and 2 percent can be persuaded to buy the book, you've sold only 883 copies—not nearly enough to make the project worthwhile for either you or a publisher.

What You'll Write

A medium-length nonfiction book, running around two-hundred printed pages, is about 80,000 words. That represents a double-spaced, typewritten manuscript of slightly more than three-hundred pages.

If your publisher is typical, your manuscript is due on the editor's desk four to nine months from the date you sign your book contract. Once you hand in the manuscript, it will take another three to six months before the books are published and distributed to bookstores.

What It Takes

Don't sit down, write a book, and then try to sell it to a publisher. It works that way for fiction. But nonfiction is different. In nonfiction, authors submit book proposals to publishing houses, and publishers decide whether they want to publish your book based on your proposal.

The book proposals I submit to publishers all contain the same basic information:

- **Title page.** The book's title and the name of the author are centered in the middle of the page. In the upper left corner, type "Book Proposal." In the bottom right, type your name, address, and phone number (or, if you have one, your agent's).

- **Overview.** Summarize what your book is about: the topic, who will read it, why it's important or interesting to your intended audience, and what makes your book different from others in the field.

- **Format.** Specify word length, number of chapters, types of illustrations or graphics to be included, and any unique organization or format (for example, is your book divided into major sections or do you use sidebars?)

- **Market.** Tell the editor who will buy your book, how many of these people exist, and why they need it or will want to read it. Use statistics to dramatize the size of the market. For example, if your book is about infertility, mention that one in six couples in the United States is infertile.

- **Promotion.** Is your book a natural for talk radio or Oprah? (Be realistic). Can it be promoted through seminars or speeches to associations and clubs? Give the publisher some of your ideas on how the book can be marketed. (Note: Phrase these as suggestions, not demands. The publisher is interested in your ideas but probably won't use most of them.)

- **Competition.** List books that are comparable to yours. Include the title, author, publisher, year of publication, number of pages, price, and format (hardcover, trade paperback, or mass market paperback). Describe each book briefly, pointing out weaknesses and areas in which your book is different and superior.

- **Author's bio.** Give a brief biography, listing your writing credentials (books and articles published), qualifications to write about the topic (for instance, for a book on popular psychology, it helps if you're a therapist), and your media experience (previous appearances on television and radio).

- **Table of contents or outline.** Offer a chapter-by-chapter outline showing the contents of your proposed book. Many editors tell me that a detailed, well-thought-out table of contents in a proposal helps sway them in favor of a book.

- **Sample chapters.** If this is your first book, you may want to include one or two sample chapters with your proposal as an example of your writing style. These sample chapters should be chapter one and whatever chapter you think is strongest. For more advice on how to write a book proposal, read Michael Larsen's *How to Write a Book Proposal*.

Another option is to self-publish your book. As the publisher, you control the design, production, and editing—and, you keep a larger share of the sales. On the other hand, you have to handle all aspects of book publishing—typesetting, cover design, printing, distribution, promotion—and not just the writing.

Getting Started

You do not need an agent to sell your book, but it does help. The large mainstream publishers are so overwhelmed with submissions that many return unagented manuscripts unopened. Others have slush piles, and rarely do manuscripts that start in the slush pile end up in the published pile (although there are exceptions).

Smaller publishers are usually more receptive to unagented submissions. Also, if you have contacts at a particular publishing house, you might be able to get your manuscript read by an editor without an agent's intervention.

Agents' fees are usually 15 percent of the money (advances and royalties) paid to you by your publisher. Most legitimate literary agents consider postage, telephone calls, and other expenses as overhead and do not pass these charges onto the client.

Additional Resources

Getting Your Book Published by Robert Bly (Roblin Press, 2000).
The Self-Publishing Manual by Dan Poynter (Para Publishing).

CHAPTER 11

Book Reviews

Overview

Thousands of new books are published every week—a staggering amount. Most books receive no review attention or extremely limited review attention. Self-published books almost never receive any reviews from professionals. The flood of new books can be viewed as hopelessly overwhelming, or as an opportunity for beginners to say something new and important about an otherwise ignored intellectual island.

Books in the catalogs of established publishers such as Random House—the books you are most likely to be assigned to review for pay—are judged by professionals at each step in the publishing process. As a result, those books should be approached with respect. While some are inevitably flawed, and deserve lukewarm or negative reviews, the default position ought to be respect. Give each book assigned for review an opportunity to prove itself worthy.

What It Pays

Nobody becomes wealthy writing book reviews. Fees for book reviews range from as low as $15 to as high as $1,500 for an essay that involves reading multiple books. Average pay is $200. The average length is 600 words.

You should read the entire book carefully—no skimming allowed when you read and write for pay. Depending on the book—its length, its complexity, whether it is fiction or nonfiction—a thorough reading usually consumes four to twelve hours. Some reviews take only an hour to write if you do most of the deep thinking and outlining while still immersed in the text. Other reviews go through multiple rewrites and consume perhaps six hours altogether.

Nuts and Bolts

Whatever the word count, the expectations of each assigning editor determine a great deal, as a reviewer learns to play to that original audience of one. Book reviews do not follow a set structure. Each is unique. So what follows in this section are suggestions, not rules. Specific editorial requirements of the publication supersede the guidelines here:

- Avoid reading reviews of the same book by other reviewers until after your own review is published.

- Do not rely on press releases, canned interviews with the author, and other material from the publisher meant to cast the book in a favorable light.

- Describe the content of the book accurately. Description is often prosaic, but mandatory.

- As word count permits, do more than regurgitate content; evaluate structure, voice, flow, thoroughness, sourcing, factual accuracy, originality, or whatever else seems relevant. To decide what to include, write extensive notes as you read the book. If you make a point that touches on material unaddressed in the book itself, you might interview the author or editor, though doing so would be the exception, not the rule.

- Whether to compare the book to others on the same topic is always an important issue to address. An older book or author named in the publicity for the book as a touchstone is not necessarily a model just because of longevity or huge sales.

- Deal honestly in the review with your preconceptions about the author, the topic, and the genre. "Preconception" is not a dirty word in the reviewing realm. You are being paid to share your opinion.

- In a relatively brief review, do not offer a quotation from the book as an example of writing style unless you are completely convinced that the quotation is representative. For example, if thousands of sentences are competently crafted or even transcendent, is it appropriate to cite one of just ten clunky sentences?

- A book might fail to live up to your expectations. Still, almost every book offers something of value. A 100 percent negative review might say more about you than the book.

- Make sure readers will be able to discern without a doubt whether you think the book is worthy of purchase or library checkout. Avoid wishy-washy evaluations.

- A review should constitute more than a thumbs-up or thumbs-down exercise. Whenever practical, the review should serve as an interesting, compelling stand-alone essay with insights beyond a simplistic grade. The *New York Review of Books*, to cite one example, regularly publishes essays that use the book as a foundation for discussion.

The assigning editor normally provides instructions about how to handle the boilerplate information, including title, subtitle, author, number of pages, price, and a brief description of you as reviewer.

What You'll Write

For daily newspapers, a word count of 500–600 is typical for a review covering just one book. More than one-thousand words is rare. In the magazines that specialize in long-form reviews and essays, such as the *Atlantic* and the *New York Review of Books*, word counts might top three thousand.

What It Takes

The question "Am I qualified to be a professional book reviewer?" can lead to endless discussion and disagreements about the credentials of reviewers. Should theater reviewers have composed plays or directed or acted? Should dance reviewers have performed on stage or choreographed a routine?

Book reviewer Steve Weinberg says, "During my sporadic tenures as an editor assigning book reviews, I prefer a published author, all other factors being equal. A biographer who has labored for years to research and write somebody else's life will bring an understanding to the genre unlikely to be matched by somebody who has never undertaken a biography."

But not every author is a superb reviewer, or even a capable reviewer, just like not every professional golfer is talented at teaching others how to play a good round. There is an argument to be made that because many books are intended for generalist readers, a review by a generalist might serve the audience well.

Potential book reviewers who have never written or edited a book can learn a great deal about the various genres through study, just like anybody can learn about corporate accounting through study. Biographers, novelists, and authors in every other book genre have shared their knowledge in easily accessible literature.

"I have never written a novel, and probably never will," says Weinberg. "But I have reviewed lots of novels nevertheless. My reviews are frequently informed by novelists' books and magazine features about how they carry out their craft."

Getting Started

If you have already published book reviews, send your clips to the editor from whom you hope to obtain an assignment. If you have never published a book review, but can show feature stories or news accounts related to books and authors, send those. If you have never published anything related to books and authors, but have published about other topics, those clips might help you obtain a review assignment.

If you have never written for publication, a well-thought-out, exquisitely composed query letter might still lead to an assignment. Maybe start your own blog, where you post reviews and other well-crafted pieces about books and authors, to serve as an inroad. You could review a current book for no reason other than sending a sample to the assigning editor. Or you can write for free at first: for a literary journal, a professional newsletter, or your local newspaper. If you can obtain a referral from a current reviewer, professional acquaintance, or social friend of the assigning editor, do so.

Lots of publications might jump at book reviews submitted by you, as long as you do not expect payment. Those outlets include small daily and weekly newspapers, little-known websites, blogs, and magazines aimed at narrow professional audiences.

Whether you agree to read and write for no payment is obviously your choice. Our best advice is to say yes, but only once or twice, and only if you need to get a few clips and credentials so that you can legitimately call yourself a published book reviewer when you seek book review assignments for pay.

Additional Resources

Get Paid to Read: Writing Book Reviews for Fun and Profit by Steve Weinberg (CTC Publishing, 2008; www.bookreviewprofits.com).

CHAPTER 12

Brochures

Overview

Writing sales brochures for businesses is a lucrative, easy-to-enter opportunity for freelancers. For every product you see advertised, there are literally hundreds that are promoted only through sales brochures. Yet this market is largely overlooked. Says freelancer Cam Foote, "Most freelancers are so oriented to soliciting agencies for ad work, they simply ignore the opportunity." As a full-time freelancer specializing in business writing, I add at least $75,000 a year to my income with brochures and related promotional pieces. While you can't expect to duplicate that figure quickly, even a single successful project can be worth $500–$3,500 or more.

What It Pays

There are two basic brochure sizes. Full-size brochures measure about 8½ x 11 inches—the same dimensions as the letter-size paper your printer uses. Fees for writing full-size brochures can be priced by the page, usually resulting in $500–$1,000 per brochure.

A slim-jim brochure, also known as a rack brochure because it fits easily in display racks at banks and travel agencies, is a letter-size or legal-size sheet folded two or three times to fit into a #10 business envelope. You can charge $750–$1,500 or more to write a slim-jim.

Some full-size brochures have a pocket on the inside back cover for holding additional sales literature. These inserts are typically 7 x 10 inch sheets printed on one or both sides. If you are already writing the main brochure, you can charge an additional $500 per side for insert sheets designed to be used with the brochure.

Nuts and Bolts

No matter what size company or project you work on, the client's expectations will be the same: a brochure that quickly communicates the essentials of a business to new customers, prospects, employees, and dealers. Brochures are primarily a medium of information; they tell prospects what the product is and what it can do for them. But most importantly, a brochure must persuade customers to purchase the client's product.

The following techniques will help you create brochures that satisfy your clients' needs.

- Put a strong selling message on the cover. Many people never get past the first page, so your reader should be able to understand what you are selling simply by glancing at the front cover. At the same time, the cover should either arouse curiosity or promise a reward for turning the page—to get the prospect to read further.

  One marketer, a mail presort service, achieved significantly better sales results simply by changing its brochure headline. The original cover featured only the company's name; the revised one read, "How to Mail a First-Class Letter for the Price of a Third-Class Stamp." Which would you rather read?

- Visualize. Whenever possible, show the reader what you mean instead of telling him. Use graphs, photos, charts, tables, diagrams, schematics, and other visual aids to tell your story. For instance, if you want to dramatize your "nationwide network of fifty repair centers," show a U.S. map with red dots representing your fifty locations.

- Organize your brochure according to the buyer's logical decision-making process. "Follow the approach a good salesperson would use," says Dick Hill, vice president of Alexander Marketing Services, a Michigan-based ad agency. "First qualify the prospect by telling him that this product is intended for his business. Then, get him interested. Then go through the features and benefits. Then, give details about selections and models."

- Ask yourself, "Does this brochure answer all the questions I'd have if I were going to buy this product?" If not, go back and add the missing details. The biggest complaint consumers and business buyers have with brochures is that they don't give enough information—especially when it comes to price. (If a client objects to adding price or other information that might "date" the brochure, put that information on a separate sheet to be inserted in the brochure.)

What You'll Write

Big companies represent the most lucrative market for your brochure-writing services. Companies with multiple divisions, departments, product lines—such as major consumer brand manufacturers, insurance firms, pharmaceutical companies, large industrial manufacturers, big technology companies like Cisco, and *Fortune* 1000 firms—likely have dozens or hundreds of different products and services, each requiring a brochure or series of brochures to promote it.

These companies have an ongoing need for many different pieces of literature, and they can afford to pay top dollar for your work. For example, one large corporate client paid me $9,000 for a major brochure with inserts; another assigned to me an extensive series of brochures that earned me more than $20,000.

Small or local firms represent an important market, too, especially for your first efforts. Such projects are typically smaller in scope, but they are still profitable assignments. I recently worked with a collection agency that paid me $1,000 for a small slim-jim brochure. It generated substantial results for the agency, which later hired me to write its ads and sales letters.

Some companies don't spend a lot of money on brochures, and represent at best only a one-shot situation. This category includes local service businesses, professionals (doctors, lawyers, accountants, dentists), self-employed business people, retailers, mail-order firms (although they will pay heavily for good sales letters), small companies run by their owners, and entrepreneurs just getting started.

What It Takes

To get assignments writing brochure copy, contact the appropriate person at the organizations described earlier. For large corporations, contact any of these: marketing manager, sales manager, advertising manager, manager of marketing communications, manager of marketing support services, director of corporate communications. You'll find them listed in such books as *The Standard Directory of Advertisers* (National Register Publishing Co.) and *Directory of Corporate Communications* (J.R. O'Dwyer and Co.), both available at your local library.

For smaller firms, contact the president, owner, or director of marketing. To get the name of the appropriate person, call the company and ask the receptionist. If none of these titles exist, ask for the person in charge of advertising. Most receptionists give this information freely. If they ask why you want it, be honest and briefly explain that you're a consultant specializing in the production of sales brochures, and you want to send information about your services.

Getting the right person's name is important. If you don't have a name, you can always write to the person by title, but this is less effective than a personal approach.

The best technique for reaching prospects is direct mail. Send a one-page sales letter describing your services. Invite the prospect to contact you to discuss a project, see samples of your work (if you have material to show), or request an initial meeting. Enclose a reply card for the prospect to respond.

Getting Started

If you're already writing for commercial clients, brochures represent an opportunity to expand your business and boost your income. Although many clients can't afford TV commercials or magazine ads, just about every organization needs printed literature to educate, inform, or sell.

Potential clients for your brochure-writing services include local small businesses, self-employed professionals, national corporations, manufacturers, service and professional firms, banks, government agencies, hospitals, colleges and universities, museums, and nonprofit institutions. You can also offer your services to ad agencies, graphic design studios, and PR firms that produce brochures for their clients.

Additional Resources

The Perfect Sales Piece by Robert Bly (Wiley, 1994).
Secrets of a Freelance Writer, Third Edition by Robert Bly (Henry Holt, 2006).

CHAPTER 13

Bumper Stickers

Overview

Promoting products and services by bumper sticker is the poor man's marketing campaign that also happens to be very effective. You only need a few words to convey your message about the product or service, and everyone who drives behind your car will see it.

Writing bumper stickers requires the use of direct and concise words to convey the message, and because of the size of the medium, words are at a premium. The fewer words used to convey the message, the better.

Bumper sticker messages cover nearly every subject in the world, and no topic is considered sacred or immune from coverage. The message must be immediately evident, as most are seen while a person is coming up behind another driver and, most likely, moving past on the left. Or the car with the message is the one moving by quickly on the viewer's left side. That means the person has about ten seconds to see the sticker, read the message, and absorb the result or impact.

Consider though that using bumper stickers is one of the most economical marketing strategies—short of free—that can be used for a business or service. If you are selling your bumper stickers on your website, then your marketing, via bumper sticker, moves up exponentially by going nationwide, even internationally, depending on your message for your product.

What It Pays

Payment is usually by the word or phrase and the strength or impact of the message. If you are writing for your own product or service, then you would obviously see a greater return through your own sales rather than just writing for someone else. You can also determine where and how your marketing is the most effective by checking sales by date and location.

Check out some of the online stores where you can build your own stickers, and study how those sites are put together and what the current range of pricing is. Most single stickers run $3.50. Having a build-it-yourself site may be the more profitable way to go, especially if you can also sell your own creations for those who don't like to design. Consider writing on subjects that people might want to buy in bulk, such as political campaigns or religious issues, and provide better discounts for these orders.

Nuts and Bolts

Bumper sticker writing requires quick delivery of message, as most readers have only five to ten seconds to read the sticker. Use simple, short, and concise words and phrases to convey the message quickly. Never use words, phrases, or accompanying graphics that readers have to strain to decipher because it only takes one to two seconds before a person turns away to look at something else.

What You'll Write

You write the final bumper sticker examples as well as any advertising to sell them by mail or online. You should have tons of notes that try out different versions of your message until you get to the final version. These notes can be saved and used for other project stickers also.

You also write any query letters to companies and publications who might be interested in purchasing your sticker slogans, although if you sell them this way, you may be giving up the right to use them for sale on your website.

What It Takes

You must sit down and take a topic apart to find words and phrases that suit the messages you want to get across. Practice saying the message in the fewest words possible, so you can make the letters larger on the sticker. Try the message in different arrangements until you find the one you like best. Test several versions on friends for impact.

Getting Started

Begin by deciding what subjects you would like to make bumper stickers for. If you are politically minded, then do stickers on the current election candidates, on bills and propositions, on issues, anything in the public eye. If you belong to a church, do stickers on events, public issues, religious concerns, anything you consider of importance for the public.

Once you have samples to show, make lists of businesses and organizations who might like to buy your stickers in bulk, and send them query letters. Humor and comedy can also go a long way in just about any subject, so don't forget to have that side developed, too.

Additional Resources

The Ultimate Bumper Sticker Book: 96 Stickers for Lockers, Notebooks, & More (Cider Mill Press, 2008).

Watch Out for the Idiot Behind Me: The Ultimate Bumper Sticker Book (Cider Mill Press, 2007).

Bumper Stickers by Bob Meehan and John A. Dahlberg (Meek Publishing, 2001).

All About Stickers: www.allaboutstickers.com.

Bumper Art: www.bumperart.com.

Bumper Talk: www.bumpertalk.com/bumpertalk.

Café Press: www.cafepress.com/buy/bumper-stickers.

Dem Store: www.demstore.com/cgi-local/SoftCart.exe/scstore/DemStore/custom/custom_bumper.html?E+scstore.

On Facebook, there is a possibility for advertising: apps.facebook.com/bumpersticker/recently_popular_stickers/list/1.

Frugal Marketing is a good marketing resource: www.frugalmarketing.com/dtb/bumper-sticker.shtml.

Mike Thomas has an article on writing bumper stickers at www.associatedcontent.com/article/243400/how_to_make_extra_money_writing_buttons.html?cat=31.

Zazzle: www.zazzle.com/custom/bumperstickers.

CHAPTER 14

Business Plans

Overview

Go ahead and Google the term "business plan writer." You'll get hundreds of results. You'll find everything from business consultants to ad agencies offering business plan writing services— even freelance business plan writers. And if you have a mind for business and can think strategically, this could be a great niche for you. Any professional business plan writer will tell you it's often fascinating and frequently lucrative.

Try this experiment. Ask a dozen friends and acquaintances who own small businesses, "Do you have a business plan?" Nine out of ten will answer in the negative. Why? Because writing business plans is taught primarily in business schools, which most entrepreneurs have never attended.

Does every small business need a plan? No. A plan isn't essential for profit. However, when a company wants to grow, a formal business plan is a must to get loans, attract venture capital and other investors, or to franchise. This is the market most professional business plan writers tackle. It's the market of businesses seeking second-round financing, and this market is big. You'll be hard pressed to find a company that doesn't want to grow—and companies seeking capital need a strong business plan to help them get the funding they seek.

What It Pays

Standard hourly rates are $40–$120. Sometimes research is charged separately per hour or per day. Or you can be like some business plan writers and charge by the word, at a rate of $1 a word—or by the manuscript page at a rate of $200 per page.

A freelance business writer can easily charge $5,000–$10,000 or more for a plan for a small business and earn in excess of $100,000 a year. If you serve small business clients as a management or marketing consultant, you can charge $1,000–$2,000 per day or more.

Most lucrative of all is to get an equity stake in your client's business. If they strike it rich, so do you! As a general rule, business plan writing can generate $20,000–$100,000 per year.

Nuts and Bolts

Writing business plans is, in some ways, an odd niche. Some argue that writers should prepare the plans, because they can present the clearest, most persuasive picture to investors of a start-up company and its vision. Others say business plans should be prepared by management consultants with MBAs or by CPAs, because these experts have financial, management, and business knowledge that many writers lack. But their writing is often turgid, and their documents can put venture capitalists to sleep.

If you decide to make business plans your primary freelance activity, you might consider going back to school for an MBA. Then, you'll offer clients the best of both worlds: business acumen combined with good writing.

What You'll Write

Business plans have six different parts: executive summary, business description and mission, market analysis, management and operational plan, marketing strategy, and financials.

- **Executive summary.** This is a summary of your entire plan, a general description of the business, and the description of the owner's qualifications to run it. Although this section is read first, it's usually written last. This gives you the opportunity to gather the detailed information you need from the different parts of your plan to create the strongest sales pitch for a business.

- **Business description.** This is where you give a detailed description of the services or products the business provides. Describe clients whether existing or anticipated. Explain how the business will market to them. Also mention the type of business organization, and include anticipated revenues.

- **Market analysis.** This is where you write about competitors. Describe the competing businesses, indicating how this business will fill a particular need. You should also address industry trends along with the planned response to these trends.

- **Management and operational plan.** This is where you discuss the nuts and bolts operation of the business. Give information about the company's background and expertise. Describe how the business will use vendors and subcontractors, if necessary. Discuss equipment and how it will be used.

- **Marketing strategy.** Explain how the business will attract clients. Describe advertising, promotional, and marketing plans. Mention the market niche the business is targeting and how it will appeal to clients in this market.

- **Financial plan.** This includes an expense worksheet, a balance sheet, and a profit-and-loss statement. The expense worksheet is usually based upon the expense summary and rate structure. It should be summarized monthly. The balance sheet is a detailed listing of all assets and liabilities. The profit-and-loss statement is a yearly summary of actual income and expenses. If the company is a start-up, indicate how it will acquire money and how it will be paid back. Be sure to include income estimates and projected increases based on expansion of the client base.

Business plan writer Linda Elkins explains the job this way:"You are basically a translator.You listen to your client's ideas, review their financial data and the other information they have gathered, and then put this information into the clearest, most direct format possible."

In addition to actually writing the plans, in some cases you'll be a consultant, and coach entrepreneurs to write the plans themselves.This is because when businesses begin seeking venture capital, some investors prefer a plan written by the business owner over one written by a professional.Then there's the start-up market. With more than 500,000 new businesses each year, this market is just as prolific.

What It Takes

As we said earlier, business plan writers fall into one of two categories: freelance writers with a head for business, and management consultants who, one would hope, can put together a clear sentence.

If you're a writer and you want to write business plans, your immediate objective should be to expand your knowledge of such key business areas as finance, management, operations, and marketing.You don't have to go back to school for your MBA (though for a full-time freelance business writer, that's not a bad idea). But you should read some basic business books and perhaps take a class or two in small business or entrepreneurship.

Getting Started

A business plan writer needs a background in business, business development, financing, or accounting. The writer has to have experience understanding financial statements and be capable of making sales and income projections.

It's also helpful to understand marketing strategy because business plan writers often have to provide market research and help develop positioning statements. Good networking skills are a plus, too. Sometimes you'll have to help your client find sources of financing. It's also important to maintain a professional appearance.

Another thing that can help is to invest in business plan software that provides templates for the plans you write. Some of these are listed in the resource section.

When you're just starting out, it's a good idea to join your local chamber of commerce and make contacts at career development centers. This way you'll mingle with established business people as well as aspiring entrepreneurs. Also contact the Better Business Bureau to get a listing of companies to contact in your area. Business plan professionals recommend honing your skills by writing a few business plans and having them critiqued by bank lending officers or merchant bankers.

Another important note: There can be a lot of liability when you're writing business plans. It's recommended you never list yourself as author of the business plan. It's also important that you consult with an attorney before setting out in this field.

Additional Resources

The Business Planning Guide by David Bangs (Dearborn, 1998).

The Elements of Business Writing by Gary Blake and Robert Bly (Longman, 1992).

All-in-One Business Planner by Christopher R. Malburg (Adams Media, 1997).

Business Plans for Dummies by Paul Tiffany and Steven Peterson (Wiley, 2004).

The Business Plan Store offers professional business plan writing and consulting services. You can read their sample business plan at: www.thebusinessplanstore.com/obraez.pdf.

The Business Writing Center offers twenty-eight online courses, writing coaching, and training manuals: www.writingtrainers.com.

You can also find resources at My Own Business: www.myownbusiness.org.

Software for business plans can be found through Business Insight (www.brs-inc.com) and Power Business Plans (www.softkey.com).

CHAPTER 15

Cartoons

Overview

Cartoon writing can be a difficult industry to succeed in. Hopeful cartoon writers are competing with more than just staff writers and other freelancers. They maneuver through the midst of artists as well. Nevertheless, there is a market for the dedicated cartoon writer. After all, humor is always in great demand.

Newspapers and magazines are the two most obvious mediums for cartoon submissions. The vast majority of cartoon writers find themselves catering to this industry. However, the exceptionally determined writer can discover opportunities through a variety of sources.

What It Pays

Single submissions generate a wide range of pay rates. Magazines pay anywhere between $10 a cartoon to as much as $500 or more; the *New Yorker* pays $675 for a single cartoon. The average pay rate is $50 a cartoon. Of course, that amount might have to be divided between the illustrator and the cartoon writer.

If you are submitting your work directly to cartoon artists, they typically pay the writer 25 percent of their profits (once they've sold the piece).

Nuts and Bolts

Cartoon writing can be approached in several ways. First, you can submit captions and ideas to a professional cartoon artist. When artists run out of material, they seek out writers to generate fresh concepts. Some of the most famous cartoonists, including Bob Thaves ("Frank and Ernest") and Bill Hoest ("Agatha Krum"), used the submissions of cartoon writers on a regular basis.

Second, you can use the Internet as a tool for selling your work. Cartoons are increasingly popular on websites. In fact, several cartoonists have made a name for themselves publishing their works solely online. (Check out Debbie Ridpath Ohi's "Inkygirl.")

Third, there are dozens of newspapers and magazines that accept freelance submissions. Several directories that list these companies are available.

Artist's & Graphic Designer's Market is an excellent resource. It does more than just list magazine publishers. It shows the average number of submissions a company receives each year, and how many it typically purchases.

Finally, cartoon writers can advertise their services directly. Local businesses, churches, and other organizations occasionally need cartoons. They are a powerful addition to newsletters, lengthy reports, ads, and presentations. Let local organizations know what you do. You may find markets you never imagined.

What You'll Write

There are three types of cartoons: single panel, comic strips, and political cartoons. The single panel (often referred to as a gag cartoon) is a simple, one frame illustration. Gag cartoons may or may not include a caption. However, the cartoon writer creates both. Captionless cartoons are the writer's humorous ideas portrayed through the drawing. When captions are used, they should be short—one line if possible.

Gag cartoons are usually lighthearted. The writer should be careful with ideas and wording; the population is becoming more easily offended. Each year, fewer and fewer topics are "safe." For this type of cartoon, steer clear of stereotypes, grouping, and potentially offensive materials.

Editorial or political cartoons contain a strong social or political message. The topics addressed in political cartoons are generally less censored than a gag cartoon. The drawings for these cartoons may be far more complex than the single panel. Your caption (if required) should stay brief.

Comic strips are similar to the single panel. Few, if any, newspapers and magazines purchase comic strips. They are generally reserved for in-house or nationally renowned cartoonists. Build your reputation, and the chance to write a weekly or even daily comic strip could be the result.

When you first start out, concentrate on single panel cartoons. They are the most frequently purchased cartoon by magazines, and are the easiest to create. Unless you are contracted to work for a cartoon artist or a business, all your work is done on spec. Single panel cartoon writing is your best bet for success.

What It Takes

An artist-writer is the ideal candidate for cartoon writing. Once there was a clear distinction, but cartoonists now need to be both writer and artist to reap the greatest profits. Not possessing artistic skills doesn't mean you can't develop them. Practice drawing on your own, or find an illustration course.

More and more artists are turning to computer graphics for their illustrations. Try it. But don't lose focus on the writing.

It doesn't take a professionally educated writer to come up with good content. However, coming up with an idea can be difficult, and the writer needs to find sources of inspiration. Of course, a background in satire, voice, and dialogue is helpful. Using hyperbole, situational comedy, a play on words, and other humorous writing techniques offer a pool of ideas to draw from.

Getting Started

As you begin your cartoon writing career, study the work of others. Great cartoons can come from a new twist on an already popular piece. You may want to consider joining a cartooning organization like Cartoon World or the National Cartoonists Society. Once you are ready to give cartoon writing a try, here are some steps to get started:

1. **Write.** Brainstorm a number of ideas. Then write the captions and drawings that should be included in the cartoon. This can be done anywhere and in a brief amount of time.

2. **Research.** Using directories or resource lists, find magazine publishers you'd like to submit your work to. Study the types of cartoons they publish and create something similar. Check their submission guidelines. If you can't find them online, call the company and request them. If you want to submit work to cartoon artists, you can usually find them through online directories. (See the resources below.)

3. **Start a website.** This is a great way to display your cartoons. Making your work available to both view and purchase is important. List all the ways companies can reach you.

4. **Find an artist.** Some companies take written work without the art, but most won't. If you can't produce your own drawings, and you plan to devote some time to cartoon writing, find someone you can collaborate with. Split everything fifty-fifty.

5. **Submit your work.** Follow the company's guidelines. Though you can send several batches of work, don't submit too many at once. The person who reads your work might get bored after a while. Just send your best pieces. Your work should include your contact information, and send a self-addressed stamped envelope (SASE) with your gags. You will not hear from the company without it.

6. **Advertise.** Don't spend very much money, but if there is a free local directory you can put your name in, do it. Put up a few flyers. Offer free cartoons with your name and contact information to local charity groups. And don't be shy about telling people what you do. Referrals are a great way to grow your business.

If you enjoy cartoons and humor, this could be your niche. Cartoon writing can be a great creative outlet. Give it a try. You just might find your cartoon in the next issue of your favorite magazine.

Additional Resources

For periodical directories, try these annuals: *The Standard Periodical Directory* (Oxbridge Communications) and *Artist's & Graphic Designer's Market* (Writer's Digest Books).

You can find cartoon markets at perower.netfirms.com.

For an online directory of freelance artists and gag writers, try Cartoon Crossroads: www.cartooncrossroads.com.

CHAPTER 16

Case Studies

Overview

In marketing, storytelling is a powerful tool for persuading prospects and customers. And there are few techniques more potent and effective than a case study.

We're not talking about a dry, academic document. Rather, case studies—also known as success stories and extended testimonials—relate the experiences of a satisfied customer who has benefited from the product or service you are marketing.

Case studies use a story format to narrate how a problem faced by a company or an individual was solved by using a particular product or service. More than just a story with a happy ending, case studies are high-powered sales collateral. By profiling a wide cross section of customers, case studies deliver information that's relevant to each target audience—and in a way they will relate to it.

What It Pays

Whether you plan to work as a specialist or add case study writing to your toolbox of capabilities, you'll find a vast market that's in constant need of good writers—and willing to pay an attractive wage.

Case studies are among the primary selling tools for lead-generating, business-to-business marketers. Considering that at least 80 percent of these companies need to generate leads on a regular basis, this represents a huge pool of opportunity for copywriters. And nice paychecks, too. In 2007, veteran marketer Chris Marlow surveyed more than three-hundred copywriters who shared their pricing for case studies and other copywriting jobs. In her e-book, *The 2007 Freelance Copywriter Fee & Compensation Survey, Volume 2*, Chris reports that the median price for writing a two-page case study is $751–$800. The highest number of responses (23.8 percent) reported $1,001–$2,000. Forty percent of writers surveyed charged $951–$3,000.

Case studies can range from short one-pagers with simple content to longer (but not too long) ones dealing with complex systems (e.g., relational databases). Fees take into account the amount of time it takes to complete a job.

Nuts and Bolts

Written properly, case studies are an excellent tool for generating leads. Because of their versatility, case studies can be used in nearly every facet of marketing. And they can be targeted at dozens of different market segments or based on industry, demographic, and geography, to name just a few.

What makes case studies so attractive to marketers and consumers alike is that they're based on real-life experiences. Case studies are viewed as credible, third-party endorsements that carry a high degree of believability. That gives case studies a big advantage over traditional advertising, which consumers often view with skepticism.

A survey by Forrester Research shows that 71 percent of buyers base their decisions on trust and believability. Relating your customers' positive experiences with your product is one of the best ways to establish credibility in the marketplace. Giving your customers confidence in what you're offering dramatically increases the likelihood they'll do business with you.

For a typical case study, the customer is interviewed by the writer and quoted about his experience with the product or service and the problems it solved. Rather than delve deeply into technical details, case studies address, in a problem-solution format, how the product or service helped the user improve his business.

An effective case study makes the reader want to learn more about your company. It's a soft-sell proposition designed to compel your prospects to request more detailed information. If you've mirrored the readers' problem successfully, the case study will propel them deeper into the sales funnel and closer to buying.

An average case study is two to three pages, or 750–1,500 words, and written in a style similar to that of a magazine feature article. The intent of a case study is not to present in-depth minutia and analytical data, but to briefly describe how a product or service can effectively address and solve a particular problem.

What You'll Write

Case studies are product success stories. As such, virtually all case studies are written according to the following outline:

1. Who is the customer?

2. What was the problem? How was it hurting the customer's business?

3. What solutions did the customer look at and ultimately reject, and why?

4. Why did the customer choose this product as the solution?

5. Describe the implementation of the product, including any problems and how they were solved.

6. How and where does the customer use the product?

7. What are the results and benefits?

8. Would the customer recommend it to others, and why?

Getting Started

Companies need and want case study writers. The challenge for both is finding each other—matching your skills with their needs. It's an involved, on-going, and often frustrating process. But in the end, it pays off.

Surprisingly, many copywriters don't even include case studies among their services. They'll list everything from sales letters to brochures to web pages, but not case studies. So, if you want to break into the field of case study writing, tell your copywriting prospects and clients that you write case studies. Better yet, recommend they incorporate case studies into their marketing. Highlight your case study writing capabilities on all your self-promotional collateral—in your sales letters, on your website, on your business cards. And make sure to mention case studies during each consultation with a client.

You can also multiply your earnings on one case study project by offering to write and revise it to fit different formats. Suggest to your client all the different ways in which a case study can be repurposed. Not only will the client get more bang for their marketing buck, but you'll get more bucks as well.

For example, once your case study is submitted, offer to write a press release on it for your client (an additional $500). Or turn it into an advertisement (another $950). Depending on the client's marketing needs and budget, you can turn a single case study into multiple opportunities for income. It seems like elementary marketing, but if you neglect to raise the issue with clients, they may simply assume you don't write case studies and are likely to look elsewhere.

A little research goes a long way when scouring the landscape for potential clients. You may want to concentrate on local clients, or stick with a particular industry and go nationwide in your search. Or a combination of both.

Whatever direction you go, start with the company's website. Familiarize yourself with what they do and how they do it. You'll come across as well informed when you contact the company, and that always makes a good first impression. Plus, looking through the site gives you a good idea if the company is a candidate for your writing services. If they feature a case study library with sharply written stories, it's obvious they're on the ball and have a solid plan in place—and case studies are integral to their marketing. Contact them to see whether they need additional writing help for more case studies. You are much more likely to get a case study writing assignment by approaching firms that regularly do case studies than by going to companies and trying to convince them they should be doing case studies.

Additional Resources

The Perfect Sales Piece by Robert Bly (Wiley, 1994).
The White Paper Marketing Handbook by Robert Bly (Thomson, 2006).

CHAPTER 17

Catalog Copywriting

Overview

Catalogs are sales tools, designed to generate either leads (as is the case with many industrial, business-to-business, and point-of-sale catalogs) or direct sales (as is the case with mail-order catalogs for consumers). Catalog writing is coming into its own as a profitable niche for writers who are building their portfolios.

This genre entails writing short, concise but colorful sentences and phrases that entice a reader to want the product. The product promises to solve a problem the reader has or satisfy a desire.

Catalogs are popular because they almost always offer products that you do not easily find on the market, in a regular store, or at a shopping mall. While a mall store can satisfy the basics, a catalog can detail many more additional products within a genre than would be found in a physical store.

The writer must show how beneficial the product is for the reader and show why the reader's life will be greatly enhanced when the product is purchased. The writer shows solutions that make life easier, and the solution is presented in such a manner that the reader feels the message was written just for him.

What It Pays

Writing catalog copy can be priced two ways, according to *2008 Writer's Market*. You can write copy for $25–$100 an hour or for $25–$350 an item. If you are a new writer, the publication will most likely set its price. When you can show that your copy sells product, then you can charge the higher end of the above fees or set your own pricing, plus request royalties.

Nuts and Bolts

Everything you write will be geared to selling, whether you are writing the front-page copy or one of the short item pieces. There should not be one wasted word—each word is part of the message to persuade the reader to buy the solution presented. You may also write the letter from the publisher or the president of the company. These letters are usually found within the first three to five pages of the catalog.

Additionally, while specifications of a product might be important for some business or manufacturer's catalogs, avoid too much tech talk, and stick with more descriptive words. Your writing tone should be friendly and conversational unless the client really wants more technical language. In that case, have a knowledgeable contact that can review your work for technical accuracy.

If your catalog copy will be posted online, incorporate the appropriate keywords into your headline and body copy. You can ask the client for a list of keywords or search for them online using a tool like www.worktracker.com. As always, the message should be geared to the reader.

What You'll Write

You write copy for each product in the client's catalog and most likely the letter from the company president, as well as the order form and front cover. You may be asked to write direct mail and advertising pieces promoting the catalog.

Writing the catalog can lead to other opportunities with the client. For instance, your client may be selling garden tilling equipment in different sizes. A video might be sent to vendors showing what each size tiller is capable of doing. You can write the script for that since you already wrote the catalog pieces and know the products. Ideally, the client will be thinking ahead to such opportunities, but chances are you will need to quiz your client about them. Make suggestions and, if you have time, provide samples to persuade your client of other methods of marketing and selling. Ultimately, catalog writing is a great way to get in the door, which may lead to other opportunities that you can suggest to the client.

What It Takes

To get into catalog copywriting, start by studying as many catalogs as you can. Study different types to see what areas or categories you may want to pursue. Visit different websites and sign up for catalogs to be sent to you. Consider renting a post-office box where you can pick up such materials, as your regular mailbox may suddenly get out of hand with tons of catalogs coming your way.

There are now some excellent courses you can take to learn how to write copy for catalogs. Try American Writers & Artists (www.awaionline. com), and sign up for their latest catalog copywriting program. Or search online for catalog copywriting to see what books and courses are available on the market.

Getting Started

After reviewing a number of catalogs and knowing what niches you want to pursue, start a list of potential clients to contact. Draw up your letter of introduction and line up your work samples. A great way to build samples is to take a few catalogs, select products from each, and create your own version to see if you can do better. Showing a before-and-after scenario is one way to show what you can do. Try to build samples in several areas, which allows you to expand your contact fields and genres.

If you take a copywriting program, you will create a sample portfolio. These programs can also provide mentors for your work who review what you've done and show you the best you can do. There is also a chance your mentors may ask you to assist in a few paying projects.

Even after you start sending samples to clients, keep creating more, as it keeps you in practice and allows you to build your portfolio, especially if you can develop more and more different genres.

Additional Resources

Catalog Copy That Sizzles by Herschel Gordon Lewis (NTC, 2000).

The Catalog Strategist's Toolkit by Katie Muldoon (Racom Communications, 2006).

Creating a Profitable Catalog by Jack Schmid (NTC, 2000).

How to Create Successful Catalogs by Maxwell Sroge (NTC, 1995).

At American Writers & Artists Inc. check out the course called Secrets of Writing for the Catalog Market: www.awaionline.com.

Multichannel Merchant: www.multichannelmerchant.com.

My report on catalog copywriting is called *World's Best-Kept Catalog Copywriting Secrets*, which can be found on my site (www.bly.com) on the Reports page.

At Marcia Yudkin's website you can find information on copywriting as well as a link to catalog writing: www.yudkin.com/catalog.htm. Also, check out her manual *73 Ways to Describe a Widget: Never Be Brain Dead Again When Having to Write Catalog Copy or Sales Material.*

CHAPTER 18

Children's Books

Overview

Americans spend more than $3 billion on children's books annually, and of course Harry Potter has helped to create a whole new generation of eager children's book readers. "It's a wonderful time to be writing for children," said Maria Witte, executive editor for *You Can Write for Children* (from *Writer's Digest* magazine), in a recent editor's letter.

Children's book sales are expected to increase to $4.3 billion a year, according to the Simba Information Report, "Children's Publishing Market Forecast 2008." The main reason for the resurgence in children's book publishing, said Witte, is the popularity of books written by notable children's writers. Even R. L. Stine, after taking an eight-year break from writing children's books, is returning to the genre with new *Goosebumps* novels.

Interest in children's picture books and rhyming books are once again on the rise, after a severe slump that began in the late 1990s. The teen market is also thriving, with sales continuing to grow every year. In 2002 alone, more than forty million teen series books were sold in the United States—an increase of more than six million books in just two years.

What It Pays

Advances for first-time children's book authors are extremely modest. According to the Society of Children's Book Writers & Illustrators (SCBWI), a typical advance for a thirty-two-page picture book might be $8,000–$12,000, which you as the writer would have to split with the illustrator. For an easy reader, the advance for a first-time author is $5,000–$8,000 against net royalties of 7–10 percent.

Nuts and Bolts

Before setting pen to paper (or your fingers to the keyboard), ask yourself: "Do I really have what it takes to write for children?" Not all writers do. Being a good or even a great writer doesn't necessarily mean you can write for children. Some of the most talented writers among us lack the most important and vital aspect needed to write stories children will love—the ability to know how a child's mind works and to think like them.

For those who don't believe that's an essential aspect of writing for children, consider beloved children's book writer Paula Danzinger. Known for her wacky outfits, zany personality, and unique ability to connect with kids in a way few adults ever can, Danzinger took her passion for storytelling, her love for children, and her unique ability to relate to them completely on their own level, and turned it into a long-lasting career spanning nearly three dozen books.

Following her death in 2004, Danzinger's editor of fifteen years at Putnam, Margaret Fritz, described her talent this way: "Paula loved her young audience and they loved her back because she was right there with them...she was one of them...Paula had a direct line into kids' hearts and funny bones."

Those aren't words you'll hear about just any writer. Those are the words describing a *children's writer.* Most struggling children's writers may never be able to connect with their readers in the way Danzinger did, though that doesn't mean you won't succeed.

What we can learn from authors such as Danzinger is the importance of staying up to date in the world of kid-think and kid-speak, and trying to remember what it felt like to be a kid in order to create characters that talk, feel, and act in the same ways as the children reading the books. Kids need to connect with the characters, or they'll quickly lose interest.

Thinking like a kid again isn't always easy. People like Danzinger may make it look natural, but it can be hard work. Children aren't just miniature adults. They can be unpredictable. They can be overly dramatic. They can be extremely honest and frustrating in their actions and attitudes. But they always have a reason for what they do, say, and feel, even if it makes little sense to the adults in their lives.

What You'll Write

The main decision every children's writer must eventually face is what age group to write for. It would be nice to cross over to all age groups, but most writers find it difficult. It takes time and experience to learn the characteristics of a specific age group, and writing for one, then another, usually doesn't work well.

Of course, some prolific and long-standing writers such as Judy Blume have managed to follow their readership as they grow older. But even she didn't cross over until she was well established within the field and had a solid readership that wanted to continue reading what she had to say, even though they had grown past her previous books.

Here is a comprehensive guide of the main age categories that publishers seek, and the types of books they want and need according to *Children's Writer's & Illustrator's Market* and Lee Wyndham's popular guide, *Writing for Children & Teenagers.* Keep in mind that while the ages listed within each group are typical for that readership, some categories may overlap due to differences in reading levels and grade levels.

- **Picture books.** The total word count of a picture book, according to Children's Book Press submission guidelines, is 750–1,000, with some publishers wanting less than six hundred and others allowing up to two-thousand words for higher quality manuscripts.

- **Beginning readers.** Nearly half of all five- to seven-year-olds are considered high frequency readers, taking nearly an hour every day to read independently, according to the Kids & Family Reading Report released by Scholastic. Beginning readers like to read primarily for fun, the report shows, with both fiction and nonfiction titles chosen among this age group.

First-word books for kindergartners may have fewer than one-hundred words for the entire book; more comprehensive books for first and second graders, such as the popular Barbara Parks series, *Junie B. Jones,* and even Mary Pope Osborne's *Magic Tree House* series, may contain as many as two-thousand words.

Genres and topics may include fiction, nonfiction, biography, science, and even history. The important thing to remember when writing for this age group is to offer "simple structure, simple word choice, and logical organization," according to senior editor Sarah L. Schuette for Capstone Press, while still managing to offer an exciting story that grabs children's attention from the first sentence.

Chapter Books and Middle Readers. With demand increasing for the eight- to twelve-year-old reading group, middle readers are finding more and more titles available in both fiction and nonfiction. Able to handle tougher vocabularies, lengthier books, and more complicated subject matter, the range of topics and styles available to middle reader writers is plentiful as you can see from these recent releases: *Grandfather's Dance* (historical fiction), *Toys Go Out* (fantasy), *The Year of the Dog* (contemporary), and *The Catlady* (humor).

Usually running 2,500–4,000 words, chapter books still provide the reader with shorter, easier to manage sentences and vocabularies, vivid descriptions and interesting plots, but stretch the child's world and imagination even further through more thought-provoking and expansive story lines. Chapter books give new writers an opportunity to tackle important issues with young elementary students in an interesting and provocative way.

Young Adult. The teen audience is getting younger all the time. As older teens turn to more sophisticated adult books for their reading enjoyment, the young adult market is now aimed at the twelve- to sixteen-year-old reader, with an emphasis on thirteen- to fifteen-year-olds.

What It Takes

Getting to know children better is an important aspect to learning how to write books they'll love to read. A love for learning new things is also important, because kids are all about experiencing new things. That's why they read. Within the pages of their favorite books, they can try new things (sometimes even dangerous things they either couldn't or wouldn't experience otherwise), meet new friends, live in new places, and experience everything they are too shy, scared, or unable to try any other way.

Getting Started

Once you've chosen an appropriate age group to target, decide on the type of story (or genre) you'd like to focus on. First-time writers often find that a story just "comes to them," and that's fine. As long as it's a good story, with a solid plot and strong characters, it doesn't matter what the genre is. When it comes time to sell it, you'll need an idea of your target audience to pitch it to an editor.

One thing that often scares new writers away from choosing a genre is fear of being pegged as a certain type of writer for the length of their career. True, if you're good at writing a specific style or tone of book, your readers will come to expect that, but that doesn't mean that you can't ever try new types of books and writing styles.

Judy Blume is a great example. She may be one of the most prolific children's writers of our generation, having written dozens of books for nearly every age level, including adults. Her sometimes quirky, sometimes serious, and always thought-provoking prose has won awards in fiction, nonfiction, and even adult literature. She's an example that screams: write what you want (as long as it's good), and it'll find a home.

Choosing a genre and sticking to it (at least in the beginning) is a great way to hone your skills and build your readership, while discovering what style of writing you're really good at and enjoy the most.

Additional Resources

Society of Children's Book Writers & Illustrators is a major organization for children's writers of all skill levels: www.scbwi.org.

CHAPTER 19

Christian Writing

Overview

The Christian marketplace is one of the hottest areas of publishing in the United States—a $7.5 billion market, with 5,600 new titles published annually.

Many people know the Bible is a bestselling book, yet it doesn't appear on any of the regular bestseller lists. As Daniel Radosh wrote in the *New Yorker* magazine, "The familiar observation that the Bible is the bestselling book of all time obscures a more startling fact: the Bible is the bestselling book of the year, every year. Calculating how many Bibles are sold in the United States is a virtually impossible task, but a conservative estimate is that in 2005 Americans purchased some twenty-five million Bibles—twice as many as the most recent *Harry Potter* book. The amount spent annually on Bibles has been put at more than half a billion dollars."

What It Pays

The Christian market pays fees and advances somewhat below the general market for articles and books. However, a number of Christian books have hit the bestseller lists to earn their authors millions. For instance, since the *Left Behind* series of novels by Tim LaHaye and Jerry B. Jenkins launched in 1995, they have sold more than sixty million copies. Shirley Dobson, wife of Dr. James Dobson at Focus on the Family, asked Bruce Wilkinson to speak at the National Prayer Breakfast in Washington D.C. Bruce talked with his publisher at Multnomah about making a little hardcover book on Jabez to give as gifts to the politicians. They created *The Prayer of Jabez*. It took off like wildfire. In 2000, the book sold eight million copies and *Publishers Weekly* called it the fastest selling nonfiction hardcover in history.

This record was short-lived, because a few years later another book eclipsed it. In 2003, Zondervan, a division of HarperCollins, published *The Purpose Driven Life* by Rick Warren. In four years, this book has sold more than thirty million copies worldwide and is now the bestselling nonfiction hardback in history. Other books like *Your Best Life Now* by Joel Osteen have also garnered millions of sales.

Nuts and Bolts

You do not have to be a Christian to write for the Christian market, though you'd enjoy it more and do it better if you were. All authors writing for the Christian market must be familiar with the basic tenets of Christian belief. For instance, Christians believe in the divine inspiration and consequent authority of the whole canonical scripture. Another key doctrine of Christianity relates to the Trinity or that God is in three persons: Father, Son, and Holy Spirit.

What You'll Write

Christian writing can take hundreds of different directions. The following is a partial list of possibilities. Note the majority of these relate to magazine writing. Many people want to write books and simply ignore the magazine market. The magazine market is far easier for the beginning writer and will reach more people. If you're stalled with your writing, consider a new direction.

- Personal experience articles
- Biographical profiles or personality profiles
- Service articles: report on a new product or service
- As-told-to articles: write the experience of someone else
- Humor articles or fillers
- Fillers
- Opinion articles
- Book reviews
- Poetry
- How-to
- Plays for your church
- Puzzles
- Short stories are often used in Sunday school take-home papers
- Children's writing (consider different age groups)
- Devotional writing
- Church news stories for your local church or newspaper
- Tracts—pamphlets with religious and inspirational messages, stories, and advice.
- Seasonal material (Easter, Father's Day, Mother's Day, Thanksgiving, Christmas)

- Bible study material
- Teaching curriculum

According to Sally E. Stuart's *Christian Writers' Market Guide 2007*, there are 740 magazines and 86 are new magazines. The top 15 adult magazines and their circulations include:

- *Guideposts,* 3 million
- *Columbia,* 1.6 million
- *Focus on the Family,* 1.5 million
- *Stewardship,* 1 million
- *Decision,* 850,000
- *Angels on Earth,* 550,000
- *Marion Helpers,* 500,000
- *Spirituality for Today,* 495,000
- *Catholic Digest,* 400,000
- *Catholic Yearbook,* 400,000
- *Positive Thinking,* 400,000
- *St. Anthony Messenger,* 324,000
- *Mature Living,* 318,000
- *Charisma,* 250,000
- *Power for Living,* 250,000

Many of the low-paying, small circulation publications in the Christian marketplace don't require a query or pitch letter. These publications prefer to see the entire manuscript instead of a pitch. In these situations, the writer has to craft the entire article for the publication (write on spec).

What It Takes

When you send a query to the magazine editor, no one asks to see your Christian membership card. While you don't have to be a Christian to write for the Christian marketplace, you do have to understand the basics of this market.

First, as noted earlier, Christians assume the Bible is true and factual, for example, God created the world in seven days. While you may not write about these facts in your article or book, you have to write with the under-standing that it is true. If you don't believe it, then make sure this perspec-tive doesn't show up in your writing. It leads to rejection.

Also you have to understand the overall purpose of a particular maga-zine. "For a couple of years, I was the associate editor at *Decision* magazine, the official publication of the Billy Graham Evangelistic Association," says Christian literary agent Terry Whalin. "One of our key purposes was to en-courage Christians and help them grow in their faith. Each of the articles were written in the first person and focused on some aspect of the Christian life." Today the focus of *Decision* has changed: the magazine is much more of an organizational publication, and each article has to be tied to a current activity in the Billy Graham organization.

In many ways, the Christian market is more open to new writers than the general marketplace. You'll have a much easier time getting published in a magazine like *Today's Christian* or *Marriage Partnership* or the *Evangel* as opposed to *Family Circle* or *Good Housekeeping* or *Woman's Day*. The market isn't as exacting or as highly demanding as the general market magazines, though it is looking for and expecting excellence. If you study the publica-tions and write the type of material the editor needs, your query letter will stand out—and you will be published.

Getting Started

Many people think they will start with a book. They attend writers confer-ences because they have written a novel or a nonfiction book. How many copies does the average book have to sell to be considered a solid performer? To the surprise of many people, most books sell ten thousand copies or less. According to the *Christian Writers' Market Guide 2007*, "The average first print-ing of a book for a new author is just under 4,600 books." Many people are surprised at these small numbers.

You reach many more people with a magazine article than with a book. A 1,500-word magazine article is much easier to write than a 50,000-word book, which is a common length for adult nonfiction. When Terry Whalin was associate editor at *Decision*, each month they printed 1.8 million copies. He says, "By far, the largest audience that I've ever reached has come from my magazine articles. I would encourage you to write for the magazine market. Besides reaching a large audience, you are also building valuable publishing experience, which can help you land a book deal. For five years, I worked as a book acquisitions editor...I was the author's advocate to try and get them a publishing deal. If the author had any publishing experience, it was something in their favor." Why? Anyone who has been published in a magazine has shown a degree of professionalism. You understand writing to a particular length and a particular audience. In some cases, because you've written for a magazine, you have a better understanding of the editorial process. You've probably been asked to revise, have some experience working with editors, and understand the editor is there to improve your work and not act as your adversary.

Additional Resources

There are several conferences focused on Christian writing, including the Blue Ridge Mountains Christian Writers Conference (www.lifeway. com/christianwriters), the Florida Christian Writers Conference (www. flwriters.org), and Mount Hermon Christian Writers Conference (www. mounthermon.org/writers).

CHAPTER 20

College Essays

Overview

There are millions of U.S. college students, and all of them write the occasional essay or term paper. Many need help writing it or have trouble meeting deadlines. That's when they turn to ghostwriters for help.

In the movie *Back to School*, Rodney Dangerfield, a millionaire who enrolls in college, has to write a term paper on Kurt Vonnegut—and promptly hires Kurt Vonnegut to ghost it for him (when Vonnegut's paper receives a B, he refuses to pay the bill). In Robert Silverberg's classic science fiction novel *Dying Inside*, the main character is a telepath who supports himself by ghostwriting term papers.

In real life, there are hundreds of essay writing firms, and possibly hundreds more independent freelance ghostwriters ready to offer their writing expertise when a time-strapped student needs an essay on the use of symbols in *Moby Dick* or bullfighting as a metaphor in Ernest Hemingway's *The Sun Also Rises* within forty-eight hours. If you like the academic style of writing, and enjoy reading and writing about literature or other subjects, you can help college students succeed and get paid to ghostwrite college essays. Whether you're personally comfortable doing so is a matter for you to decide. Some students want help with writing their college essays. Some parents hire writers to essentially write the whole application essay for them. As for term papers, it's okay for a tutor or consultant to look over the student's work, suggest sources, and help them cite their sources correctly so that they don't get accused of plagiarism. But colleges can expel students who hand in ghostwritten term papers as their own work.

What It Pays

College essay ghostwriters can make anywhere from $5–$10 per page. Many essay companies charge a flat fee of $14.95–$40, depending on how quickly the student needs the completed paper and the degree level for which the paper is meant. Some ghostwriters sell the same papers again and again, though the practice is considered fraud by some. Students who purchase such a paper can get in trouble for plagiarism.

Nuts and Bolts

Most academic essays and term papers follow the same basic structure: a title, an introductory paragraph of three to five sentences detailing the thesis, or what the paper is about, the body, a closing paragraph that reiterates what was just discussed, and a works cited page. References are cited in accordance with a particular style guide, discussed later in this chapter.

Legally, ghostwriting college essays isn't considered academic fraud. The fraud only occurs when the student submits the purchased paper as his own, which essay services advise against.

Universities have developed ways to fight this type of fraud, such as having professors require students to submit their papers electronically, so that they can be checked against a database of known plagiarized papers. Instructors who suspect a student of turning in someone else's work can also quiz the student on the paper's content. If they are unfamiliar with their own paper, they can be accused of academic fraud.

Some ghostwriting services knowingly sell the same papers over and over again, and don't worry about what the student does with them once they are sold. These companies are known as essay mills, a derogatory term, and are considered disreputable. Many individual ghostwriters, as well as ghostwriting companies, work hard to stay above board by guaranteeing that each paper produced for a student is completely original and do not sell the same paper twice. Others overcome this by offering only to review completed papers and help students with citations and final edits. There are a lot of disreputable companies out there, and you must decide what you will and will not do for the ghostwriting companies and students who hire you.

What You'll Write

You may write college entrance essays, book reviews, theses and term papers, and, if you have the qualifications, doctoral dissertations. Subjects can include everything from astrophysics to women's studies.

Some ghostwriters offer additional services including résumé and curriculum vitae (CV) writing, as well as editing and proofreading services. You can also conduct essay reviews, in which you simply look over a student's completed paper, suggesting sources and making sure their sources are cited properly.

What It Takes

Since you're writing and assisting with college-level work, you need at least a bachelor's degree in English or the subject you're writing about. In order to help students at a master's level, you need a master's degree.

You also need to be both familiar with Modern Language Association (MLA) style and have a copy of the latest MLA style guide on hand. If you're qualified to write about history- or psychology-related subjects, you'll need to know Chicago style or American Psychological Association (APA) style. Staying up to date on these styles is important, especially all the ways in which electronic information on websites and other media is cited in academic papers.

Getting Started

Dust off those old college essays, and start with sites like Elance (elance.com) and Freelancewritingjobs.com to find students who need papers written. Set up a simple website and market yourself as a ghostwriter, and promote yourself in blogs and forums where college students hang out online. You can even establish yourself as a term paper writing expert by writing and posting articles online about how to write college papers, such as rules for proper grammar and formatting and citation guidelines.

You can also offer your services to essay ghostwriting companies. Visit their websites and see if they hire ghostwriters. Tell them your qualifications, send a few samples, and you'll probably get assignments.

Additional Resources

Academia Research: www.academia-research.com.
American Psychological Association: apastyle.apa.org.
Buylance: www.buylance.com.
The Chicago Manual of Style: www.chicagomanualofstyle.org/contents.html.
Essaywriters.net: www.essaywriters.net.
eSWO: www.eswo.net.
Go Freelance: www.gofreelance.com.
Modern Language Association: www.mla.org.
Rent a Ghostwriter: www.rentaghostwriter.com.

CHAPTER 21

Coloring Books

Overview

Coloring books are usually the first interactive books children use. While some are created after children's movie characters and stories, others are developed to teach young children how to read, spell, and do math.

Children can also use coloring books to learn how to draw and use colors in different combinations. This provides a child an introduction to artistic creativity. Several sites like www.crayola.com also provide a child a chance to create one's own coloring picture that can be printed for coloring or can be colored online using an interactive pallet of crayons.

Writing text for coloring books requires writing the fewest possible words while still holding a child's interest. The writing must refer 100 percent to the picture, yet barely be noticeable in the overall view.

The age group targeted by the coloring book determines the word count. For the youngest just learning to read, single words such as "rabbit," along with a colorable picture of a rabbit, goes a long way in teaching a youngster how to read. For the next level of reader, you can start writing phrases that tell a story about the picture of the rabbit, like "Peter Rabbit eats a carrot."

To educate young children about fire ants, Ortho has produced a coloring book that depicts ants and parts of ants, like the antenna, head, stinger, and legs. Along with the labels, there are descriptions of what the ant uses those parts for. Later, there are puzzles that pertain to ants and playing outside. It is a clever piece of interactive advertising aimed at both the parents and the children, and includes safety notes to parents about ant stings and how to safely use Ortho products.

Coloring books can also help children develop their motor skills and retrain them after they have been in accidents or through serious illnesses. By creating books that depict an image along with a corresponding word or phrase, a counselor can pose questions to the child that requires him to select another image and word, or phrase, that answers the question.

What It Pays

Writing coloring books is not lucrative unless you are well known in a certain area such as Hollywood. Ideally, you team up with an illustrator to do a book and then present it to a publishing company. When you can present a complete package to an editor, it is then easier to sell the project, especially if it fits a current market need. That is also why it is important to do your own market research before creating your book, as you want your subject matter to be timely.

You can also query an editor to find out if writers are needed for any current coloring book projects. Your initial contract might be for an advance against sales, but if you are not well known, then it may not be a substantial amount.

Nuts and Bolts

If you move into this market, you must have the ability to connect with children. As there is usually very little writing on each page, an editor may pay you by the word or by the page, and throw in royalties. There are no wasted words in a coloring book, as you will be writing maybe one to ten words per page, depending on the target age group.

You can always ask a group of children to test out your coloring pages to see how they react to them. Check out your neighbors, church and Sunday school, and local elementary school, and see if they are willing to test your pages.

What You'll Write

You write all captions for each illustration in a coloring book. If you are just writing for a coloring book but have no illustrations to show, then you may also write a summary of the story that provides more background than is given within the captions. Additionally, you can also write any promotional pieces to help sell the package, not only to an editor, but to help promote and sell the book in stores and online.

What It Takes

Write your story using descriptive words. Practice conveying a lot with fewer words. Use your dictionary and thesaurus, and most of all, study the coloring books out there on the market.

Think of new ways to do a coloring book that helps children learn and also develop their imagination. The more you can make your project stand out from the crowd because it is unique, the more likely you can sell it to an editor and the public.

Getting Started

Start by visiting local bookstores to see what they carry on the shelves and also talking to the sales people who can give you a good idea of what's selling the most. Not only can you find out which coloring books are selling, but also what children are interested in the most. Build your books on subjects likely to catch their interest.

Search online for "writing coloring books," and explore the different sites that promote interactive coloring books as opposed to the traditional hardcopy. Having an online site for coloring books or pages may provide a venue for creating a paying subscription membership offering different activities and products. You must ensure your membership area is safe for kids and that the parents trust you with their children's well being.

Additional Resources

Writing Children's Books for Dummies by Lisa Buccieri and Peter Economy (Wiley, 2005). Includes information on writing coloring books.

Doodles by Taro Gomi (Chronicle Books, 2006). A great example of a coloring book that is also instructive.

Beautiful Doodles by Nellie Ryan (Michael O'Mara Books, 2007). Another great example of a coloring book that offers additional drawing creativity as well as coloring.

Crayola's website for online coloring pages is www.crayola.com. You can also find information about the Crayola magazine for kids.

Mimi Bee is a good site to review what is appropriate for kids: www.mimibee.com.

Creativity Portal is a great site for kids' activities: www.creativity-portal.com/becreative/activities.

CHAPTER 22

Comic Books

Overview

Comic books have been around for decades, and are read by millions of people young and old. Many of the medium's most famous characters are now household names, the subjects of blockbuster movies and TV series, their faces emblazoned on everything from T-shirts to bed sheets.

Comic books hold an iconic place in American culture, and superheroes teach us about good and evil. From Spider-Man we learned that with great power comes great responsibility, and from Superman we learned to always seek truth, justice, and the American way. Comics are one of the few truly American art forms, even though their tales of powerful beings mirror the stories of earlier cultures, like those of Hercules, Gilgamesh, and Beowulf.

In this time of uncertainty and untrustworthy athletes, politicians, and other celebrities, people turn to comics for larger-than-life people who they can still count on to save the day, to never falter, and to always fight the good fight. If you love comics, you can make your mark on the field by writing new comic book stories for pay.

What It Pays

There are three basic pay structures in comic book creation, depending on the publisher who gives you the assignment. There's a fee per page, which is a flat fee that is usually a royalty or an advance against royalties (though few comics ever pay any royalties), a flat fee per issue, or a profit split, in which the net profits are split between the publisher and the creator(s).

Nuts and Bolts

The creation process for comics is generally handled in one of two ways. In one method, the writer writes the basic outline of a plot, and then hands it off to the artist, who draws the story before the writer adds dialogue. This method of collaboration has been dubbed the "Marvel Way," because it was developed by Stan Lee and Jack Kirby at Marvel Comics.

In the second method, the writer writes a full script, complete with guidelines for the artist, such as how many panels per page, details on point of view, what the characters are doing, much like a screenplay. Then the artist takes the script and produces the artwork and hands it back to the writer to enter dialogue text into the word balloons, as well as any narration.

Both methods have advantages and drawbacks, depending on who you talk to. The "Marvel Way" offers the most collaboration between the writer and artist, but the writer may be surprised by what the artist hands back, and may not like the interpretation. The writer might also have to rewrite some of the dialogue to fit into the word balloons the artist drew. A long working relationship and a good rapport with an artist you trust, who knows what you're thinking, are the keys to making this procedure work for you. Depending on whom you work with, you will probably end up using both methods.

What You'll Write

Comic books are about more than superheroes, and you'll find virtually every type of story: biographies, detective, horror, mystery, and science fiction, even adaptations of classic stories from literature and the latest motion pictures. You can write the adventures of popular characters like Batman and Iron Man, or create your own character.

Within these genres, you might be called upon to write anything from a story spanning only one issue that isn't part of a series, called a one-shot, to a monthly series, to a large graphic novel. You might also write a full script, or only a barebones plot that will be scripted by another writer.

What It Takes

The comic book is a visual medium, so you need to visualize what your story should look like on the page. Also, comic book editors look for the proven ability to tell a story, so if you've written and published any fiction, say so.

Also, comics are created largely by committee, so you must work well with the artist, editor, and other creative staff, under tight deadlines. Everyone involved likely has several issues of different books they are working on at any given time, and the writer may have scripts, plot summaries, and finished artwork in various stages of completion. So organization and time management skills are very important.

Getting Started

The traditional route is to write a script, then look up the submission guidelines for the companies you want to write for. Some accept unsolicited submissions, while a few, like DC, prefer to meet potential writers and artists at one of the major comic book conventions for a portfolio review. If that's what it takes for a chance to write for your favorite characters, traveling to a convention to meet the editors is well worth it.

An even better way to get your foot in the door is to create your own comic book. This can be done easily these days, thanks to the Internet and print-on-demand publishing. If you can't draw, search the Internet for comic book artists looking for writers.

Put your comic together, print a few copies in color or black and white (black and white is cheaper, and both are acceptable), and go to a large comic book convention where you know editors are on hand to review your work. You can also take it a step further by contacting Diamond Comics Distributors (www.diamondcomics.com) to see if they will distribute your comic.

Additional Resources

Dark Horse: www.darkhorse.com/company/guidelines.php.

DC Comics: www.dccomics.com/about/?action=submissions.

You can find artists looking for writers at www.digitalwebbing.com.

Marvel: www.marvel.com/company/index.htm?sub=submissions_current. htm.

Major comic book conventions include San Diego Comic Con (www. comic-con.org) and Wizard World Chicago (www.wizardworld.com/ chicago.html).

Write Now! focuses on the art and craft of comic book storytelling: www. twomorrows.com.

CHAPTER 23

Cookbooks and Recipes

Overview

Writing cookbooks might not make you a whole lot of money, but if you love to cook, then you will probably enjoy writing all your recipes down into one collection. Recipes are a window into different cultures and family heritages.

Readers can learn a lot about a culture by studying cookbooks because there is always more information in such a book than just the recipe. There should be a section on appropriate cookware, instructions on how to prepare and use each piece of cookware, a section on traditionally used spices and what foods they are used with, how sauces are made, and so on.

A good example of a well-defined cookbook is Diana Kennedy's *The Art of Mexican Cooking*. Now in a new edition from the original 1989 version, Kennedy's cookbook is considered the top of the line for Mexican cooking and information. Not only does she give a history of a particular recipe, but she also, on one page, sets a scene of a Mexican street corner at sunset and the smells of evening food being prepared such as *antojtos*, known as "little whims," snacks made of corn tortilla dough that can be filled with any number of goodies.

With that example, decide if your strength is in cooking but perhaps not in writing, which means you might want to hire a ghostwriter to help you put it all together. A good cookbook represents not only the texture, smells, and taste sensations of the food, but brings those aspects to life for the reader and new cook. If you do not have a talent for descriptive writing, then leave it to someone who can do that for you. There are tons of cookbooks out there and yours needs to be distinctive, informative, and fun to read.

What It Pays

You can write articles about food for many different magazines. *Bon Appétit* is a well-known publication for the upper class who dine out often and worldwide. *2008 Writer's Market* shows that they accept about fifty manuscripts per year and pay from $100 up. You need to query first.

Another magazine, *Gourmet*, also hires writers and pays expenses. Again, you need to query. Article length can be 200–3,000 words. Be warned: it's rough to break into writing for the food magazines without considerable experience either as a chef, professional cook, restauranteur, or food writer. You might start with *Taste of Home* or *Cook's County*, two magazines more open to reader-generated recipes.

Nuts and Bolts

Aside from being a good storyteller of recipes, you must also give background information on ingredients, types of food used, where they are grown or cultivated, and how foods are cooked and why.

Be mindful that you cannot copy recipes from another publication, but you can rework a published recipe to be your own. Say you have a recipe to bake chicken in the oven for twenty-five minutes at 300°F using paprika, cumin, and a touch of garlic. Sally's recipe calls for fifteen minutes at 350°F and ¼ teaspoon of paprika, but you use ½ teaspoon plus you have added in cardamom seeds, ginger, black pepper, and made a tomato sauce that goes over the chicken. That would be enough difference to say this recipe was yours, but to be safe, you can always reference where you found the original version.

What You'll Write

There are the recipes themselves, as well as stories about the spices, vegetables, and any foods or produce that are grown in certain areas. Historical background is always interesting to most cookbook readers, as recipes reflect cultural heritage. "Throughout human history, people have paid attention to what they eat," says Daphne Derven, director of the American Center for Wine, Food, and the Arts. "Food is a necessity, but also something we choose to devote an extraordinary amount of care and thought to. It's part of who we are."

You can also write teaser articles for magazines that talk about your upcoming book by referring to a particular recipe and how it came into being. You could sell a story to *Organic Gardening* magazine about the tomatoes you grow for a recipe for an Italian pasta dish.

What It Takes

You need to be descriptive in your writing to keep your reader's attention. Write your book using as many of the senses as possible. Describe the wonderful heady smell of garlic. Or perhaps the musky smell of cilantro. Or the slight bitterness of ginger root. Make the reader smell and taste what you have smelled and tasted. You have to sell your recipes to the reader and chances are they will sit down and read your book first, at a store, before buying.

Getting Started

If you have a favorite type of cooking, then look at all the cookbooks on the market to see what's out there and how you can make yours stand out from those already published. Make a list of publishers who have put out books like the one you plan to write, and research the editors. Find their submission guidelines on their website.

Start gathering your recipes together, cook each one of them to make sure there are no mistakes (really important!), and then develop more information to accompany each recipe and make it entertaining for the reader and cook.

Additional Resources

Will Write for Food: The Complete Guide to Writing Cookbooks, Restaurant Reviews, Articles, Memoir, Fiction and More by Dianne Jacob (Marlowe, 2005).

The Recipe Writer's Handbook by Barbara Gibbs Ostmann and Jane Baker (Wiley, 2001).

Make Money as a Food Writer in Six Lessons by Pamela White (www.food-writing.com, 2006).

The International Association of Culinary Professionals has a good site, with information about cooking, health benefits for professionals, jobs, etc.: www.iacp.com.

O Chef is a good place for recipes and information: www.ochef.com.

CHAPTER 24

Copyediting

Overview

You may be wondering what copy editors actually do. It's not just a case of checking spelling and basic grammar. The copy editor is expected to make sure the writing is clear and well organized, that it makes sense and is easy to understand, and that it is both accurate and up to date. You also ensure consistency in tone and style, using a style book such as *The Chicago Manual of Style*, *Publication Manual of the American Psychological Association*, or *Scientific Style and Format*. If you are editing news copy, then you use the latest version of the *Associated Press Stylebook and Libel Manual* as well as the *Merriam-Webster Collegiate Dictionary*.

Copy editors use standard symbols within the copy to indicate corrections or to question the writer on word usage or to double-check information that is in question. More substantial queries and comments are typically made on the hard copy manuscript using sticky notes. When editing electronic documents, copy editors use the Track Changes feature to delete, reposition, or add text. When the change must be made by the author, the copy editor notes her comments, recommendations, and instructions using the Comments feature. The copy editor also indicates where there are inconsistencies in information. While copy editors are not responsible for factual errors, they should query a writer if they see something they know is incorrect.

There is nothing romantic about being a copy editor, as you do not write stories yourself; you just correct them. But while copy editing isn't writing, it does offer a view into the publishing world and the publishing process, as well as an opportunity to see how other authors handle certain types of subject matter.

What It Pays

If copyediting a manuscript for a nonfiction book publisher, you might earn $20–$75 per hour, or $1–$6 per page, or $2,000–$5,500 per project, according to *2008 Writer's Market*. If you are editing for a more technical project (such as engineering or medical), you can be paid more, particularly if you are an acknowledged expert in that field.

Nuts and Bolts

Know your grammar and styles guides as best as you can. When in doubt, check your reference books, dictionary, and thesaurus. Reading books from good writers, especially those in your field, really helps you to see with a trained eye when there is something wrong in a preliminary manuscript or story. Know how to do quick online research and support your work, too.

What You'll Write

You don't necessarily write much of anything. But you do make corrections and give directions to the writer on how to make changes to a piece so that it flows better or is more technically correct. You edit the main manuscript, sometimes along with the jacket copy, press release, and any other supplemental documents that accompany the book.

What It Takes

Becoming a grammar expert is a good way to begin. If you haven't studied grammar since elementary school, dig out the latest primer and buy one of the major style guides, such as *The Chicago Manual of Style*. If you do a lot of work for a particular company and they have a stylebook, then learn it inside and out. Consider working as an in-house copy editor for a year or two to gain experience before going freelance. It teaches you the craft and gives you valuable credentials. Your freelance livelihood depends on it.

Getting Started

Start with clients in a genre that you feel comfortable in, so you can get work and samples lined up in your portfolio. Know as much as you can before you move into another genre. Make a list of potential clients, like publishing houses, and send introduction letters notifying them of your availability as a freelance copy editor.

Writing and publishing a free online newsletter on copyediting is a great promotion for building a list of potential copyediting customers. Get potential clients to sign up for your free online newsletter by offering them a bribe, such as a downloadable PDF tip sheet, "Seven Copyediting Secrets."

Additional Resources

The Copyeditor's Handbook, Second Edition by Amy Einsohn (University of California Press, 2006).

Copyediting & Proofreading for Dummies by Suzanne Gilad (Wiley, 2007).

Copyediting by Karen Judd (Crisp Learning, 2001).

The Concise Guide to Copy Editing by Paul LaRocque (Marion Street Press, 2003).

Proofreading, Revising, & Editing (Learning Express, 2003).

The McGraw-Hill Desk Reference for Editors, Writers, and Proofreaders by K. C. Sullivan and Merilee Eggleston (McGraw-Hill, 2006).

CHAPTER 25

Corporate Histories

Overview

A corporate history gives a historical overview of a company and the people who have developed and led it over the years from its inception. Histories lead with those who have been instrumental in bringing the company to where it is today. You create small biographies of those at the top level, such as the president or CEO, vice presidents, financial officers, and all members of the company board.

A basic outline for a company history is:

- A one-page statement about the company and its market vision

- A pictorial section of the company in physical residence from the beginning to now

- Biographies of corporate members from the top level on down

- A section on products, including the one main product or service the company is known for in the market

- A financial overview, including graphs and charts of how the company has improved over the years, with different steps taken to raise the return on investments

- A section on where the company is headed in the future

These sections do not have to be in the order listed above. You can get a company's previous history if it exists, and find out if they want the same focus. As this is a front-end marketing piece for the company, it may want you to focus on the new fighter jet being built, which is also helping the local economy with more jobs and money flowing through the area. The product area may be the first thing the reader sees, which definitively establishes the corporate identity. Then your next section may be the biographies and photos section for all the key players in the company. Third might be the company's mission statement.

If you are writing the corporate history, you can suggest that you create a website as well, since you already have all the information needed to set up the pages. The arrangement of information may be different from what is outlined in the printed book, but the core information remains the same. The only difference may be links to extended information and products and services.

What It Pays

For corporate histories, *Writer's Market* lists $1,000 on the low end, $12,500 as midlevel, and $35,000 on the high end. If charging by the hour, then $35 on the low end, $87 at midlevel, and $180 on the high end. You can also charge by the word, about $1–$2 per word. Ask what the budget is before stating any fees, as that will help you evaluate what to charge. If you can, always have your client give a number first, then do the negotiating after that.

Nuts and Bolts

You should have the skills to write a good story with entertaining sidebars, pictures, and other attention-grabbing information. This is a marketing piece for the company, so this is not the time to mention the latest failure or any other negative information associated with the company.

You also do not want to make things up. Stick to all the positive accomplishments and aspects of your client and what they have to offer the community.

What You'll Write

You write the full story for the company history. You create the biographies and any side stories or sidebars of information included in the corporate history. As mentioned before, offer to write the website copy, as you have all the information to develop the site.

What It Takes

You must have a talent for writing stories and using descriptive language without distorting the truth, though your angle will be one-sided. You must have correct spelling and grammar, proof all copy, and be sure of all facts presented. Double-check your quotes.

Getting Started

Visit websites of big companies and request hard copies of their corporate histories. Spend time reading them, then visit the website and see how the history is outlined there. You can compare the information on the sites with that in the book, and see what is emphasized differently in each version.

Once you have a good idea of how to write one, offer to do one or two on speculation for several companies so that you can start building a professional portfolio. Also offer to do any marketing pieces when they get ready to send the histories out to potential customers.

Additional Resources

The Copywriter's Handbook, Third Edition by Robert Bly (Holt, 2006).

Write to the Top: Writing for Corporate Success by Deborah Dumaine (Random House, 2004).

Writing for the Corporate Market by George Sorenson (Mid-List Press, 1990).

Student Workbook for Public Relations Writing by Donald and Jill Treadwell (Sage Publications, 2005).

CHAPTER 26

Crossword Puzzles

Overview

Crosswords are one of the most popular puzzles in the world. A reported forty million people in the United States solve a crossword every day. Many major newspapers publish crosswords, and there are entire magazines devoted to them.

The crossword was first created in England in the nineteenth century, and was patterned after an ancient puzzle form called a word square, which consists of five rows of five-letter words that can each be read forwards, backwards, up, and down. Originally called a "word-cross" puzzle, these puzzles were first published in book form in 1924 by Simon & Schuster, launching a craze that continues to this day. You can become a part of this stimulating hobby when you write your own crossword puzzles for profit.

What It Pays

Pay rates for the *New York Times* are $125 for daily puzzles (15 x 15 inches) and $600 for the Sunday edition (21 x 21 inches). The payment for diagramless puzzles is $150, and the rate for cryptics and novelty puzzles is $200. Crossword puzzle magazine pay rates are usually based on the size of the puzzle.

Nuts and Bolts

Crossword puzzles follow a complex set of well-established rules. They must fit within one of five square grid sizes (15, 17, 19, 21, or 23 inches). Many publications also accept 13 inches and smaller, but 15 inches is the most common puzzle size, especially for newspapers that run crosswords.

The placement of black squares within the grid must be diagonally symmetrical. For example, if there is a black square in the upper left-hand corner, there must be one in the bottom right-hand corner.

There are other limitations as well. Two-letter words are not allowed, and three-letter words may only be included sparingly. Also, each letter square must be part of words that go both across and down.

A good crossword puzzle is challenging and fun to solve, without using words that are too complex or clues that are so obscure few people can figure them out. About one-third of the clues should be rather straightforward ("great white" for "shark"), while another third should be a clever ("carries its trunk" for "elephant").

The rest can be a mixture of fill-in-the-blank ("The Empire Strikes _____"), name clues ("Novelist King" for "Stephen"), clues for theme words, and so-called "crosswordese," which includes bizarre clues such as animals, genuses, and weights and measures. Such words are found mainly in crossword puzzles, and are familiar to longtime crossword enthusiasts. Every clue must be available in some reference work, whether in print or online. You can't make up words.

What You'll Write

Theme-based puzzles are popular these days, and they are fun to create and challenging for crossword lovers to solve. There is also an advanced type of crossword called diagramless, in which the black squares aren't filled in and the clue squares aren't numbered. Puzzle solvers have to fill in this information themselves, making them very challenging to solve.

You'll write crossword puzzles, of course, but you could also branch out into other types of puzzles, such as word searches and Sudoku, if you have an interest. You write puzzles for newspapers, such as the *New York Times* or *Washington Post*, as well as the many specialty puzzle magazines published each month.

What It Takes

Since many crossword puzzles are based on a particular subject, a thorough knowledge of one or more topics is helpful in formulating puzzles. This can also make it more fun for the writer. You can write a crossword puzzle on almost any subject, so a good imagination is also helpful. Crossword puzzles are a perfect way for people to share their love of Aaron Burr or *Buffy the Vampire Slayer* with the world.

A crossword writer also needs crossword puzzle software to create puzzles. You can find many good crossword puzzle creators on the Internet for free, but since you're writing puzzles for publication, you should invest in a more robust version that produces professional quality puzzles. A good crossword puzzle dictionary also comes in handy.

Finally, you need patience, especially in the beginning. Solving a crossword is one thing, but writing your own can be difficult. If you stick with it, you'll soon be writing challenging puzzles that are fun to solve.

Getting Started

The first thing you should do is get some crossword puzzle software (see re-sources below). Once you become skilled at using the software, it will make creating puzzles a snap. You should use the software and not create puzzles by hand, because developing words and clues that correspond to the accepted crossword formats can be too complex to do on your own.

Once you have your software, start creating. Then check out the *New York Times* and other major newspapers, as well as crossword puzzle magazines, for places to submit your puzzles.

Additional Resources

You can find crossword puzzle rules at barelybad.com/xwdrules.htm.

There are various crossword puzzle creation software, including Armored Penguin (www.armoredpenguin.com/crossword), Crossword Express (www.crauswords.com), and Crossword Weaver (www.crossword weaver.com).

A good online crossword puzzle community is Cruciverb: www.cruciverb.com.

Crossword publishers include Penny Press (www.pennypress.com) and Dell (www.dellmagazines.com).

CHAPTER 27

Direct Mail

Overview

Direct response, also known as direct marketing, refers to any marketing that generates a direct inquiry for—or sale of—a product or service. In the old days, before the Internet, it was often called mail order. You'd rent a mailing list, send out long-copy sales letters, and get back orders and checks in the mail. This is in sharp contrast to general advertising, which seeks to build brand awareness but does not directly generate a sale or other action. For instance, when you hear a Coca-Cola commercial on the radio, there is no number to call to buy a case of it.

Direct-response clients mainly care about one thing: can you write copy that beats their control? A control is their direct mail package they currently use to sell the product. It is the best-performing mail piece they have created to date, which is precisely why they are mailing it and not other mail pieces.

Direct mail is considered the workhorse of direct marketing, but there are many other types of direct-response promotions. Offline, we have TV and radio commercials, magazine and newspaper ads, inserts, and telemarketing. Online we use banner ads, e-newsletters, email marketing, and landing pages.

The mind-set of much Madison Avenue advertising seems to be: How clever, funny, or creative can I make my commercial, and is it original enough to win an advertising award? The mind-set of corporate marketing communications (marcom) managers seems to be: how can I find a vendor who can turn things around quickly and provide the administrative and project management capabilities that will make my life easier? The mind-set of direct marketers is: how can I write the strongest copy possible to sell this product and increase my response rates while remaining legally compliant (e.g., no false claims).

A recent study by the Direct Marketing Association found that nearly 70 percent of consumers prefer to receive announcements and information on new products from companies they are familiar with via conventional mail, versus less than 20 percent who prefer email notification. According to the

Winterberry Group, spending on direct mail in the United States was $58.4 billion in 2007, up 5 percent from 2006.

What It Pays

While fees are all over the lot, a novice direct response writer could charge as little as $1,000 for a one-page sales letter to generate leads. Experienced direct mail copywriters can charge $5,000–$10,000 or more to write a full-blown direct mail package (outer envelope, long sales letter, order form, sales brochure). Top copywriters can earn $100,000–$400,000 a year or more. A few earn seven figures.

Nuts and Bolts

The expression "copywriting is salesmanship in print" has been quoted more times than I can count. But it's not really true for many forms of copywriting. Much corporate communication and marcom really seems to be explaining or describing products, but not really selling them—not asking for the order. The salesperson does that.

With classic direct response, there *is* no salesperson. Your sales letter must gain the reader's attention, engage his interest, create desire for the product, answer any objections, and get him to give you a check or his credit card number. This requires considerably more skill than writing, say, a press release announcing your quarterly results.

What You'll Write

The true workhorse of this traditional marketing channel is the direct mail package: a sales letter, a brochure, and a reply element mailed in a standard-size No. 10 business envelope, with teaser copy printed on the outer envelope. The teaser is designed to entice recipients to find out what's inside. You may want to test your teaser copy against a plain envelope.

Another popular direct mail format is the magalog. A magalog is a self-mailer designed to look like a magazine, with the same page size (7 x 10 inch). Magalogs are used to sell mail-order products, such as stock market and health newsletters, nutritional supplements, and household appliances (e.g., water purification systems and juicers). Magalogs are typically twelve to twenty-four pages long. Fees for magalog copywriting are $7,500–$15,000 and up.

What It Takes

To be a direct response copywriter, you must focus on sales, not creativity. Forget branding, conversation, community, and other warm and fuzzy concepts.

You have to get inside the mind of the prospect, tap into powerful core emotions, and motivate them to pick up the phone and give you their credit card number. This is why direct response copywriters are in demand and command the highest fees.

The trick of direct mail or any other kind of writing is that, for one, you've got to be either good or able to get good at it, which requires a certain kind of overly inquisitive personality and a whole lot of time just stringing words together. But there aren't many shortcuts other than doing a lot of writing and a lot of reading.

"Ultimately, for me, it worked out that advertising writing—copywriting—was what paid best and what I enjoyed doing," says direct mail copywriter John Forde, "particularly in direct mail advertising. Because I specialize in writing direct mail for publishers, I get to write about some big ideas for information products, in a creative and involved way. And because it's in direct response, where long copy tends to do better than short copy, my tendency toward being a windbag is actually an asset."

Getting Started

Major direct marketers such as Publishers Clearinghouse and Omaha Steaks are looking for copywriters with experience and a track record of writing successful direct mail promotions.

For a novice, one way to break in is to volunteer to write fund-raising letters for local nonprofits, such as the YMCA or county animal shelter. Small businesses in your town—dentists, plumbers, chiropractors—may also need a sales letter or postcard written, and because their budgets are too small for them to afford a top direct mail writer, they are open to working with less experienced writers.

Additional Resources

A number of trade publications cover the direct response industry; the ones with heaviest coverage of direct mail are *Direct* (directmag.com), *DM News* (www.dmnews.com), and *Target Marketing* (www.targetmarketing mag.com).

eBay

Overview

If you can write persuasive ads, you can make money by writing eBay ads for eBay marketers or for yourself, selling products you own or buy on eBay. Today eBay has 210 million registered users worldwide, trading items worth a total of $12.6 billion.

What It Pays

You can't charge a fortune just for writing an eBay ad for a business or individual client—maybe $50 or so. An alternative is to charge 10 percent of the revenue the ad generates. An even better idea is to not only write the ad, but handle the entire transaction: writing the ad, taking and posting the digital picture of the product, managing the auction. For this, you might charge from 10 to 25 percent of the revenue generated by the sale.

eBay is an online auction site with all the excitement of a real live auction. You bid. You hold your breath while someone outbids you. You bid again. You wait for your opponent's next move. For the seller, it is equally exciting as you create a pricing strategy, put a product up for bid, and watch the action. Easily addictive, buying and selling on eBay can be both fun and profitable.

The requirements are simple. Registration and set up take a matter of minutes. No special tools or software are required, and there is a wealth of information online to help you determine the price at which you should buy or sell products. On the eBay site, you are even able to search to see what sold successfully and the price that was paid.

Nuts and Bolts

Digital pictures are essential when selling a product on eBay. Since the buyer is not able to see and touch your product, it is critical that they have a vivid picture of what they are buying online. One picture is allowed at no cost, and there is a small fee for additional pictures. With thousands of items to choose from, buyers almost always prefer the items with pictures.

If you don't have access to a digital camera, look online (e.g., a Google Image search) for pictures of the items you are selling. Make sure that the picture is not copyrighted; if necessary, request permission to use their picture.

What You'll Write

When writing product descriptions for eBay, provide enough detail that the customer understands exactly what you are selling. If someone is interested in your product, they want as much information as possible before making a purchase. The bottom line: tell more to sell more.

For example, you may want to provide:

- the year your product was made
- the model number
- the size
- the color
- the exact product name
- the condition (any flaws)
- functionality
- technical specifications
- any unique characteristics (differentiate from competitors)

Include features as well as benefits. For example, if you are selling a GPS system, in addition to listing the features of the system, you may also want to mention the time saved by always having accurate directions and not getting lost. Always answer, "What's in it for me?" when crafting your description. The benefits should be concrete and easy for the buyer to understand.

Be honest about the condition of your product. eBay sellers and buyers receive feedback. If your product does not meet the expectations of your buyer, you could receive negative feedback that future buyers can view. Put yourself in the buyer's shoes and include all of the information that you would want to know if you were buying a similar product. Describe any flaws or imperfections. A satisfied buyer is one who gets what she expects or something better.

What It Takes

What can you sell on eBay? Everything imaginable, from the obscure to the ordinary. There are many categories of items that sell successfully. Choosing the correct category for your product is critical to a successful sale. The first step, as mentioned in the previous section, is to check out the Completed Listings. To do this, click on Advanced Search at the top of the screen. It will take you to a page where you have the option in the middle of the page to select Completed Listings and fill in your category.

Of those items similar to yours, determine which sold (marked in green) and which got the highest price (show listing from high to low). Then, you can look at the detail for the listing and see what category or categories it was placed in. This is a good starting point. For increased exposure (for a fee), you can place your item in more than one category.

Below is a list of item categories that sell well on eBay:

- antiques
- art
- books
- business and industrial
- clothing, shoes, and accessories
- coins
- collectibles
- computers and networking
- consumer electronics
- dolls and bears
- DVDs
- eBay Motors (vehicles)
- health and beauty
- home goods
- jewelry
- music
- musical instruments
- photo (cameras and camcorders)
- pottery and glass
- real estate
- sporting goods and fan memorabilia
- sports cards

- stamps
- tickets
- toys and hobbies
- travel
- video games

Getting Started

While the process of selling on eBay is easy, don't forget to research your product by looking at the Completed Listings on eBay. When the price is marked in green on a Completed Listing, it means the item sold at that price. This will give you an idea of what you can typically buy or sell in a particular price range. Completed Listings also show you the techniques that sell including effective pictures, pricing strategies, descriptions, keywords, and appropriate categories.

Additional Resources

You can find information on how to effectively market products on eBay at www.auctiontrainingcourse.com.

CHAPTER 29

E-books

Overview

The simplest information product to develop is the e-book (electronic book). And it is as close to a "perfect product" for Internet marketers as you can get. An e-book is an information product often formatted as a downloadable PDF (Portable Document Format) file. E-books typically vary in length from twenty to a hundred pages (though some are longer), and prices also vary, usually $19–$79, and occasionally higher. Thousands of e-books are published every year. They are written on everything people want to learn how to do and search for information over the Internet.

The topics for e-books are almost limitless. You can write one about anything, but the bestselling e-books are usually oriented toward being instructional, informational, and how-to. You know something that interests other people, and you can publish and sell an e-book sharing your knowledge for profit and fun.

An e-book costs nothing to print because it is an electronic file. That also means that your e-book takes no physical room to store. There is no inventory, no hard copy, no printing, and no handling. The buyer can read it on the screen or print a hard copy, but that does not concern you—YOU do not print it.

What It Pays

Three good places to look for e-book writing assignments are Craigslist (www.craigslist.com), Guru (www.guru.com), and Elance (www.elance.com). One advantage to using these services is that the clients tell you how much money they have budgeted to have their e-book written.

All three services allow writers to bid on projects. In the case of Craigslist, the entire service is free—for you and the client. Guru and Elance charge the writers for using the services.

When publishers post e-book writing projects, they can either set a budget or ask writers to submit a bid. Writers submit a bid based on the information and criteria supplied in the project post. The publisher's post includes a description of the project (what they want you to produce), tells the writers what information will be supplied, whether the publisher wants to see samples of your writing, and a deadline.

You can receive $300–$700 for an e-book with 10,000–20,000 words. This includes doing research for the e-book and completing two rewrites of the e-book. (A rewrite means incorporating any changes or edits requested by the client.)

Note that most e-books are written as work for hire. This means that once you are paid for your work, you surrender all rights to the e-book you have written, now and forever. The publisher owns all the rights, and the e-book is copyrighted in the name of the publishing company.

If you think $300–$700 seems like a small fee for so much work, you are right. The real money to be made here is writing, publishing, and selling your own e-books online—not writing e-books for others.

Nuts and Bolts

The best style for writing e-books is a simple style. Write clearly and simply. While you are writing, avoid using jargon or really big words. You want your work to be friendly and easy to read, so work at writing the same way you speak. It's called conversational writing, and it allows you freedom in building your sentences. You can't quite throw grammar out the window, but you can be a little more relaxed about it. Your topic, like computers, might have jargon that is unavoidable. In that case, part of your task as a writer is to help your readers become more familiar with the jargon associated with your topic. You do that by introducing and explaining terms and using them in context. The trick is to do this sparingly and include a glossary. Your readers will appreciate it, the glossary adds authority to your e-book, and it is a great selling feature to add to your sales page.

A good e-book on conversational writing, written by Scott McDougal, is *How to Write Better and Faster* at www.writebetterandfaster.com. This can help you improve your writing skills.

What You'll Write

Start your e-book writing career by choosing a specific, targeted topic for your first e-book—a topic that people are actively searching for more information on. Ideally, you are not just choosing the topic for your first e-book. You are selecting the niche upon which you will build your entire information marketing empire. All your future information products will hopefully relate to this topic in some way. For example, the topic for my first e-book was hiring a contractor you can trust. It's the first in what will be a full line of information products on residential renovations—a huge, evergreen market.

People who buy your first e-book have proven that they are interested in the topic and that they accept you as a source of information on that topic.

This position of authority is both why and how you will produce an entire line of related information products.

What It Takes

Aside from writing skill, an e-book author must be a good researcher. Publishers—mainly independent Internet marketers—expect you to provide the content and may only help minimally in that regard. Research means getting the information you need to write a valuable e-book your buyers will find useful and well worth the price they paid.

Start a research file for each new e-book. This is going to serve two purposes. One is for your research right now, and the other is for later, when you want to publish an updated version of your e-book.

The best thing to use is a hanging file with the title of the e-book. Within that hanging file, place one file folder for each chapter (with the number and title of each chapter on the tab).

As your research uncovers new material, drop clippings and printouts into the relevant folder for that chapter. This allows you to sort information as you collect it, and keep it all in one spot. As soon as you have the file folder system, you will find yourself frequently coming across item after item in your reading that you can drop into the chapter files. This is not luck. Making the folder gives the topic more importance in your mind. Your mind becomes more attuned to the topic, pays more attention, and is unconsciously on the lookout for information on that topic. Start a research file as soon as you get the idea for an e-book—even if you are not contracted to write it yet. By the time you decide it is time to write, you will have almost all the research materials you need *before* you even start actively looking.

Getting Started

The first step is to create an outline. The outline is a road map for getting from blank pages to a finished book. Even if the publisher does not request it, show your outline to the publisher and get his approval before proceeding to write the first draft.

Decide how you want to organize the information. Every outline should include a table of contents that uses chapter divisions. Dividing your e-book into chapters makes it easier for your readers to find information. It also breaks the material into smaller pieces that are easier for readers (and you) to handle. As you add information, and the e-book becomes more detailed, you can decide whether to add subdivisions to your chapters.

One way to organize an outline is to use the steps in the process you are writing about. Whether the subject is goal setting, selling a house, or refinishing furniture, each follows a process with distinct steps that can be described. An example of a process or steps book is *Getting Your Book Published* (Roblin Press). It walks you through eight proven, essential steps to getting a nonfiction book published. Those steps are also arranged in the order I recommend that you follow; that is the distinctive feature of the process outline. Each step became the title of a chapter. It doesn't matter how long, or short, each chapter is.

This outline type is more likely to result in the use of subdivisions within chapters. There is often more than one way to accomplish each step of a process, just as there is more than one way to set up an outline.

Additional Resources

For a beginner's course on how to get started in Internet marketing, visit www.theinternetmarketingplan.com.

You can learn how to write and sell e-books online at www.myveryfirst ebook.com.

CHAPTER 30

Email

Overview

The Internet has revolutionized marketing, and one of the most effective Internet marketing methods is email marketing. According to an article in *Internet Retailer* in October 2007, email marketing is the best method of generating traffic to e-commerce websites, used by 91 percent of online marketers. Other methods of driving traffic to websites and landing pages include pay-per-click advertising (used by 88 percent of Internet marketers), affiliate marketing (67 percent), and search engine optimization (51 percent).

What It Pays

Fees for writing email marketing messages are all over the map. My clients routinely pay me $1,000–$2,500 per message to write short promotional emails they distribute to their customers and prospects online. But some writers I know charge as little as $500 per email marketing message.

Even though email marketing messages can be very short, that doesn't mean they are easy to write. Your client can precisely measure the results produced by your email copy, and know whether it was successful within twenty-four hours of distributing your copy to their email list. Therefore, if you can generate consistently high results, you can command fees at the upper end of the scale. On the other hand, if few people respond to your email copy, you have more to learn, and until you master the format, clients will not pay you top dollar.

Nuts and Bolts

There are a number of different business models for making money online. In my own Internet marketing business, I follow what is known as the organic model or Agora model (because it was pioneered by newsletter publishing giant Agora Publishing). In the Agora model, you build—using various traffic-generation methods, including pay-per-click ads and organic search—a large opt-in list of subscribers to a free e-newsletter you publish. (The different methods of building such a list are described in detail in my list-building program at www.buildyourlistfast.net.)

You then send email marketing messages to your list. The frequency depends in part on the frequency of your e-newsletter. I publish a monthly e-newsletter, and send an email marketing message to my list weekly, sometimes twice weekly.

Your email marketing messages typically promote one of your products, and have a link to the landing page or order page for that product. A small number of people on your list click on the link. If 1,345 people do this, then the email has generated 1,345 "clicks." This number is known as the click-through rate (CTR), and can range from 1 to 15 percent or even higher. Of those who go to the landing page, a small percentage actually buy the product. This is known as the conversion rate or "conversions," which can range from 2 to 15 percent or more.

What You'll Write

There are several types of email messages that companies send to their prospects and customers. For example, transaction emails notify the customer of the status of their order or account. You will most likely write solo email marketing messages, which are emails promoting a specific product. Some companies also hire writers to create their monthly or weekly e-newsletters.

Most email marketing messages are five-hundred words or less, and some are considerably shorter. When writing an email message for a client, ask to see copies of the e-newsletter and other emails regularly sent to their list. If those other emails are mostly text, yours should be text, too. On the other hand, if most of them are HTML emails (emails with pictures and graphics), yours should be, too.

Your job is to write the text, not create the HTML design. However, when writing an HTML email, you should include a rough sketch of how you want the elements to look. An example is provided on page 114.

What It Takes

Writing an email marketing message is similar to writing a sales letter, except the copy is usually shorter. In the email you have a link the reader can click to visit the landing page. I usually repeat these links several times, even in a short email message, because I have found it increases click-through rates.

Keep in mind that the purpose of your email is not to sell the product, but to drive as much traffic to the landing page as possible. It is the landing page copy, not the email, that sells the product and persuades the reader to order.

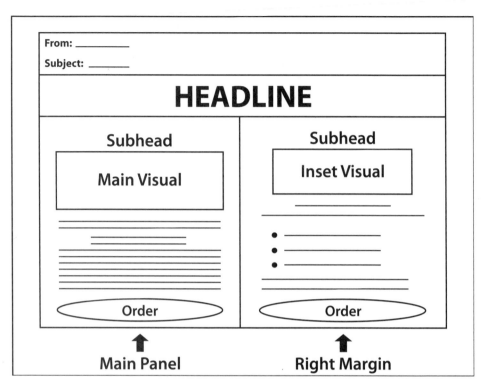

To learn how to write effective email marketing messages, you should study advertising copywriting and other media. The principles are the same. But in addition, pay attention to the email marketing messages you get every day, particularly those that seem interesting and persuasive.

When a company approaches you about writing an email, ask to see samples of their more successful email marketing campaigns. Ask the client if there are any keywords in the subject lines or body copy that work particularly well for their offers, and use those same keywords in your copy, too.

Getting Started

Almost every company does at least some online marketing, and nearly every company uses email messages as part of their total marketing effort. Big corporations typically use short HTML emails to generate leads and build brands online. Smaller Internet marketers sell products (merchandise or information) directly off the Web using microsites or landing pages. A microsite or landing page is a small website dedicated to selling only a single product (see www.thelandingpageguru.com for an explanation). Email messages are sent to e-newsletter subscribers to drive traffic to the landing pages. On the landing page, the user can read about the product and order it online.

To get assignments writing email marketing messages, set up a simple Web site offering your services as a freelance copywriter specializing in Internet marketing. Write and offer a free special report, as a downloadable PDF file, on how to maximize email marketing response rates. Follow-up with people who request the free report to see if they need to have email marketing campaigns written or improved.

Additional Resources

The Online Copywriter's Handbook by Robert Bly (McGraw-Hill, 2002).

The Official Get Rich Guide to Information Marketing by Dan Kennedy, et. al (Entrepreneur Press, 2007).

You can order my book on email marketing messages, *Bob Bly's Million-Dollar Email Swipe File* at www.emailswipefile.com.

CHAPTER 31

Employee Communications

Overview

Employee communication is one aspect of business writing. Being able to continually communicate with employees is imperative to a company's success. Even companies with in-house writers occasionally need to employ the services of a freelancer for fresh and engaging writing or overflow work.

What It Pays

The average writer can expect to make $50–$100 per hour. If you would like a scale to follow, the annual *Writer's Market* includes a guide of what you should charge. Most corporations expect to be given a flat rate for each assignment. The freelance writer should calculate their time, overhead costs, and any other expenses to determine the fee.

Nuts and Bolts

Employee communications have two major purposes: education of personnel and motivation. Corporations expect their written communication to be informative and to create a positive culture for the company.

First, corporations must regularly educate their employees about company policies, benefits, procedures, training, and government regulated issues. The information included in this communication must be factual and accurate. When changes occur in a corporation or the government releases new business laws, the employees need to know. This is usually done through some form of written communication. Serious consequences can occur when a corporation fails to adequately inform or train their employees.

Second, strong employee relations can be critical to reducing the amount of turnover a corporation experiences, increasing self-esteem (and thereby production) in employees, and improving customer relations. Well-written communications can create a more positive atmosphere in a company. Sincere communication can help employees feel understood and content in their positions.

The written communication a writer produces can significantly impact the dynamics of an organization. Being able to effectively communicate information and provide a feeling of camaraderie among employees is critical.

What You'll Write

Employee communication might include something as simple as a one-page news release to the employees or something as complicated as a manual. If this is an area of interest, be prepared to do any or all of the following: manuals, newsletters, online newsletters, booklets, emails, articles, speeches, training programs, reports, presentations, videos. All writing for employee communications, whether informative or entertaining, needs to be clear, concise, and engaging.

What It Takes

Between government policies and corporate jargon, written communication can be difficult to understand. It is the responsibility of the writer to clarify all meanings and convey information in a simple format. For this reason, training in technical writing is important. Employee communications should also provide a strong foundation for improving executive-to-employee relationships. Background in communications is helpful. Finally, a writer might find a niche in an area of business they are already familiar with. Otherwise, the writer should gain some education in whichever area of business they intend to target.

Large corporations have human resources (HR) departments. Your potential client for employee communications writing could be the HR manager, training manager, or employee communications manager. If the company has any kind of employee newsletter, get a hold of a copy. The editor, usually listed in the masthead, would be another person to approach about freelance work.

Getting Started

These tips will help you get off the ground.

1. **Join the chamber of commerce.** Networking and referrals are the fastest means of building your client list. Attending these meetings help you see what companies are looking for and get you in direct contact with those companies.

2. **Contact local and small companies.** Small and local companies are more willing to give newer writers a chance. Larger organizations look for experience and want writing samples before they even talk to you. By starting small, you can build your portfolio. (Of course, smaller companies don't usually have as much money to spend on freelance work. But it's a good place to start.)

3. **Research companies.** Once you're ready to contact larger or national corporations, do a little research. Everyone wants to know what you can do specifically for their company. Having a knowledge base of the company and what they do helps you get your foot in the door. Also, make sure you contact the right person. Most large companies have an employee communications department. You might also try a directory such as the *Standard Directory for Advertisers* to find major corporation information (such as key personnel).

4. **Contact larger corporations.** Larger corporations generally have more money to spend on their outsourced work. If you have a strong portfolio, try to obtain work from bigger organizations.

5. **Keep networking.** Once you have established your name with a corporation, they will most likely call you again. However, work is always uncertain, and you should continually be building your clientele.

Writing employee communications can be challenging. You are responsible for not only providing necessary information to employees, but building a positive atmosphere as well. Companies are often as particular about the communications they send to employees as they are about their advertising to outside audiences. Nevertheless, it's a great way to build your freelance business and keep you writing for years.

Additional Resources

Careers for Writers and Others Who Have a Way with Words by Robert Bly (VGM Career Books, 2003).

Untechnical Writing by Michael Bremer (Untechnical Press, 1999).

The $100,000 Writer by Nancy Flynn (Adams Media, 2000). Flynn is a successful freelance writer whose specialty is employee communications.

For an article on corporate writing with several links to other sources, try "Freelance Writer Market: Find Jobs and Clientele": riri.essortment. com/freelancewriter_rsdw.htm.

CHAPTER 32

Erotica

Overview

Do Americans like sex? Well, they certainly like to read about it. Sales of erotic fiction in the United States exceed $1 billion annually. Writing erotica is similar to writing romance novels, but uses more direct and explicit imagery. The difference between erotica and pornography is the choice of words and graphic depiction. Pornography is more graphic, raw, and hard-core, without romance or tenderness. Erotica is more sensual, uses words that elicit warmth and passion, and generally teases the reader into a state of wanting mental and physical satisfaction by seeing what comes next.

There are different types of erotic writing, such as stories for gay and lesbian readers or those written strictly for women. Stories written for men tend to be more hard-core and pornographic in focus. Each type has its own style, and the best way to study these differences is to read widely in each area.

What It Pays

The pay scales in erotica range from pitiful to passable. Most erotica writers enjoy the writing and say their part-time erotica writing earns them a little extra cash. A few of the more productive report being able to pay their living expenses; but almost no one is getting rich. For specific fee data, consult *The Erotica Writer's Market Guide,* available from The Circlet Press Collective in Cambridge, Massachusetts.

In general, first-time authors receive only royalties from book sales, but if the book does well, the publisher may pay an advance for the next book, especially in a sequel situation.

If writing stories for magazines, check their guidelines or websites, which usually indicate what they pay, based on story length.

Nuts and Bolts

Practice your sensory writing, using different levels of erotic words until you find your comfort level. When you find it, be consistent with that level. Using hard-core language one moment and more passionate, soft words in the next will result in a disconnect.

Read bestselling erotica authors for a good overview on how to write for this market. Join an erotica writers group and talk with others who write these stories.

What You'll Write

You write the story itself, perhaps an outline to develop the story while writing it, and sometimes marketing materials to sell the story. Depending on what style of erotica you write, you should outline a plot first, along with some character sketches. In the character-driven story, develop your characters first, as that will be your focal point in the piece.

Plot-driven stories usually begin with a trigger event and allow for the characters' interactions to be a part of the plot. For the character-driven story, development of the characters as people through their actions and cause-and-effect situations are the focus.

What It Takes

You must have a vivid imagination and a free-spirited approach. If you feel embarrassed while writing intimate scenarios, that will spill over into the story and the reader will sense that and lose interest. If you feel too much embarrassment writing erotica, but really want to do it anyway, consider using a pseudonym.

Getting Started

Read magazines that publish erotica to get a feel for their style and what these magazines are looking for in the stories they buy. Start writing your stories and compile several for your sample portfolio, then start querying editors.

Additional Resources

You can find information and resources on erotica writing at www. erotica-writers.com.

You can take a free online course on writing erotica at Suite 101: www. suite101.com.

The Virginia Romance Writers offer links to helpful sites at www.virginia romancewriters.com/Links/erotica.html.

CHAPTER 33

Essays

Overview

You hear the word "essay" and you might have an adverse reaction, a leftover feeling of dread from your school years when you had to write essays as part of an exam. Back in school, you were given a question about a subject you studied in class, and you were expected to develop a written thought process that took the question and moved step by step through a series of supporting arguments to reach the final answer.

While it's still the same thing now, if you are out of school, you get to choose the question, which makes it easier to develop the arguments leading to the solution or final outcome. In this kind of writing, you do state your opinion (without wild emotion, however) and provide information to back it up. You should also discuss the common arguments you may have heard about this subject and offer your evidence for or against it.

Pick something you are passionate about or interested in. If you find the material boring, then your work will be boring for the reader as well. For instance, you might be interested in art history, then narrow it down to Impressionist painters, which then is whittled down to Vincent van Gogh and his use of vibrant color. Your topic could be his use of those colors as opposed to the other Impressionist painters, why he used them, and how the style of his brush strokes led to the Expressionist era.

What It Pays

Essays, most likely, are written for editorials, school, and business projects, and can also be collected in book form. You can sell essays to trade magazines, particularly as a sidebar to a main article about a larger event. Using the Vincent van Gogh example, if there is a van Gogh exhibit in town, a newspaper or magazine may run an article or review about the show and might also like to have that essay as additional reading for the interested consumer. Most fees will be small, but it is a great byline to have in your portfolio. At the bottom of the scale, one local publication focusing on parenting in New Jersey, *The Parenting Paper,* paid me with a gift basket of books, toys, and coupons for kids products. At the high end, *Newsweek* pays $1,000 for essays for its *My Turn* section. I have done better with publishing my essays in a book: a major publisher paid me a $20,000 advance for a small collection of my essays, *Count Your Blessings*.

Nuts and Bolts

You must be articulate and able to outline your work. Observe the headline and opening statement rules so that the reader knows exactly what you are writing about in the first two sentences.

The same principles from news editorial writing apply: use concise writing with no wasted words while persuading readers to your way of thinking. You must follow through from topic to conclusion to have a successful essay.

What You'll Write

You write the main topic header and opening statement in the first paragraph. You outline your arguments throughout the piece, with a consolidation of findings leading to a conclusion. Every argument needs to tie together, and there should never be an abrupt disconnect from the theme.

What It Takes

Writing essays takes a linear approach with a progression from the opening statement to the conclusion. You must be able to lead your readers from one section to the next, and convince the reader of your opinions and convictions. Study the methodology of writers you find convincing in their arguments and analyze how they did it.

Getting Started

First decide what areas you want to write about, then narrow it down to specific topics. You can get ideas about subject matter from the media. Make a list of where you would like to submit your essays or consider publishing them on your own website. You need to write a convincing query letter if you plan to submit to a publication.

Additional Resources

Schaum's Quick Guide to Writing Great Essays by Molly McClain and Jacqueline Roth (McGraw-Hill, 1999).

At Associated Content, you can read about Essaywriters.net, a site freelancers can join for writing essays and other projects: www.associatedcontent. com/article/343727/essaywritersnet_lets_you_pursue_your.html.

CHAPTER 34

E-newsletters

Overview

Thousands of companies use short online newsletters, also called e-newsletters or e-zines, to regularly communicate with their customers and others at virtually no cost. Corporations publish e-newsletters for a variety of applications, and many larger corporations publish multiple e-newsletters each month. They may have one for employee communications, a second for technical and customer service personnel, and a third for customers and prospects. Or, they may have a separate e-newsletter for each market they serve or each division or product line.

What It Pays

Small companies pay little or nothing for e-zine articles, but some of the *Fortune* 500 and other large corporations pay writers $500–$3,000 per issue to research and write brief articles.

Before the Internet, corporations published quarterly newsletters or magazines at great expense, and paid handsome fees to their writers. So they are accustomed to paying respectable fees for newsletter articles, and pay writers well whether their newsletters are print, online, or both.

Thousands of small businesses now publish online newsletters that never published newsletters before the Internet era. They only started newsletters once the Internet made it cheap to do so. So small businesses often do not pay writers a fair wage for writing online newsletters. They may write it themselves or hire the cheapest writer they can find.

Nuts and Bolts

Many people tell me they do not create e-newsletters for their business because they simply do not have the time. It only takes me two hours or less per month, and those two hours are some of my highest return-on-investment hours.

I hate to waste time, so I have come up with a simple formula for writing e-newsletters that anyone can follow. I write five to seven short articles about a topic, about one to three paragraphs each. You want the reader to get through each story in less than a minute. You do not have an unlimited amount of time with your reader, so make sure he can read your entire issue in about five minutes.

The next little tip might seem insignificant, but I think it is vitally important. Do not put any links to a site with more of the story; you do not want to give the reader's mind a chance to wander while they wait for another page to load. A lot of e-newsletters like to give a brief description of the article, then ask you to click on a link to read the whole article. That's just too many hoops to jump through. So I like to write short articles and include the entire article in the e-newsletter itself, not a teaser.

So here, it is in simple form:

1. Five to seven stories

2. One to three paragraphs each

3. Less than one minute per story and five minutes reading time per issue

4. Include full stories, no links

What You'll Write

Some clients assign specific article topics to their freelance writers, while others are less certain as to what they want in the issue. The most difficult situation is the client who hires you to write an issue of their newsletter and then has no idea what to put in it. Writers in this situation often panic. To help you get around this stumbling block, here are thirty-two topics to get going:

1. **Product stories.** New products, improvements to existing products, new models, new accessories, new options, and new applications

2. **News.** Joint ventures, mergers and acquisitions, new divisions formed, new departments, industry news, analysis of events and trends

3. **Tips.** Tips on product selection, installation, maintenance, repair, and troubleshooting

4. **How-to articles.** How to use the product, how to design a system, how to select the right type or model

5. **Previews and reports on special events.** Trade shows, conferences, sales meetings, seminars and presentations, press conferences

6. **Case histories.** Either in-depth or brief reporting, product application success stories, service successes

7. **People.** Company promotions, new hires, transfers, awards, anniversaries, employee profiles, customer profiles, human-interest stories, unusual jobs, hobbies

8. **Milestones.** One-thousand units shipped, sales reach $1 million mark, division celebrates tenth anniversary

9. **Sales news.** New customer bids accepted, contracts renewed, satisfied customer reports

10. **Research and development.** New products and technologies, new patents, technology awards, inventions, innovations, breakthroughs

11. **Publications.** New brochures available, new ad campaigns, technical papers presented, reprints available, new or updated manual, announcements of other recently published literature

12. **Explanatory articles.** How a product works, industry overview, background information on applications and technologies

13. **Customer stories.** Interviews with customers, photos, customer news and profiles, guest articles by customers about their industries, applications and positive experiences with the product or service

14. **Financial news.** Quarterly and annual report highlights, presentations to financial analysts, earnings in dividend news

15. **Photos with captions.** People, facilities, product, events

16. **Columns.** President's letters, letters to the editor, guest columns, regular features such as tech talk or FAQs

17. **Excerpts.** Reprints, condensed versions of press releases, executive speeches, journal articles, technical papers, company seminars

18. **Quality-control stories.** Quality circles, employee suggestion program, new quality assurance methods, success rate, case histories

19. **Productivity stories.** New programs, methods, and systems to cut waste and boost efficiency

20. **Manufacturing stories.** New techniques, equipment, production line successes, detailed explanations of manufacturing processes

21. **Community affairs.** Fund-raisers, special events, support for the arts, scholarship programs, social responsibility programs, environmental programs, employee or corporate participation in local, regional, or national events

22. **Data processing stories.** New computer hardware and software systems, improved data processing and its benefits to customers, new data processing applications, explanations of how systems serve customers

23. **Overseas activities.** Reports on the company's international activities, profiles of facilities, people, markets

24. **Service.** Background company service facilities, case histories of outstanding service activities, new services for customers, new hotlines

25. **History.** Articles on company, industry, product, community history

26. **Human resources.** Company benefits, announcements of new benefits and training, explanations of company policies

27. **Interviews.** With company key employees, engineers, service personnel; with customers; with suppliers (to illustrate the quality of materials going into your company's products)

28. **Forums.** Top managers answer customer complaints and concerns, service managers discuss customer needs, customers share favorable experiences with company products and services

29. **Gimmicks.** Contests, quizzes, puzzles, games, cartoons

30. **Reviews.** Important books in the industry

31. **Links.** Point to relevant sites

32. **Free downloads.**

What It Takes

While writing solo email marketing messages to sell products is similar to writing direct mail letters or classified ads, writing e-newsletter articles has more in common with journalism. If you can write a good magazine article, you can write for e-newsletters. One major difference between writing magazine and e-newsletter articles is word length. Magazine articles are typically 800–1,500 words, while e-newsletter articles are 250–500 words.

Because of the length constraints, e-newsletter articles have to be tighter and more to the point. No cute or colorful leads, wandering off on a tangent to tell an interesting story, or lengthy quotes from interviews. E-newsletter readers want practical news and tips in a pithy, no-nonsense, straight-to-the-point style.

Getting Started

For writers who want to get paid, focus on writing articles for corporate e-newsletters. Corporations regularly hire freelance writers to contribute articles, for pay, to both online and offline newsletters. Do not pursue writing articles for small businesses, entrepreneurs, and independent Internet marketers. They typically do not pay for articles. Other Internet marketers are eager to give articles for free in exchange for the exposure it gives their own e-zines. So these small businesses have no reason or incentive to buy an article from you.

Additional Resources

Visit Alexandria Brown, the e-zine queen: www.alexandriabrown.com.

I offer a book, *Ready Made E-Zines*, that you can order at www.emailswipefile.com.

CHAPTER 35

Fantasy

Overview

Fantasy tales have existed throughout world history, and such stories have been passed down from one generation to the next as a way to delight and entertain. Today, fantasy has evolved into an exceedingly versatile genre that is in high demand from writers who have vivid imaginations and a gift with the written word. According to Simba Information, sales of science fiction and fantasy books reached $495 million in 2006. Fashionable fantasy offers a dazzling array of settings and characters, where a writer can indulge his imagination and set his creative spirit aflutter for a rewarding income.

What It Pays

Thanks to the ever increasing popularity of the fantasy market, demand is growing. Many print and online publications are calling for short story fantasy submissions. While you should always strive to submit to the best-paying publications, which pay five cents a word or more, publications that pay one to four cents a word can still be a good starting place, as you gain experience and confidence to compete for the sought after and higher paying assignments.

Another possibility is the lucrative international market. Across the globe people enjoy a great fantasy story, too. And publishers pay good money to fill the demand for the written version of something otherworldly.

Nuts and Bolts

Writing fantasy doesn't usually follow a particular pattern or formula. A fantasy story can include any other genre type, such as romance, horror, or mystery. The basic components of the story classify where it falls into a particular subgenre. Some examples of these are:

- **Science fantasy.** Where magic and science coexist, or where science is enhanced to include magical properties.
- **Historical fantasy.** Set in a historical period.

- **Heroic and epic fantasy.** Good versus evil battles or quest scenarios.
- **Urban and contemporary fantasy.** Real world setting, but with magical elements or aspects of fantasy.
- **Humorous fantasy.** Fantasy stories with lighthearted humor.
- **Mythic fiction.** Inspired by fairy tales, folklore, or myth.

Fantasy gives writers the freedom to blend genres and craft an entertaining story where the reader can lose themselves in a world of wonder, to escape their real-life worries, if only for a few chapters at a time.

What You'll Write

Fantasy stories must include all the elements of good old-fashioned storytelling, such as characterization, description, plot, and dialogue. Another important aspect in writing fantasy is world building. World building is designing the world where your characters live and your story world exists. This world-building process is essential in creating the overall structure and providing a solid background to your story. This can be as simple as integrating mythical elements into contemporary life, or as difficult as crafting an entire language, history, geography, and culture of a world that exists only within your own imagination, but must be transferred to paper and effectively described.

What It Takes

The first approach to writing fantasy is to research and study the fantasy market. Read popular books on the subject of fantasy. Study and take notes on the nuances in the writing style, paying particular attention to how the setting is developed for the story, to get an idea of how an effective world is crafted.

Remember, imagination is the key element in storytelling. Fantasy is a whimsical venue to express yourself in, as well as being entertaining for others. Hopefully, with the resources listed here, you'll ignite stories that not only pay well, but also thrill your readers.

Getting Started

After you've done your thorough market research and studied fantasy story writing styles, you should be confident enough to write a masterful fantasy story of your own. Once you find the fantasy publication(s) or publisher(s) you wish to write for, review their websites and submission guidelines. Based on their requirements, write and send a well-crafted query letter.

Additional Resources

Novel & Short Story Writer's Market (Writer's Digest Books) is an annual guide of markets.

Ralan's Webstravaganza: www.ralan.com.

The Writer Gazette: www.writergazette.com.

CHAPTER 36

Fund-Raising

Overview

Total giving to charitable organizations was $295 billion in 2006, an increase of 4.2 percent over 2005, a positive trend seen for the last fifty years. Americans are a nation of generous givers, with 70–80 percent of U.S. households making monetary contributions to charitable organizations averaging more than a thousand dollars annually. There are 1.48 million nonprofit organizations in the United States competing for these donations, and they depend on fund-raising—and fund-raising writers—to get their share.

What It Pays

Even though your clients are nonprofits, that doesn't mean writers don't get paid. After all, the director or executive who hires you is getting a salary, so they expect to pay you as well. However, at the local level, many organizations are run by volunteers, so writers are expected to donate their services or work for a greatly reduced wage. Therefore, professional fund-raising writers concentrate almost exclusively on working with clients at the national level.

Rates for projects vary according to the experience of the writer, but more so based on the type of letter you are writing. A two- to four-page direct mail letter sent to a mailing list to acquire new donors might pay $650–$2,000 or more. If you come up with the concept for the mailing and write all elements—letter, outer envelope copy, response devices, inserts—you might be able to charge as much as $5,000 per mailing package.

There may be times when you're asked to write a series of follow-up letters, asking an organization's existing donors (this list is called the "donor file") to give once again. In that case, you might charge $2,500–$5,000 for a series of three to five letters to donors or members.

With each successive time you write for that client, your time goes down, but your pay doesn't. Let's say you get paid only $500 to write your first donor appeal. Your hourly rate the first time with twenty hours of work is a measly $25 per hour. With a bit of experience, your actual writing time on a donor appeal for that same client could easily drop to five hours, for a handsome $100 per hour rate.

Large and frequent mailers may send material on a monthly basis to their house lists, test acquisitions several times a year to drum up new donors, and perhaps do a few special appeals on top of that. If you become the writer of choice for perhaps four frequent mailers, and they mail between ten and fifteen packages per year each, you will be a busy writer!

For a writer with two to three medium-to-large mailers and four to six clients who mail in smaller quantities, you could make $50,000 annually on only part-time hours. For those of us with short attention spans and the need for great flexibility, the niche can be both rewarding and profitable.

Nuts and Bolts

Fund-raising copywriting may be the most challenging type of direct mail copywriting on the planet. In ordinary direct mail, the prospect sends a check, and gets a product in return. In fund-raising, prospects are asked to send money and get nothing in return.

The copywriter's job is to tap into the core human emotion that motivates people to give. Do not assume that core emotion is always guilt, which is the emotion many beginning fund-raising copywriters mistakenly focus on to the exclusion of all others. Guilt is only one of the reasons people donate to charity, and it is often not the primary motivator.

So what is? It seems to be a basic part of human nature that we all want to leave the world a little better than we found it. That common compelling motivator is to leave a legacy and make things better for future generations. By giving, donors claim a personal stake in making the world a better place and feed their deep desire to be part of solutions to the world's problems.

Donors also give simply because it feels good to help others and to feel like they belong. They continue to give after the initial donation because they like to be loyal. They may give to vent their own anger at an injustice or to do their part to right a wrong. And yes, sometimes, they give primarily to get the free DVD or tote bag or other gift that is given with a donation.

What You'll Write

Traditionally, fund-raising targeted at a mass audience has been accomplished through direct mail. Fund-raising direct mail packages are usually standard business size (#10 envelopes) or smaller. The letters are usually shorter than direct mail letters that sell vitamins, investment advice, or other consumer products. The average fund-raising letter is one to four pages long. While consumer direct mail packages selling products may have many multiple elements (think Publishers Clearinghouse), fund-raising mailings are usually simpler and cleaner in design: an outer envelope, sales letter, reply form, reply envelope, and maybe an insert.

Because fund-raising direct mail packages are often shorter and simpler than commercial direct mail, time frames are often tighter. "I like to give copywriters two weeks, but sometimes the time lines get tighter—one week or less," says Mikaela King of the Creative Direct Response Fund-raising Group. "To become one of our regular writers, you've got to write passionately and persuasively about the organization's issues, and you've got to deliver copy on time."

The best-paying assignment in fund-raising copywriting is to write an acquisition package. This is a letter mailed to rented mailing lists to persuade people to give to an organization they have not contributed to before. A donor appeal is a letter or series of letters sent to a mailing list of people who have already donated to the organization, asking them for another contribution.

Fund-raising also takes place on the Internet, though the nonprofit sector lags behind for-profit marketers in making money online. Natural disasters, such as Hurricane Katrina, spurred many organizations to rapidly evolve their websites from an informational focus to an interactive, relationship-building, e-commerce tool. On the more advanced side, donors may receive personalized content and newsletters tailored to their interests, based on data and preferences they've shared with the organization.

Getting Started

Start with nonprofits with which you have some kind of personal connection or affinity. For instance, one writer we know has a wife with multiple sclerosis, so it might make sense for him to start freelancing for MS organizations. Check your mailbox. What fund-raising appeals do you receive? What organizations and causes do you support with your own charitable dollars? Are you an animal rights activist? Do you support a political party or candidate? With so many worthy and fascinating causes, start with those where you already have a deeper understanding of what makes their donors and supporters tick.

Additional Resources

Open Immediately! Straight Talk on Direct Mail Fundraising by Stephen Hitchcock (Emerson & Church, 2004).

Fundraising on the Internet, Second Edition by Mal Warwick (Jossey-Bass, 2001).

How to Write Successful Fundraising Letters, Second Edition by Mal Warnick (Jossey-Bass, 2008).

Raising Thousands (If Not Tens of Thousands) of Dollars with Email by Madeline Stanionis (Emerson & Church).

Fundraising Success Magazine: www.fundraisingsuccessmag.com.

Association of Fundraising Professionals: www.afpnet.org.

Alliance of Nonprofit Mailers: www.nonprofitmailers.org.

American Institute of Philanthropy: www.charitywatch.org.

Charity Navigator: www.charitynavigator.org.

BBB Wise Giving Alliance: www.us.bbb.org.

Direct Marketing Association: www.the-dma.org.

DMA Nonprofit Association: www.the-dma.org/nonprofitfederation.

DMA of Washington: www.dmaw.org.

Marketing Sherpa: www.marketingsherpa.com.

Nonprofit Technology Network: www.nten.org.

United Way: www.unitedway.org.

CHAPTER 37

Ghostwriting

Overview

Celebrities from Lee Iacocca to Bill O'Reilly pay ghostwriters handsome fees to write their books for them; noncelebrity individuals and companies also hire ghostwriters to produce books, articles, speeches, and more.

A *ghostwriter* is a professional writer who is paid to write books, articles, stories, or reports *that are officially credited to another person*. Celebrities, executives, and political leaders often hire ghostwriters to draft or edit autobiographies, magazine articles, or other written material. The ghostwriter is sometimes (but not always) acknowledged by the author or publisher for his assistance.

What It Pays

Ghostwriting fees are all over the map, and methods of payment are just as varied. Some ghostwriters charge $25–$100 per hour, depending on the project and the client. I know several book ghostwriters who charge by the page, with fees of $75–$150 per page (that's per book page, which is about 300–400 words). A per-page rate makes sense when ghostwriting a book the author plans to self-publish, as there are no advances or royalties, and no accurate way to track sales (many self-published authors give their books away as promotions).

Another method of compensation is for the client and ghostwriter to split the advance and royalties on the book; this works when the book is sold to a mainstream publishing house. An ideal split for the writer is fifty-fifty, though many clients will push for sixty-forty or something even more favorable to them.

"There really is no standard way in which ghosts charge for their work," says ghostwriter David Kohn. "Sometimes how ghosts came to be paired with their coauthors has an effect. If someone comes to the ghost looking for a writer, the ghost often will charge a fee for doing the proposal. If the book is bought, then the writer may charge an additional fee for writing the book, get a healthy cut of the advance, or both."

Writers have also been known to have a charge per chapter fee instead of a flat fee for the overall book. Once the chapter is done, the author pays for it. Sometimes the author ends up paying the writer more than the amount of the advance. That outcome becomes more likely in this era of shrinking advances. Almost always there's a royalty split as well, if the book is being published by a royalty publisher.

"To write, reorganize, edit, coauthor—whatever—a book, I get $3,000 up front against my hourly rate of $70," says ghostwriter Warren Jamison. "I keep close records of time worked on each project, which I supply the client on request. When the first payment is used up, I bill the client for additional upfront money. I never write on speculation, which I would be doing if I billed after doing the work."

If the writer approaches the expert, often, but not always, the writer will not charge for the proposal and will take a healthy cut from the advance and royalties, possibly adding an additional fee if the advance is small. But there are all kinds of exceptions.

At least one additional factor has to be taken into consideration. If a collaborator is a true ghost—no name on the cover or title page, just a mention in the acknowledgments—that invisibility can mean that the author will have to pay the writer more than if the writer's name were on the cover. Again, there's no hard and fast rule here.

Nuts and Bolts

As a ghostwriter, consult an attorney before signing any contract. There is at least one collaboration rule set in concrete: no ghost should ever, ever, ever sit down at the keyboard until he or she has signed a contract with the co-author. That contract should specify everything from how many words the writer will write to the nature of the research. Some writers organizations have model ghosting contracts.

Sometimes the ghostwriter will receive partial credit on a book, signified by the phrase "with" or "as told to" on the cover. Credit for the ghostwriter may also be provided as a thank-you in a foreword or introduction. For nonfiction books, the ghostwriter may be credited as a contributor or research assistant.

In other cases, the ghostwriter receives no official credit for writing a book or article. In cases where the credited author or the publisher or both wish to conceal the ghostwriter's role, the ghostwriter may be asked to sign a non-disclosure contract that forbids them from revealing their involvement.

What You'll Write

Ghostwriters primarily write books. Ghosting, of course, can also be done for articles, white papers, columns, corporate work, and speeches. These pieces generally are done by flat fee or hourly rates.

The degree of involvement of the ghostwriter in nonfiction writing projects ranges from minor to substantial. In some cases, a ghostwriter may be called just to clean up, edit, and polish a rough draft. In other cases, the ghostwriter will write an entire book or article based on information, stories, notes, and an outline, provided by the celebrity or public figure. The credited author also indicates to the ghostwriter what type of style, tone, or voice they want in the book (that is, colloquial, serious, or sarcastic, for example).

It is rare for a ghostwriter to prepare a book or article with *no input* from the credited author. At a minimum, the credited author usually provides a basic framework of ideas at the outset or reads and comments on the ghostwriter's final draft.

What It Takes

"Ghostwriting is like most other writing gigs," says Kohn. "A few writers do great, some do so-so, and it goes down from there. There aren't nearly as many ghosts as there are writers who do other things, so that is a big plus in its favor. I've heard of people who do corporate ghosting—and that includes speechwriting, by the way—making very, very good money. I do know of one ghost who has no corporate work and has done more than one-hundred books who seems to be doing quite well indeed."

If you are considering becoming a ghostwriter, somewhere along the way you've come to the conclusion that you *are* a writer, first and foremost. Perhaps you're already earning a living as a writer in some other field, or are a published (if not paid) author. If so, you've most likely got the organizational skills of an accomplished writer:

1. You can set a deadline and stick to it.

2. You easily break down a project into component elements: interviewing, archival research, writing, editing—and execute each part in a timely way.

3. You are flexible and open to new directions in a project.

To determine whether you have the personality characteristics of a successful ghostwriter, ask yourself the following questions:

- Are you accepting of other people's beliefs and opinions?
- Are you the one to lead in discussions?
- Are you a team player?
- Can you be accepting of revision requests?
- Can you talk articulately with anyone, from any walk of life?
- Can you accept criticism?
- Can you separate facts from feelings?
- Do you have an inquisitive nature—are you curious about the world around you?
- Can you stand your ground with someone?
- Can you put your ego in check and let someone else take center stage?

Getting Started

Assignments may come from word of mouth, judicious advertising in select publications, referrals from writers organizations, or relationships with literary agents who call on you when they have an author in need of a writer. Writers also can take a more active approach and seek out people with a platform or a great story to tell. Some ghostwriters run small classified display ads offering their ghostwriting services in writers magazines, literary magazines, and even the book review sections of major newspapers. If you are really interested in getting opportunities to ghostwrite books, there are two steps to get you there faster.

First, get an agent to represent you, and then let your agent know you are available and eager to do ghostwriting. Agents are routinely approached by authors and publishers in need of ghostwriters, and these agents are often searching for writers to recommend (for a percentage of your fee, of course).

Second, find an interesting celebrity, semi-celebrity, or subject matter expert with knowledge, experience, or a story that you think would make a great book. Approach that person and suggest doing the book together. If the story is interesting enough, or the person famous enough, a publisher may be interested in the project you jointly propose.

A book ghosting gig also can come out of working for an existing client. For many writers, ghosting is something they do on top of other, shorter writing work.

Additional Resources

Ghostwriting for Fun & Profit by Eva Shaw (Writerrific, 2003).

Take a look at ghostwriters' websites and see how others promote themselves:
editor-ghostwriter.com.

www.becomeanauthor.com.

www.bookdoctor.com/index.html.

www.coverscript.com.

www.freelanceghost.com.

www.ghostwords.com/ghostwriting-ghostwriters.html.

www.ghostwriters.in.

www.ghostwriterscentral.com.

www.pegr.com.

www.ronwatkins.net.

www.storysolver.com/indexnew.html.

www.theghostinthemachine.com.

www.theghostwriter.net.

www.thewritersforhire.com/ghostwriting.

www.writerservices.net.

CHAPTER 38

Google AdWords

Overview

Pay-per-click (PPC) advertising is an underserved niche market for copywriters; clients need PPC ads that generate lots of traffic at low cost. Although a number of search engines permit PPC advertising, the king of paid search is Google AdWords.

PPC advertising is an online advertising method in which advertisers place paid ads that appear alongside keyword search engine results. Search engines that accept PPC ads include Google and Yahoo. But instead of a traditional display ad, which costs the advertiser money every time it is displayed, PPC ads only cost the advertiser when someone clicks on their ad.

Also, marketers can decide how much to spend, setting a daily budget and the cost per click, for example, $5 per day and 10 cents per click. You can also set a maximum total budget, instructing Google to cut off your campaign when the cost reaches $1,000 or another dollar limit preset by you.

The more popular keywords cost more per click than unpopular ones. The reason is that more users search on them, so your ad will be seen by more people, and therefore generate more clicks to your website.

What It Pays

Fees for writing PPC ad campaigns vary widely. One copywriter I know charges $3,000 to write and manage a Google AdWords campaign for a product. Other copywriters, like me, just write the copy but do not manage the campaign.

Since Google AdWords PPC ads are so short, and can be tested so easily, you should offer your client a price for a package of ads for the same product or offer. I have charged $500 for a package of three to five PPC ads. I have also included a few PPC ads at no extra charge when a client hired me to write a bigger project, such as a landing page or website.

Nuts and Bolts

Each Google ad is made up of four lines and up to 130 characters. The first line is a blue hyperlinked headline of up to twenty-five characters.

The next two lines are descriptive copy of up to thirty-five characters per line. The last line is a link to your website's display URL of up to thirty-five characters. Total length is 130 characters, including the website URL link.

Note that the display URL can be different from the actual destination URL. This is because only the display URL will show up in the ad, but when a viewer clicks on it, the ad will take them to your destination URL. For example, if the page you want to send visitors to has a really long URL, like www.crazyquilts.com/quilts/patterns/index/home.htm, you could give it a shorter display URL, like www.discountquilts.com. The people viewing your ad will only see the display URL, while clicking on the ad takes the visitor to the longer destination URL.

What You'll Write

As many professional copywriters will tell you, a PPC ad is one of the hardest pieces of advertising to write, but in this chapter, we'll go through the steps of creating a workable PPC ad, whether you're using Google AdWords, Yahoo! Search Marketing, or some other PPC program.

According to copywriter Steve Slaunwhite in his book *The Everything Guide to Writing Copy*, a PPC ad is made up of a headline, two short lines of body copy, and a link. Here is an example:

Become a Freelance Writer
Earn great money working from home
Free booklet shows you how
www.becomeawriter.com

That's it. Sounds simple enough, doesn't it? But let's take a look at what is going on here. The first line is the ad's headline. This is the ad for your ad. To craft a supereffective headline, include your keywords. According to AdWords guru Perry Marshall, more people click on ads when the headline includes the keyword they're searching for.

The second line is usually a benefit of your product or service, followed by the third line, which is usually a feature or offer. In the case of the above ad, the second line is a benefit and the third an offer. This is usually the standard across most markets, but Perry Marshall suggests you test the order for maximum effect.

The fourth line is your display URL. This is the website address people will see. The display URL doesn't have to be the same address as the one it points to. In fact, for best results, you should always send the viewer to a special page that's tailor made for this specific search. Consider this another line of your ad copy. Ideally, you have a domain name that contains a keyword or other selling phrase instead of one that has no meaning. For example, for my home-study course on list building, the URL is www.buildyourlistfast.net— so it is both a URL and a line of sell copy!

What It Takes

Study your competition. By that, we mean search for your top five to ten keywords and print the results pages. Study them. They may represent hundreds of hours and tens of thousands of dollars of market research and testing. In short, your competitors have already done all the work for you. Jot down your thoughts about each of the ads, asking yourself questions such as:

- What's the big promise?
- What's the tone?
- What's the emotional appeal?
- What's the logical difference?
- How does each ad position itself as different from the rest?
- What features are highlighted?
- What proof is offered?
- What's the call to action?

Only by answering these questions will you be able to write a highly effective ad that beats the pants off your competition.

If appropriate and whenever possible, use the keyword in your headline. Including a keyword in your headline often increases click-through rates— the percentage of people reading the ad who click on the link in the last line. For example, an ad with the headline "Homebrew for Beginners" achieved a 3.88 percent click-through rate with the keyword "homebrew" (as one word) but pulled only 1.01 percent with the keyword "home brew" (as a two-word phrase). The reason? Because matching the ad to the exact keyword sends the message to your prospects that you understand them. In Google's case, the site bolds keywords on its results page, so when people type in, say, "natural remedy," ads in Google with that phrase in the headline will stand out, inviting more clicks.

Getting Started

Until recently, writing PPC advertising wasn't a specialty in itself. Rather, copywriters who do websites and landing pages also offered PPC ad copy to clients needing to drive traffic to those sites or pages. Now, a number of writers are choosing to specialize in writing and managing Google ad campaigns. They not only write the copy, but also place the ads online for the client, set up copy tests, track the results, and otherwise manage the complete campaign. One writer I know charges $3,000 per ad campaign for this service.

To get these assignments, you can ask existing copywriting clients whether they need PPC ads written to increase unique visitors and registrations on their websites. You should also add a page to your own writer's website talking about your Google AdWords copy and campaign management services.

To create your Google AdWords account, go to adwords.google.com. Ad-Words has a starter and standard edition, and you choose the one you want to sign up for. There are no price differences between the two editions. The starter edition has a limited range of features and is for inexperienced online advertisers who only want to market one product or service and who may not already have a website. If you sign up for this edition, you can upgrade later. For now, choose the starter edition if:

- You only have one product and one web page
- You want to sell to just one region
- You don't want to deal with complex reporting
- You only want to use text ads
- You want simple keyword bidding

If you have more than one product (T-shirts in both red and blue) or sales funnel (for example, you sell T-shirts to college students and soccer moms), the starter edition will be too limited for you. You also won't be able to bid higher for some keywords than others. The standard edition is designed for experienced Internet marketers and offers the full range of features, including the ability to track multiple campaigns. You must have a website to sign up for the standard edition.

Because you should have a working website, we recommend diving right into the standard.

Additional Resources

AdWords for Dummies by Howie Jacobson (Wiley, 2007). Askhowie.com is the companion website. Contains more info, articles, video tutorials, and a blog. He also offers a keyword tool that gives you the top one-hundred searches for a given keyword and a free split-testing tool.

Ultimate Guide to Google AdWords by Perry Marshall and Bryan Todd (Entrepreneur Media, 2007).

Google offers an AdWords Learning Center, with text and multimedia AdWords lessons. This site allows you to watch short videos, take quizzes, and even become a Qualified Google Advertising Professional: www.google.com/adwords/learningcenter.

You can use a free keyword tool at loweryourbidprice.com/freekeywords.

For an AdWords Coaching Program, visit Perry Marshall's site at www.perrymarshall.com/adwords/coaching.htm.

CHAPTER 39

Grant Writing

Overview

Most freelance writers don't say, "Hey, I think I'll write grants for a living." But maybe they should. Grant writing is big business. Just think about it for a moment. Almost every nonprofit company or foundation needs money from grants, and they need a writer to secure it for them. And grant writing doesn't stop with nonprofit organizations. Businesses of all kinds scramble for the free money grants provide. So do entrepreneurs, educators, scientists, artists, and many others.

What It Pays

Hourly rates are $30–$100 an hour and up. A typical grant writing project could require 10–50 hours of your time. Some of the larger ones take more. Instead of an hourly rate, some writers charge by the project. Fees can be $2,000–$10,000, and writers are paid regardless of whether the grant is awarded. A few writers go for the big money and work on commission. They get paid only if the grant is awarded. For example, they charge 3 percent of the full grant. So, for a $500,000 grant, payment would be $15,000.

Nuts and Bolts

A grant is a gift of money or property and never has to be paid back. (At most, the recipient could be required to provide periodic reports to the grant source describing its use.) A grant can come from local, state, or federal sources, as well as from foundations or corporations. Grants are only given to fulfill a specific purpose. The recipient must demonstrate they can fulfill this purpose in order to get the grant through a grant proposal. These proposals can be lengthy, but they're often formulaic.

What You'll Write

Every grant proposal should include:

- a cover letter

- proposal summary

- introduction to the organization

- statement of problem or need

- project goals and objectives

- methods and schedule

- evaluation criteria and process

- budget

The cover letter shouldn't be longer than a page. It should briefly explain the purpose of the grant-seeking organization. It should also include basics like contact information. The proposal summary should also be a page. It should explain why the group needs the money. What's the purpose of the project? You can get into some of the specifics of how the problem will be solved. The letter should also include the total budget amount the group needs.

The introduction describes the organization's history, purpose, goals, and objectives as they relate to the specific project the group is seeking money for. It can also include the group's accomplishments as well as service areas and the number of people served.

The statement of problem or need is the biggie. What's the problem this project will address? How will a solution benefit a community or society at large? Grant writers often use a funnel approach here. They start with the generalized problem, move into its conditions, then get into specifically how the project will solve the problem.

The project goals and objectives explain specific project goals and how progress reports, if any, will be made. The methods and schedule tell how these goals will be met. What specific steps will be taken, when, and by whom? The evaluation criteria and process describe how progress will be evaluated and monitored to ensure success.

The budget is how much money you are asking for. More detail is better here. Don't round out numbers. Be very specific. And don't pad the budget. Include all sources of support. We'll get to those in a second.

What It Takes
Now let's look at what you need to become a grant writer.

- To begin with, grant writers must be detail oriented. Organizations go over proposals with a fine-tooth comb and yours must withstand scrutiny.

- Grant writers must be creative. Some grant proposals are as dry as reading a cereal box. Creativity is a bonus and can help you win the grant.

- Grant writers must work well with other people. Most grant writers work directly with a committee or group within the organization they are trying to secure the grant for.

- Grant writers shouldn't mind working on long-term projects. The actual writing of the grant might not take that long, but the process can. Between project inception, research proposal submission, and review, months can go by. The grant writer must have commitment and patience.

Getting Started

First, study the grant writing process. Conduct grant searches to identify funding sources. Become familiar with what they offer. Many send guidelines upon request. Learn how they pick and choose grant awardees. When are their deadlines? Begin your search online; look for "grant writing" or "grant writing jobs." Also use the resources listed at the end of this chapter.

Then get your feet wet. Call the nonprofits in your area. Tell them you're interested in learning how to write grants. Ask if you can talk to their grant writer. You never know, you might even get an assignment. And remember, like other areas of freelance writing, don't focus too much on what you charge at the outset. It's more important to gain experience.

An important note about working on commission: this fee arrangement has forever been debated in the grant writing community. Some professionals won't work on commission. They feel they should be paid for their time and expertise, regardless of whether it wins the grant. Others want the gamble and big money lure of working on a percentage.

The National Society of Fund Raising Executives (NSFRE) Code of Ethics disallows charging a fee based on a percentage of the money awarded. They feel it causes donors to perceive that the grant request is padded to cover the fee. However, outside of the nonprofit sector, many grant writers do work on commission. It depends upon the entity. It's a good idea to investigate both hourly rates and percentage fees if you choose to get involved in grant writing

Additional Resources

The Grantsmanship Center, a leading source of information for grant writers: www.tgci.com/index.shtml.

The Foundation Center offers a free, short course in grant writing: fdncenter. org/learn/shortcourse/prop1.html.

Grant search and information site with useful links: www.silcom.com/~paladin/promaster.html. The National Center for Outreach offers an introduction to grant writing in a variety of sectors: www.nationaloutreach.org/Conference2002/Presentations/GrantWritingIntro_Linfield.pdf

The *Philanthropy News Digest*: foundationcenter.org/pnd.

Philanthropy.com offers free job listings for nonprofit professionals.

ProposalWriter.com is the site of a freelance grant writer.

University of Wisconsin Grants Information Center: grants.library.wisc.edu.

American Association of Grant Professionals: www.go-aagp.org.

A U.S. government site with lots of grant writing resources: www.govspot.com/features/grants.htm.

CHAPTER 40

Greeting Cards

Overview

The next time you walk down the greeting card aisle at a grocery store, you might be seeing more than just paper. You could be seeing dollar bills. In a single year, more than seven billion greetings cards will be sent in the United States alone. Those cards generate more than $7.5 billion dollars in retail sales. About one-third of all greeting cards are written by freelance writers. However, few writers take the time to explore this potentially lucrative market, so the possibility of breaking into the card writing scene is encouraging.

What It Pays

A greeting card may not pay as much as a magazine or newspaper article, but most greeting card companies pay a flat fee of $25–$200 for a single card. The few companies that pay their writers royalties offer about 2–10% of the wholesale price. Expect to receive $35–$50 per card. Once you establish yourself as a successful greeting card writer, you can command more money.

Nuts and Bolts

Don't be fooled with misconceptions about the greeting card industry. You may have already picked up a card and declared, "I could write this," but greeting card writing is more difficult than it appears. A typical card runs between two and ten lines. But those few lines are a concise masterpiece. A writer should understand the importance of voice before submitting any work.

Every greeting card must accomplish two main goals: grab the attention of the buyer in 1.5 seconds and perfectly convey the emotion of the sender. You must produce a strong me-to-you connection between the sender of the card and the receiver.

If a direct, personal message is not included, the sender will never buy your card. If the wording is too vague and doesn't use enough personal pronouns, the receiver will not feel special. In either case, your card has failed in its purpose.

Remember, there is one more person involved in this intimate exchange: you. Think of yourself as merely the silent messenger. Cards are not meant to display your phenomenal command of the English language or force your worldview on others. Just deliver the message intended, whether wishing for a quick recovery from an illness or sharing the joy of college graduation. Keep it simple, and keep yourself out of the picture as much as possible. If you have a strong control of voice, greeting card writing may be your niche.

What You'll Write

There are three basic types of greeting cards: traditional, contemporary, and humorous. Traditional includes poetry or prose and allows for more written lines. Contemporary includes all messages in a conversational tone. Humorous cards include a wide range of possibilities, and they also pay the most. Greeting card companies have an equal demand for all three styles.

Until your name is well known at a particular company, all your projects are written on spec. So what you write is entirely up to you. You have no set structure to follow. Be creative. Experiment with all styles and occasions.

What It Takes

Theoretically, anyone can write a greeting card. Unlike other publishers, greeting card companies don't care about your past writing experience (even if you don't have any). They don't want you to send a résumé or other writing samples. All they care about is the work you submit. That being said, skilled writers have the greatest advantage in this industry. With a firm grasp of voice, their work is more likely to be accepted.

But greeting card writing is a skill that can be acquired. The best way to learn greeting card writing, particularly what sells, is to browse the card aisles of any store. Read as many cards as you can. Study additional greeting card resources (at the end of this chapter) for tips and ideas on how to improve your writing. Then keep trying. Eventually, you can become an expert in the industry.

Getting Started

1. **Write.** Jot down your ideas. One great aspect of greeting card writing is that it can be done anywhere. If you have five minutes, grab a pen and brainstorm.

2. **Request guidelines.** There are dozens of greeting card publishers in the United States, some of which you can find online at www.writerswrite.com/greeting cards/publish.htm. Contact the publisher, president, or creative director. Many companies have their submission guidelines available online. If not, send the company a polite request for their guidelines, along with a self-addressed,

stamped envelope. Focus on midsize companies. Large companies do not accept unsolicited materials.

3. **Research.** Publishers tend to produce similar cards; browse their cards on their websites if not at the store. Get an idea of what they're selling and make sure your cards match. Like any other industry, greeting cards follow trends. Know what those trends focus on before submitting any work.

4. **Type your work.** No matter what format the company requires, always type your work. Include your name and address on the top left-hand corner of all your submissions.

5. **Send your submission.** Make sure everything you send includes your personal contact information and a #10 self-addressed, stamped envelope. The easier it is for a company to contact you, the more likely the sell. Send six to twenty submissions at one time, and resist sending simultaneous submissions to other companies. Once you have submitted your work, sit back and wait. It could take several weeks or months for a publisher to send a reply.

If you are serious about greeting card writing, there are a few resources listed below to consider. Good luck, and happy birthday, or Merry Christmas, or whatever.

Additional Resources

Write Well and Sell: Greeting Cards by Sandra Louden (Jam Packed Press, 1998).

Visit the Greeting Card Association: www.greetingcard.org.

For an industry directory, visit www.writerswrite.com/greetingcards/publish.htm.

CHAPTER 41

Help Screens

Overview

You're working with a word processing program, and you just can't get the merge function to work. So who do you to turn to when you don't have a software manual? Nearly every software program on the market has a help section that offers step-by-step instructions or explanations, usually searchable by keyword. Did you ever wonder who put all that information there for you to use? Writers just like you.

What It Pays

The *2008 Writer's Market* suggests a fee of $60–$165 an hour. You must determine how involved and technical your writing will be for the given project. If you are writing code as well as the help guide, then charge more to cover the time spent testing your work.

Nuts and Bolts

You should be comfortable with software and computers before attempting to write any software help information. This is not for the technology beginner or faint of heart. You must be exact in helping a consumer who knows much less than you.

Writing help screens requires that you know the program on a very technical level. You work with a program and its developer for quite some time in order to understand how a program behaves under different conditions or keystrokes.

If you are writing for a brand-new program, then you create the help information from scratch or from notes made by the programmer during the software development. If you are writing the upgrade notes, then you can work from the previous version's information as the starting point, and consolidate all the new information from the new version.

The best way to begin documenting function steps is to determine first what the program is supposed to accomplish for the user and proceed from that point to more targeted functions.

You need to test the program for each set of instructions you write, so you can be sure you present the correct steps for each function. Additionally, you need to include keywords in your help information that allows the software to tag the specific information when a query is made for it.

What You'll Write

You write all the information for the screens and possibly assist in writing the hard copy manual as well, if there is one. With the knowledge you have on the project and the actual software, you are in a good position to also suggest advertising pieces, direct mail packages, or an online user survey.

What It Takes

You must think in a linear manner and keep all the steps straight. You must also have a talent for understanding software and its functions.

Getting Started

Start a list of some of the smaller software companies, or contact those companies with software that you are already familiar with, so that writing help information won't be a stretch of your efforts. Wait to have a few projects under your belt before you tackle writing help for brand-new software.

When approaching software companies about writing assignments, show them samples of any software documentation you've worked on, not just help screens. If you don't have samples just yet, take a process from a software program you currently use at home and write a sample step-by-step function procedure.

Additional Resources

Writing Software Documentation by Thomas Barker (Longman, 2002).

Technical Writing 101 by Alan Pringle and Sarah O'Keefe (Scriptorium Press, 2003).

How to Create Zero-Search-Time Computer Documentation by Peter Scherer (Carioles Group Books, 2000).

Writing Software Manuals: A Practical Guide by Martyn Thirlway (Prentice Hall, 1995).

CHAPTER 42

Horoscopes and Astrology

Overview

According to Bloomberg News, Americans spend $200 million on astrology each year. There are 10,000 full-time and 175,000 part-time astrologers working in the United States. A Harris Poll shows nearly one in three Americans believes in astrology, and Amazon.com carries more than 48,000 book titles that touch on astrology. Divination through astrological signs and reading charts has been around a long time but regained popularity in the 1970s. Many writers have made a decent—even handsome—living off of writing daily horoscopes, especially in syndicated markets that reach thousands of readers. With the arrival of the Internet, more writers have found ways to open their own business online and reach a worldwide audience. However, having such a business does entail a good amount of research and knowledge of the subject, as today's readers are more sophisticated than those from the 1970s.

If you can create charts based on a person's birth date and write entertaining and believable readings, then you can do well. The business of astrology is very professional, so knowing as much as you can about your subject matter is critical.

What It Pays

The ideal arrangement is syndication, particularly if you write a column for a newspaper, as you receive fees from each outside market that subscribes to your column. Individually, newspapers pay you according to the column's importance, whether it's a daily column, weekly, or monthly arrangement.

Nuts and Bolts

Study websites offering astrology readings, as you need to match the level of expertise that many of these people demonstrate. If you don't know how to build a chart, then take classes and online seminars to learn how. Charting can be very complex due to the nature of knowing the planets, houses of the zodiac, what each sign represents, and then how to relate the signs to the twelve different houses in the chart.

Study other methods of divination, such as runes, tarot cards, angel cards, numerology, palmistry, and decide which of these you are most comfortable with. Offer them on your website as extended services to your astrology writings.

What You'll Write

For a full horoscope reading, you write a general synopsis, then elaborate on the different aspects of the chart, such as the sun sign meaning, what house the moon was in at birth, and also what house the rising sign is in. You also describe the houses that the chart's planets are in and how they affect the person's life overall and also for the current moment.

While you can write a full overall life reading, you can also write off-shoot horoscopes for business ventures, a love interest, health, careers, and anything else a person might want to know about in their life.

When writing a column, especially a daily horoscope column, you create a reading for each day for each sign. You may also be required to offer a weekly, monthly, and overall year forecasting.

What It Takes

Read books on astrology and horoscopes, take classes, and learn how to do interpretations. Consider ways to present these charts and readings to clients in a creative manner to keep it interesting. Interview successful astrologers to learn how they got started in the field.

Work on your presentation style, as you must be believable; otherwise you will lose your readers. Believability comes from knowledge of your subject, but also the way you connect with readers to make them feel you wrote the column just for them. They see themselves in the information you have presented. If they feel you have accurately captured their traits and tendencies, they will come back for more.

Getting Started

As with many writing genres, writing for astrology has two basic requirements: a knowledge of the subject and the ability to write clearly and engagingly.

Start getting educated if you currently have no background in astrology or divination. Try your local colleges for their adult education classes and also the local YMCA and any other community-oriented organization. I suppose you could make a living writing about astrology from a skeptic's point of view, but it would be tough going: the main market for astrology writings is people who either believe in it or are at least interested in it. So if you want to write for this market, become an enthusiast. Know your sign and what it means. Read your daily horoscope.

If I wanted to break into astrology writing, I'd put up a website where people could get their horoscopes free, and spend money on Google advertising and email to drive traffic. Offer a free daily horoscope by email and get visitors to sign up for a subscription. When you have many thousands of subscribers—a feat easier to achieve than it sounds—you will have a credential and platform that will gain the attention of both newspaper editors and book publishers looking for astrology content.

Call up local readers to see if they will train you.

Additional Resources

The General Principles of Astrology by Aleister Crowley and Evangeline Smith Adams (Weiser Books, 2002).

Astrology for Dummies by Rae Orion (Wiley, 2007).

The Textbook of Astrology by A. John Pearce (American Federation of Astrologers, 2006).

Astrolabe offers astrology reference information and software: www.alabe. com.

Chaos Astrology offers information on astrology and a free reading: www. chaosastrology.net/freeastrologyreports.cfm.

The International Society for Astrological Research offers certification as a professional consultant in astrology: www.isarastrology.com.

Star IQ is a writing resource for astrology: www.stariq.com/Main/writefor. htm.

CHAPTER 43

Horror

Overview

In our modern lives, we still crave the thrill of being frightened. We look for safe scares in magazines, books, and movies. The horror market is booming, and demand for horror writers is evidenced in the numerous publications calling for short story submissions.

What It Pays

The Horror Writers Association suggests submitting to publications that pay at least 5 cents a word. This amount is considered to be the professional market rate. Advances for first horror novels range from $2,000 to $5,000, but top horror novelists get considerably more. Dean Koontz, for instance, can command $6 million per book.

Nuts and Bolts

Horror appeals to the morbid fascination we have with violence and death. These days horror can be anything that frightens us, but the traditional, long-standing horror stories are about ghosts, monsters, and vampires. Modern horror stories apply those basics to complex characters and suspenseful plots.

Horror stories offer a safety valve where we can exercise, in the words of Stephen King, "those antisocial emotions which society demands we keep stoppered up...for society's and our own good." This kind of genre story is very appealing to adolescents because horror, like rock music, is an antisocial anthem teens can relate to while experimenting with their emerging emotional extremes.

Horror writing is about evoking fear. It pushes us to examine our deepest fears, and to confront ourselves and see what lies inside.

What You'll Write

The top three qualities of a good scary story are suspense, character development, and setting. To keep your readers on the edge of their seats, you must incorporate elements of anticipation, dread, and uncertainty. Suspense should continue throughout the story, and provide a satisfying ending that leads to an unexpected or shocking twist.

Believable characters hold a horror story together. Readers want to be feel for the characters, their pain, fears, and triumphs. "You have got to love the people," says King, because "that allows horror to be possible."

A vivid, believable setting gives readers a clear picture of where all the action is happening, so they can feel present and involved. Use of the fantastic or supernatural increases the importance of first establishing the reality of the story's world.

What It Takes

If you're just starting out, write for the many online and print horror publications that offer short story contests. This way, you can see if this writing style is something you enjoy and have a talent for.

In writing good horror, it is essential to research the market. Borrow, buy, and read classic and contemporary books by the masters of horror, like Stephen King and H. P. Lovecraft.

Take online courses to educate you on the mechanics of crafting a frightening horror story from beginning to end.

Getting Started

There are fewer than a handful of horror magazines that actually pay writers for stories, and of those that do, the pay is peanuts. Worse, they have only a few thousand subscribers, so even if you break into the horror magazines, few readers will see your work. For the horror writer, it makes more sense to start with a novel, which will likely be a mass market paperback original. Consult *Writer's Market* for a listing of book publishers that publish horror fiction.

Unfortunately, as a first time horror novelist, you are not going to be able to sell your book on a proposal or chapter outline. You must actually write the novel, find a literary agent, or shop it directly to publishers; having an agent exponentially increases your odds of making a sale. Don't be discouraged: Stephen King wrote three unpublished horror novels before finally making his first sale.

Additional Resources

Dark Markets: www.darkmarkets.com.
Horror Writers Association: www.horror.org.
Ralan's Webstravaganza: www.ralan.com.

CHAPTER 44

How-To Writing

Overview

In a TV interview, historian and writer David McCullough expressed the opinion that, as a genre, how-to books are of limited value, saying,"You learn to play the piano by playing the piano, not by reading a book on how to play the piano."Yet each year, thousands of how-to books, DVDs, and audio learning programs are published, ranging from home improvement to finding a mate.

What It Pays

Spend some time browsing *Writer's Market*, the annual guide to the magazine and book marketplace. There you will find hundreds of editors who buy how-to articles, also known in the magazine publishing trade as"service articles." Magazines covering niche areas are especially looking for how-to material. Every issue of *Modern Bride* is filled with articles on how to plan a wedding. And the women's magazines publish how-to on everything from how to get a raise to how to have multiple orgasms. For how-to articles of 500–1,500 words, fees can range from a few hundred dollars to a thousand dollars or more per article.

Visit your local bookstore and notice all the how-to titles in categories ranging from baking and cooking, to investing and personal finance, to finding a mate and getting a divorce, to succeeding in your career and starting a small business. For most of these how-to authors, the pay scales are modest, with advances of $5,000–$25,000 or more. Those who establish themselves as a name in their field and build a large platform—speaking to large groups at conferences or having their own TV show—can earn more.

Nuts and Bolts

How-to writing must be specific, detailed, clear, and accurate. If you make an error in an article to be read for entertainment, you may be embarrassed, but nobody is harmed (in most cases) by the error. But if your how-to instructions are wrong, the reader cannot complete the project and will be frustrated and angry.

How-to writing must also have an organizational theme. A book on how to build a log cabin should be organized sequentially according to the steps involved in the planning and construction.

In addition to being well-organized, accurate, and clear, how-to writing must also be motivating. If the reader gets discouraged and puts the book aside, you have failed him in some way. A writer of how-to computer books once told me that, ideally, the voice used should be that of a patient, friendly teacher looking over the reader's shoulder.

Finally, how-to books should be entertaining, interesting, or at least not dull and boring. If you bore the reader, he will quickly give up on the reading and on the tasks you teach, and again you will have failed him.

What You'll Write

There are many formats for how-to writing. They include books, magazine and newspaper articles, special reports, booklets, e-books, audio programs, instructional DVDs—you name it. You can write for traditional book and magazine publishers, specialized companies selling how-to information products, or self-publish your how-to materials and sell them online.

What It Takes

What your customers want is solid how-to information that tells them how to do something, whether it's saving money on a new car or becoming a freelance copywriter. The mistake many how-to writers make is that they have written a "what-to" piece instead of the "how-to" book or article the buyer wants.

To live up to the customer's expectation of getting great how-to information, your book really has to tell the customer how to do the thing you are writing about. That means specific step-by-step instructions, recommended tools and resources, and strategies, tips, and techniques for doing the thing better and faster.

Many how-to books I see tell the reader what to do—but not how to do it. For instance, one small business advertising guide recommended advertising on billboards. That's advice on what to do, which is fine as it goes, but not enough. When a reader buys your book, he also wants you to tell him *how* to advertise on billboards. What are the dimensions of a typical billboard? What's the most effective word length for billboard copy? The recommended size of the letters painted on the board to for maximum readability? How can I find the billboards in my area where I can advertise? Who do I contact about renting them? What's a reasonable cost I can expect to pay? Can that be negotiated?

"What-to-do" is easy to write, because you present only the big picture (what to do), and not the niggling details (how to do it). But it cheats the reader. In most instances, the reader already has some idea of what to do. He is buying your book because he expects you to go in-depth and tell him exactly how to do it.

I tell the writer: the reason the reader is paying for our e-book is because he expects *us* to have done the research and present the results. Telling your reader to conduct an online search is the sign of a lazy writer who has not done his homework—and a sin I will always ask my writers to correct. While you can point people toward Google searches to find additional resources, your work itself should explain the how-to steps of the process itself.

Getting Started

One of the easiest ways to break into how-to writing is to teach a how-to course at a local adult education center, at the YMCA, or at a similar venue for low or no pay. Once you have taught the course and have that experience under your belt, approach the editor of your local newspaper about writing a how-to article and use your instructorship at the local venue as your credential. Once you have a few of those articles completed, send clips to magazine editors with query letters proposing articles on your topic.

Additional Resources

Writing Successful Self-Help and How-To Books by Jean Marie Stine (Wiley, 1997).

CHAPTER 45

Indexing

Overview

Any nonfiction work is made more useful as a reference with a comprehensive index. Some authors index their own work, but that is usually not the case. Publishers and packagers (who proofread, edit, and index books) may have a few in-house indexers. But the truth is that the bulk of indexing work is accomplished by freelancers, most working from home.

Indexing databases is another opportunity, involving physics, information technology, psychology, linguistics, and mathematics. What you should know is that skilled, traditional book indexers are moving into this area to assist the skilled technology experts with indexing. Indexers are working to teach information technology specialists that search engines need real people to create user-friendly indexes that actually work. These are often full-time jobs or full-time consulting enterprises.

What It Pays

Freelance book indexers price themselves either by page or by entry. Publishers that want specific detail in the index will generally pay by entry. Experienced indexers are compensated at a higher rate than those just starting out. A freelancer offering an estimate typically charges $50 per hour, $4–$5 per page, or 80 cents an entry.

Over the past eight years, the demand for database and technology indexers has grown substantially. A full-time employee with eight or more years of experience, either in-house or as a consultant, earns well over $100,000 a year.

Nuts and Bolts

Probably the best way to begin a freelance job in indexing is to start with books. The experience gained in vocabulary, intuition, and other basic indexing skills are worth it before jumping into database and search engine projects. (To learn more about web and database indexing, check out the resources below.)

For book index projects, you will receive, from the editor, page proofs for the book. These are the actual pages of the book, formatted and page numbered the way in which the book will be bound. Your task is to write the entries and subentries for queries on any subject discussed in the book.

What You Will Write

You need to anticipate a reader's quest for particular information. The indexer reads the book, makes headings and subheadings for the index while working, and notes the page number of each reference word.

What It Takes

If you are meticulous in your work, pay attention to detail, and exercise patience in working through material—thoroughly, to completion—you could be an indexer. You need to work rapidly, under a time crunch, as indexers are handed their work often at the last possible minute before printing. Being patient with impatient people, being graceful under pressure, and being diligent to meet tight deadlines are all qualities of a good indexer.

You should know that in the rush to get books to print, it is not likely that anyone will remark on your work, and will often not thank you adequately for it. If you are the kind of person who enjoys getting positive feedback for a job well done, indexing might not be for you.

Indexers do not need degrees, although a technical background is needed for some specific kinds of writing. A good indexer is generally intelligent and well read. A good library science course at a college or university is helpful, as is a good workshop.

Getting Started

1. Read books and check out their indices. Are some books indexed better than others? How would you do an index job differently for some of these books?

2. Take a course offered by the American Society for Indexing.

3. Apprentice with an experienced indexer. Some require a training fee. Use him or her as a reference to acquire more work.

4. Network by becoming a member of The American Society for Indexing.

5. Read or subscribe to *The Indexer,* an industry journal.

6. List your services as a freelance indexer in *Literary Marketplace* or *Books in Print.*

7. Contact publishers and indexing companies directly. Send a résumé and cover letter.

Additional Resources

The Indexing Companion by Glenda Brown and Jon Jeremy (Cambridge University Press, 2007).

American Society for Indexing: www.asindexing.org.

www.indexstudents.com.

CHAPTER 46

Instructional Writing

Overview

You bought an item from the store recently. The item was cheap, the parts were not identifiable, or the instructions were not clear—or all of the above. You have to go back and redo half of it because you missed something in step C. This is called poor technical writing.

Some technical writing is going overseas, along with product manufacturing. Even English-speaking technicians who write these instructions have a long way to go in their writing skills. That's where you come in. It's time to make companies aware that you can save their reputations and convince customers that it is safe to purchase their wares again.

What It Takes

Technical writers, who typically write other items besides instructional inserts, make more than $100,000 a year, depending on geographic location, expertise, experience, and the complexity of the job.

Lynn Wasnak of njcreatives.org recommends $60–$110 per hour for technical writers. However, the Society of Technical Communication advises freelance instructional writers to get away from an hourly rate because clients get nervous when their total cost is open ended. You may prefer to give a price for a project and include a clear scope of work. If the work goes beyond that scope, you receive additional compensation.

Nuts and Bolts

A company gives you the item or items and a few basic written materials about the device and its components. You need to sometimes decipher complex technical information and winnow it down to the basics in layman's terms.

An instructional insert can be a small card or a 100-page manual, depending on the complexity, and usually the expense, of the device. When you buy a new car, for example, a lengthy manual describing its use and care accompanies the purchase. Parts of instructional inserts may include the following:

- A few sentences highlighting the features of the product and the benefits to the user. This is part of advertising. Some prospective customers review the product information before purchasing the item. A good instruction insert sells the product to customers who scrutinize it carefully. This also reduces buyer's remorse later on.

- Equipment and supplies, a checklist to ensure that the package arrives with all necessary parts, plus a checklist of needed or optional components, such as batteries

- A diagram of the object and its labeled component parts

- A list of the functions and features of each part

- Assembly instructions to accompany the diagram

- Special notices or cautions about using or replacing some of the parts

- How and under what conditions to use the item

- How to maximize its enjoyment

- Interesting, optional, or artistic features

- Instructions for cleaning, care, and storage

- Warranty for parts or services

- Company contact information

- Product registration information

Your writing should reflect an element of excitement and enjoyment, as when one unwraps a gift—not just, "Here's your stuff. Good luck with that."

What You Will Write

Instructional inserts may have multiple documents for different components of the product. In addition to instruction manuals or leaflets, you may be asked to write sales brochures (sometimes these can be technical), manuals, technical reports, and feedback for the manufacturer. You may get assignments to work on technical manufacturing documents, if your expertise can meet the challenge.

The most important element of all technical writing, including instruction manuals, is that you assume your reader knows little to nothing. Don't talk down to your reader, but do start at zero and work up. For some of your users, English might be a second language. If your instructions are labeled correctly with appropriate headings, more savvy buyers will know how to scan your document to get just the information they need. They will not be put off by your elementary approach.

The second most important thing to remember is that all terms must be defined. Avoid abbreviations or define them regularly in your documents. Using industry jargon will alienate most readers.

What It Takes

You do not need to be technically gifted to write instructional inserts. You should be comfortable with the technology and able to ask questions. If you want to write instructional materials, you should:

- Have a logical, mechanically intuitive mind
- Enjoy problem solving
- Love writing and have a clear writing style that is precise, leaving no room for ambiguity
- Like to create order out of complexity and sometimes chaos
- Be comfortable reading technical information
- Be able to communicate with technical specialists
- Be able to empathize with a very untechnical reader
- Desire, work for, and write for the success of your client

Getting Started

The best preparation for this niche is to read a lot of instructional inserts. You probably have a drawer or file full of them at home. Could you do a better job than some of those writers? Debbie Swanson of *Writers Weekly* offers these suggestions for finding technical writing work, which includes work for instructional inserts:

- Look for start-up companies.
- Share your work, tips, and leads with other peers in the industry.
- Network with other technical writers in membership associations, at seminars, or online.
- Teach. Offering to do so makes you an expert. Offer to teach community courses or offer training services to companies.

Additional Resources

The Elements of Technical Writing by Gary Blake and Robert W. Bly (Longman, 2000).

The Instruction Writer's Guide: How to Explain How to Do Anything! by Marilyn Haight (Worded Write, 2008).

An online textbook for technical writing: www.io.com/~hcexres/textbook/instrux.html.

Society of Technical Communication: www.stc.org.

CHAPTER 47

Investor Relations

Overview

Delivering positive news to the media while downplaying the impact of negative news is the job of a company's investor relations department. It is a public relations interface with investors.

When Martha Stewart Living (the company) faced scandal due to inside trading by Martha Stewart (the person), the investor relations department of the company brought forth financial data to communicate with investors that the company was still solid. But the stock for Martha Stewart Living fell anyway. Without the efforts of the investor relations team, it could have suffered an even worse blow.

If you pursue a career in investor relations (IR), you have two main responsibilities: to excite investors and to put out fires. The role of developing good investor relations is more than just having a silver tongue, though. Your words need solid financial and legal backing, as well as an in-depth understanding of trading regulations.

What It Pays

Although freelancing for investor relations is not common practice, it is certainly possible. Generally, though, most companies either have their own investor relations department or subcontract out that responsibility to an investor relations firm. Once you settle into a firm and gain the trust of your co-workers, your hours can be flexible. Freelancing, consulting, or starting your own IR firm are always possibilities later on.

An entry-level position in this arena generally pulls in $45,000–$60,000 a year. IR senior management (for which you can be eligible if you have eight solid years of experience on your résumé) can rake in $107,000–$250,000 a year, making it one of the most lucrative staff positions for writers. Freelance IR writers are highly compensated as well. For instance, I am regularly hired by firms going public to write reports promoting their stocks—mostly microcaps, small caps, and penny stocks—to individual investors. For a twelve- to sixteen-page special report on a single stock, I get $10,000–$12,500 per assignment. In recent months, I have written IR reports on topics ranging from solar energy and wind power to gold mining and natural gas.

According to the U.S. Department of Labor, demand for public relations jobs is projected to grow over the next ten years, but competition is fierce at the entry level.

Nuts and Bolts

A company's investor relations department usually partners up with newswire services to get information to investors in a timely manner. The Federal Trade Commission and Securities Exchange Commission have guidelines for accurate and fair dispensing of company news. The framing and phrasing of the financial information is the job of the investor relations team. These company announcements go out over the newswire, and quickly thereafter, the newswire agencies funnel the information to newspapers and online business news services.

What You Will Write

Whether staff or freelance, the investor relations writer may be responsible for the following:

- financial information that stays in-house
- press releases
- company announcements
- questions and answers about the company's financial standing
- events coordination, for example, investor meetings (some of these are online) and annual reports
- corporate presentations for industry and investor conferences
- the monitoring of analyst models and estimates. Analysts are professional, independent financial institutions that project through the news agencies the company's future financial performance, based on a number of criteria.

Dominic Jones, of irwebreport.com, draws attention to the technical aspects of writing for the web. "Long tracts of gray text are unattractive in any format," he says, "but they are wholly off-putting on the web." He's right. If you check out investor relations sites, some of them have this penchant for writing their memos in a corporate gray. What's up with that? You want to create online reading that is easy for investors, not problematic.

Eye-tracking studies, he goes on, at the Poynter Institute at Stanford University, have verified the understanding that people are picky about what they choose to read on a screen. Anything that looks like an advertisement is skipped over, and the eye gravitates to text. So writing in a large, readable font, in an informative style, is the best bet for posting company announcements online.

What It Takes

Linda R. Press, a senior IR executive at PondelWilkinson, an investor relations firm, says in an interview with Career Exposure, "Computer skills are imperative at every level. A strong knowledge of disclosure requirements [SEC and FTC regulations] for public companies is essential for all but entry-level professionals." She goes on, "Professionals in investor relations and financial/corporate communications come from a wide variety of backgrounds including Wall Street, accounting, finance, journalism, marketing, strategic planning, public relations, and law. Educational backgrounds are just as diverse, but as a minimum require a bachelor's degree in preferably business or economics. An MBA, CFA, or master's in communications is additive."

Finally, and most importantly, "The most important skills in investor relations and financial communications are a strong understanding of Wall Street, finance, and financial journalism, along with well-honed writing and communications skills. As a consultant, business development and relationship-building become critical to advancing one's career."

Getting Started

1. Read investor relations releases. You will find them in news magazines, both hard copy and online, and on company websites. Could you do a better job in presenting the same information? How?

2. Get a bachelor's degree in a related field.

3. Get accredited. The ABC certification (Accredited Business Communicator) indicates that you have achieved a certain rank of proficiency in communicating financial data. This includes knowledge of FTC and SEC regulations.

4. Join NIRI (National Investor Relations Institute), a membership education and networking organization.

5. "Pay attention to what's going on in the business world," says Linda Press. "Religiously read business publications and websites, watch financial news, and get out there and meet business people through professional groups, alumni associations, and social events."

6. Journals such as *Investor Relations* and *Crisis Manager* can only help you.

7. Learn about XBRL (eXtensible Business Reporting Language), a financial reporting language that the SEC or FTC may require soon. If you are knowledgeable, you will have an edge.

8. Get two to three years of experience in-house before exploring subcontracting or entrepreneurial endeavors.

Additional Resources

Investor Relations: The Comprehensive Guide by Stephen Bragg (Accounting Tools, 2008).

"Writing for IR Websites" by Dominic Jones is at: www.irwebreport.com/features/features010303.htm.

An interview with Linda Press, IR executive with PondelWilkinson is at: cms.careerexposure.com/upclose/upclose_detail.jsp?siteid=3&DS=up close-lindapress.

IR101: www.ir101.com has general information about investor relations.

An IR job description can be found at jobs.iabc.com/c/job.cfm?site_id=65&jb=4359354.

CHAPTER 48

Jokes

Overview

Although some don't admit it, many professional comics buy jokes from free-lancers; fees start at $25–$100 per joke, more if you have a track record or write for a superstar. If you're self-motivated and have a funny bone, you can explore a career writing jokes or gags for stand-up comics. Like fuel that runs a car, new and fresh jokes keep comics and their careers flourishing. They can never get enough of them. But they have to be great jokes. No filler or bombs allowed.

What It Pays

As a beginner you can expect $25–$50 a joke. When you get more clients and get more established and comics start to use your material on television, you can charge more (especially if your joke killed on *Letterman*.) However, you might write fifteen to thirty jokes, and a professional comic may buy only three. If they do, you're lucky. Comedians are a picky bunch.

And realize once the comic buys a joke from you, it's his. You lose all exclusivity to it. And you can't sell it to another comic. If you do, and the performers find out, your reputation as a joke writer is ruined.

Nuts and Bolts

Television eats up material quicker than sharks do chum. That's why there is always a need for a terrific gag writer. Once you get proficient at gag writing, and word gets out, there's a strong chance other comedians might want to work with you. But be forewarned: comedians can be a desperate, competitive breed of entertainer. If you write sure-fire, killer jokes for one comedian, he might want to keep you all to himself. Comedians in general want their brethren and public to think that they're geniuses who came up with their great jokes all by themselves.

What You'll Write

As a joke writer, you'll write—what else!—jokes. But jokes about what? Well, while you should write on a variety of topics that interest you, they have to be of interest to the audience as well. There are many different styles of gags. What's important is that you should never let the audience know where you're going with a joke. Never let them get ahead of you. Comedy is built on surprise. Here is an example of a joke from comic Peter Fogel that uses misdirection.

"Man, if anyone is thinking of going to their high school reunion—don't. Big disappointment. People change. I saw this one former schoolmate. The gray in the beard, the beer belly, the thinning hair…and that was the Prom Queen."

Just as in writing sitcoms, jokes have their own structure, too. It's a craft and you have to learn it.

In writing jokes you want to get to the punch line using the fewest words possible. Exceptions of course are the jokes with the long setup, like "This topless nun walks into a biker bar…."

Remember when writing a story joke, you're using a long premise with the hopes of painting a picture in the audience's mind. They're going along for the ride, so don't disappoint them. Audiences as a rule don't like to think too much and usually demand instant gratification (at least a drunken audience does.) If you don't think it's funny, then the audience won't. Joke writer Gene Perret says, "Writing comedy is a seat of the pants thing."

What It Takes

Don't overanalyze your jokes too much. Just write, edit, write, edit. Show your work to your friends and family (except jokes about them). Get their consensus on which ones are funny. If a joke gets a decent response, see if you can tweak it and make it funnier. Shorten the premise, change the punch line. Play around with it. Never get married to a joke you like. If it doesn't work, and it's a dog, lose it.

And above all don't defend the ones you've discarded. Don't get defensive and admonish your buddy, "Hey, man, you don't get it, see the dwarf was…" No, he gets it. It just wasn't that funny. So move on.

After you've alienated your loved ones with your material, go after another audience. A paying one. And the best way to see if you've mined some gold is to actually perform your material yourself—at an open mike at a local comedy club. Baptism under fire. What is so gratifying is that you'll know immediately if a particular joke is working.

But for now, you have some homework to do. If you see a particular established comic on a late show, and you think he's funny, study him. Each comic has a unique voice, certain hook, or some intangible that makes him stand out, whether it's his outlook on life (perhaps he does topical material) or maybe it's the character or persona he's created. Either way the public relates to them for a reason and laughs at what they say. From Rodney Dangerfield's "I don't get no respect" to Joan Rivers's "Can we talk?" their persona, style, or delivery makes them unique.

Getting Started

If you see a particular comedian on television that you really like, focus on his material and style. Figure out what you think he thinks is funny, and what the audiences laughs at. Does he lash out at society's injustices (Lewis Black)? Is he self-deprecating (Richard Lewis)? Perhaps he does observational material (Jerry Seinfeld).

Next, try to find out when he's going to appear at your local club. Watch his performance and try to meet him after the show. Explain that you're not only an admirer, but also a comedy writer. Ask him if he's interested in buying some jokes from you. Most comics are very approachable and won't mind looking at your material. (It never hurts to ask.) And better yet, if you worked on specific jokes for his (or her) particular persona, he'll be even more flattered and more apt to look at what you have.

If the comedian has some notoriety and is doing television on a regular basis, there's a strong chance he is getting paid decent bucks. You don't want to approach the opening or middle act. They can't afford to buy material yet. But the headliner who's a draw at the club can. If the entertainer likes your material, he might commission you to write some jokes for him on spec. If he can use them, he'll buy them. Simple as that. And don't be afraid to ask him what arena to concentrate on. The usual favorites are kids, family, sex, dating, and politics. (The last three work hand in hand.)

And realize that this performer will try to get you cheap. It's the nature of the beast. You're hungry, and he knows it. A comedian is running a business: himself. He has an overhead and possibly an ex-wife somewhere who is probably draining him big time.

If you've written for some established comics, you're confident, and you're ready for the big time (e.g., Chris Rock or Joan Rivers), then you have to contact "their people" and see if the star accepts freelance submissions of jokes. Stars guard their privacy, so you have to be a little inventive. (Please, no stalking here.)

Stars are all members of the American Federation of Television and Radio Artists (www.aftra.org) or the Screen Actors Guild (www.sag.org). Contact their union (request membership), and ask for the star's agent or publicist's name and phone number. If you end up calling the agent first, be prepared.

They usually don't want to be bothered and will most likely give you to the publicist or the client's manager.

Once you contact the publicist, briefly explain your intention. Remember: you can't come off as a fan. You're a professional comedy writer, so act accordingly. Hopefully they tell you how to sell comedy material to their client (if indeed they are buying). You might get a cheat sheet telling you the type of material the star is looking for. But before you submit any jokes, you will have to sign a release form. It states that if the star buys the material, they own it.

You probably won't get a chance to meet your client in the beginning. If things go well and you prove yourself, there's a chance you might get a call from him down the road.

As far as sending jokes to late night television shows, it is not recommended. It's very difficult to break in, and they have paid staff writers or use freelancers who they've had relationships with for years.

Additional Resources

Comedy Writing Workbook by Gene Perret (Scarecrow Press, 1994).

CHAPTER 49

Landing Pages

Overview

A landing page is essentially a long-copy sales letter posted on the Web and dedicated to selling a single product. The objective is to convert unique visits to orders. Why do online marketers need landing pages? Well, blogs, social networking, search engine optimization, viral videos, online ads, and a dozen other Internet marketing methods can drive traffic. But what do you do with that traffic once you get it?

That's where your landing pages come in. A powerfully written, well-designed, and scientifically tested landing page is the one tool that can convert all that expensive traffic to leads and sales. Double or triple your landing page conversion rates, and you can double or triple your subscriber list, revenues, and profits.

One of the biggest mistakes you can make in online marketing is to simply put up a landing page for a product and accept whatever conversion rate it generates as the final number—or the best you can do. A good copywriter who can write persuasive online copy can help companies that market products on the Internet to squeeze more incremental performance, conversion, and sales out of their important landing pages and other websites.

What It Pays

There are two basic types of landing pages. A lead-generation landing page is a web page where the visitor can sign up for a free offer. The offer might be downloading a white paper or registering for a free webinar. Because the offer is free, these free-offer landing pages are usually short, and therefore there's a limit to how much a writer can charge. Fees for a landing page making a free offer typically are $1,000–$1,500.

When you sell a product directly from a landing page (for instance, www.myveryfirstebook.com), you ask the visitor to make a purchase online with their credit card, so you need a lot more copy. For a long-copy landing page, fees are all over the lot. Beginners write these landing pages for $1,000. More experienced copywriters charge $5,000–$7,500.

Nuts and Bolts

The headline of a landing page is similar to the headline of ad. It grabs the reader's attention so that they read the subhead below it.

Michael Masterson's 4U formula can help you write stronger headlines for landing pages and other advertising. The 4U formula says that headlines should be:

❏ urgent

❏ useful

❏ unique

❏ ultra-specific

The headline should give your customers a promise that is big, and it must have an emotional appeal. For instance, the headline on the landing page for my e-book on email marketing reads:

Triple Your Email Marketing Results in 90 Days—or Your Money Back!

This is a dual promise: you will get results, and there is no risk to you.

Why did it work? Every person using email marketing wants to get better results. Better response rates translate directly into increased revenue. Even successful, experienced online marketers want to triple their results.

Here's the headline for a landing page selling a viral video marketing e-book:

How a "Bionic Hamburger" Made Len F. a Rich Man

This headline combines a dual promise with curiosity. What is a bionic hamburger? The sales copy answers that question, and tells you how it made Len F. a rich man. The idea of a bionic hamburger makes readers curious; they want to know what it is. What draws readers in is that discovering that answer could make them wealthy, too.

The headline gets the reader's attention. The subhead expands on the idea in the headline to draw the reader into—and get him to start reading—the body copy. The subhead for the landing page selling the e-book on viral video marketing says:

Everybody's talking about YouTube, Facebook, and MySpace. More important, they're sharing videos and pictures on these

sites with their friends, colleagues, and neighbors. *The good news is: now it's easy and cheap to make your own short video… post it all over the Internet…and advertise your product or service to thousands of eager customers—virtually for free!*

Notice the one thing this subhead doesn't do. It doesn't satisfy the reader's curiosity about a bionic hamburger. In fact, the curiosity is increased by suggesting the bionic hamburger has something to do with a video. What the subhead does do is show the reader that the videos are part of what made Len F. rich, that the videos are popular, and that they are easy and cheap to make.

Aside from the headline and subheads, the most important part of the landing page copy is the lead. The lead runs from the salutation to the first subhead inside the letter. You can use the lead to identify a problem or need, make an emotional appeal, or make a big promise. How you use it is determined in large part by your headline and subhead. The lead has to relate to what you introduced in the headline and subhead, or the reader will feel misled. Here's the lead for the landing page on my email marketing e-book:

Dear Marketer:

Whether you are an Internet marketer…or simply use the Internet as part of your overall marketing mix…

Your success online depends in large part on email marketing— and in particular, on writing and broadcasting email marketing campaigns that get delivered to—opened—read—and responded to by your prospects and customers.

The bad news is: it's tough today to write email marketing messages that comply with CAN SPAM laws…and aren't blocked by ISPs and spam filters.

It's even tougher to get your prospect's attention…stop her from deleting your marketing emails…and get her to open, read, and respond to your message.

The good news is: proven solutions to all of your email marketing problems exist.

Now, you can download these email marketing "best practices" immediately—and watch your open rates, click-through rates, and conversions soar.

This lead starts by making the reader aware of a huge problem in online marketing today: email deliverability. It then focuses on the topic of email marketing and how to make your email marketing efforts successful. You are encouraged to continue reading not simply because you will get a solution. You will be getting proven solutions—more than one. It also promises you can have the solutions immediately and see immediate improvement in your marketing results.

What You'll Write

Here are some variations of response-oriented web pages that clients typically ask you to write:

Landing page

Any web page designed to generate conversion or other direct action, as opposed to a page that just provides content or links to more content. Example: www.theinternetmarketingretirementplan.com

Name squeeze page

A landing page, usually brief, designed to capture the user's email address, either in exchange for an offer of free content or as a condition of allowing the reader to access a copy on a landing page or other web page. Also known as a squeeze page; see www.bly.com/reports as an example.

Order page

When you click the Order Now button on a landing page, you are taken to an order page describing the offer and allowing you to place your order online.

Pop-over

A page that pops up on the screen when you visit a website or landing page, meant to capture the email address of the visitor, usually by offering free content.

Pop-under

A page that pops up on the screen when you attempt to leave a landing page or website without placing an order, meant to capture the email address of the visitor, usually by offering free content.

Floater

Similar to a pop-over or pop-under, except it is not blocked by pop-up blockers because it is part of the web page or landing page HTML code. The floater is used to capture the visitor's email address, usually by offering free content.

What It Takes

Writing a winning landing page is much closer to writing a traditional direct mail sales letter or mail-order ad than writing the short-copy descriptive web pages you find on most corporate sites. Those short pages are often merely descriptive.

But the landing page's purpose is to make a sale. Specifically, it is to convince as many visitors as possible to purchase the product being promoted on that page. Writing strong-selling copy to generate an order takes more skill and talent than writing ordinary descriptive copy; therefore, a good copywriter with a track record in landing pages can charge a premium price.

One thing you need not worry about (at least not too much) is optimizing your landing pages with keywords and phrases. Google typically gives low rankings to sales pages, and landing pages are sales pages. While I do advise you to use keywords in landing page headlines and body copy, it is not nearly as critical as with regular websites.

Getting Started

The plum assignment in writing landing pages is long-copy landing pages that sell a product directly off the website, and there's absolutely no reason even a beginner can't start with that. It's where I would start, since there is very little money in writing short-copy, free-offer landing pages.

The companies that need long-copy landing pages range from tiny mom-and-pop Internet marketing entrepreneurs to midsize companies to large direct marketers and publishers. You can approach any of these, since there is a shortage of copywriters who specialize in landing pages. You can do your first few assignments at the low end of the pay scale ($1,000 for a landing page) to overcome the fact that you don't have a lot of experience.

Small independent online marketers in particular are willing to hire a new copywriter as long as the price is within their budget. Once you have a couple of successful landing pages working online, you can point potential clients to those and gradually raise your fees.

Additional Resources

Dedicated to marketing online with landing pages: www.thelandingpage guru.com.

CHAPTER 50

Love Letters

Overview

A love letter attempts to find reason in the madness—and express it eloquently. It is the written desire to bring someone who is already close even closer. And sometimes it is the desire to gently part ways. For writers, this process comes easily because the written word is our strength and preferred mode of communication.

For some people, however, writing a love letter, especially at a pivotal moment in a relationship, is awkward at best and a crisis at worst. Couple that awkwardness with a large population of singles (thanks in part to a national divorce rate of over 50 percent) what you have is the growing need and desire for people to have someone else do the writing for them. According to Emilie Johnston, president of libraryonline.com, "A lot of people who struggle with letter writing can't make it flow. They have random thoughts thrown all over the place. We're piecing it together. We're giving you the flow."

There is demand for people with excellent written communication skills, and businesses specializing in writing are forming at a rapid rate to meet that need—even where personal writing is concerned. Are you are talented at crafting a love letter, a really good love letter? You can be paid for your gift.

What It Pays

One writing service, www.letterlover.net charges a $50 flat rate for a letter. LibraryOnline.com charges an annual membership fee of $40, which allows subscribers to peruse love letter templates covering all kinds and stages of relationships. Members can download a letter or letters of their choosing at any time during the year, do their own editing, and send it to their significant other, who will not likely know about the ghostwriting involved. Passionup. com writes the letters, puts them in template form, makes them available for free, and makes money through advertising. Another way to make money in this industry is through how-to manuals, books, or workshops. Some people just want to hone their own skills.

Nuts and Bolts

There are different genres of love letters:

- secret romances
- long distance
- love at first sight
- Internet courtship
- apologies
- breakups

If you write custom love letters, the best way to send them to your client is via email attachment, so your client may handwrite them on stationery of their choosing. Or you might offer a variety of stationery options as part of your cost or for an added fee. Don't forget to offer other personal letters, which can be as endearing as love letters. What about these occasions and milestones?

- apology letters (nonromantic)
- thank-you notes that require more than a few words
- groom to his bride on their wedding day, or vice versa
- the grateful daughter to her parents on their golden wedding anniversary
- the grandparents to a grandchild for a bat or bar mitzvah
- the letter from Santa Claus ("I like the way you are sharing with your sister")
- parents to a child leaving for college or the military

Here is your opportunity to create some heirloom-quality letters—or to teach people how to write them—ones that the recipient will treasure and pass onto the next generation.

What You Will Write

Many professional letter writers have noted that the writer of love letters usually wants to take the relationship up a notch. He or she wants to get closer and deeper. Even in the nonromantic categories of personal writing, there is a desire to form a closer connection.

There is a word for that. It's called *intimacy*. The best way to create intimacy with a reader is for the writer to disclose something about himself. Sharing significant feelings that one normally keeps close to the heart and does not readily blurt out creates tenderness and closeness. A connection is formed. Often the recipient will respond with disclosure, too. Sharing those feelings involves risk, and sometimes coming up with the words is daunting. That's where you come in.

What about dreams, goals, plans for the future? Having loving feelings toward someone does not propel the relationship forward unless there is a plan. Perhaps the message is that together we are better than the sum of our parts.

The other thing that is needed is appreciation and admiration. True love is not greedy and does not pursue its own ends. If you want to craft an enduring love letter, the "writer" should note profound qualities in the recipient that have nothing to do with infatuation. How do his talents contribute to the world at large? How does she contribute to the happiness of everyone around her—not just you?

What It Takes

Writing classical letters is becoming a lost art. If you already craft letters for the people you love, you are perfect for this job. You need empathy in order to assist your client to disclose some pretty emotional information. Your skills in listening and counseling will come in handy. If you want to take your heirloom-quality love letters to the next level, sign up for a calligraphy class.

Getting Started

1. Read classical love letters. There are plenty of examples online. Because letter writing is becoming a lost art, go back in time a little to get a good grasp on what is needed. Emilie Johnston of onlinelibrary.com gets inspiration from the letters former president Ronald Reagan wrote to Nancy. "They're unbelievably touching," Johnston says. "Ronald Reagan had the gift of writing."

2. Read books about the art of writing love letters.

3. Practice, practice. Write up several examples to promote yourself.

4. Set up an online letter writing service.

5. Offer to custom craft each letter or provide templates.

6. Offer workshops in your community. Become the expert.

7. Write a good book or how-to manual on love letters. Self-publish or submit to a publishing house.

Additional Resources

For the Love of Letters: A 21st-Century Guide to the Art of Letter Writing by Samara O'Shea (Collins, 2007).

Read "Streetside Letter Writing Service" at scarletconspiracy.blogspot.com/2007/05/streetside-letter-writing-service.html.

www.letterlover.net/order.

spec.lib.vt.edu/cwlove.

www.wendy.com/letterwriting.

www.wordsru.com/letter-writing-service.php.

CHAPTER 51

Medical Writing

Overview

Employment opportunities for medical writers are expected to increase by 25–35 percent (according to www.healthcareers.com) through the year 2010. Medical writing communicates clinical and scientific data and information to a range of audiences in a wide variety of formats. A medical writer is a specialized writer. The medical writer's job is to understand the content and make it clear to the reader. Your readers could be health professionals, students, or even the general public. Though the medical content that needs to reach these diverse groups are somewhat the same, the format, tone, and style in which it has to be written is totally different for each of these groups. It should be more technical for health professionals and nontechnical, without any medical jargon, for the general public. The medical writer's job is to know the audience and write accordingly.

What It Pays

According to the 2004 salary survey of the American Medical Writers Association (AMWA), the median income of writers working full time for a company was $75,000 a year. The mean gross income of freelance medical writers in the 2004 survey was $103,432, with a net income of $77,529. The mean hourly rate for freelance medical writers was $85.

Nuts and Bolts

Medical writers compile information and present it in a concise and clear format to the audience, mostly the public, and sometimes health professionals. Sometimes medical writers may write articles for journals, which are written in a prescribed format and guidelines.

Though the American Medical Writers Association has been around since 1940, the practice of pharmaceutical companies employing medical writers specifically to write clinical study reports, study protocols, and other documents needed for submission to the FDA for drug approval has become common only in the past few decades.

There are several reasons for the demand for medical writers. Pharmaceutical companies want to get new drugs to market as quickly as possible. They want the information about the drugs to reach the health-care professional so that they can start prescribing them to their patients. At the same time, they also want the general public to know about the arrival of a new drug to market and the benefits of the drug.

The pharmaceutical companies face tough competition, but it is a lucrative business as well. So these companies always want to make use of opportunities very efficiently. They use the services of the medical writer to compile data about the new drug. The medical writer's job is to assimilate all the information and put it in clear and concise language before it reaches the target audience.

Finally, people constantly seek information about how to stay healthy and about diseases they might be suffering from. People have access to medical websites, online medical journals, health education websites, drug information websites, and health discussion forums. These websites are constantly updated. A medical writer is needed to write the content for these websites and sometimes serve as a moderator in the discussion forums.

The following clients need medical writers who may work as in-house writers or freelance writers:

- Academic medical centers hire medical writers for writing course materials.

- Contract research organizations involve medical writers on projects outsourced to them by the pharmaceutical companies. The projects include writing investigative brochures, clinical trial protocols and reports, and sales copy.

- Doctors hire medical writers to write newsletters, health information materials for patients, articles for their websites, and materials for scientific paper presentations at conferences.

- Foundations like Global Neuroscience Initiative Foundation (www.gnif.org) hire medical writers for proposal writing and educational medical writing.

- Hospitals and health-care systems hire medical writers to write articles for their websites, to write about the services they provide, and to write materials for patients.

- Medical device manufacturers hire medical writers to write website content, brochures, sales copy, newsletters, and informational materials.

- Pharmaceutical companies hire medical writers to write investigator's brochures, clinical trial protocols and reports, sales copy, and informational materials for patients and physicians.

- Publishers hire either an in-house medical writer or a freelancer to write medical articles and medical books. News magazines may hire medical writers as science journalists.

- Websites belonging to pharmaceutical companies, medical device managers, doctors, hospitals, and academic institutions hire medical writers to write about their products and services.

What You'll Write

Tasks range from writing TV commercials and magazine ads to sales presentations and formulary kits selling drugs to doctors. A formulary kit is a folder of information given to pharmacists and doctors when a new drug gets approved.

One of the best-paying assignments in medical writing is the monograph. Usually, a monograph summarizes all the scientific and clinical data known about a new drug, particularly data that has been published in journals or scientific meeting abstracts. Monographs can be sixteen to twenty-four pages, or can become longer, forty to sixty pages (usually standard letter-size pages). A typical content flow is (1) overview of the disease and current treatment strategies; (2) overview of the new drug, its category, mechanism of action, pharmacokinetics, pharmacodynamics, etc.; (3) preclinical studies; and (4) clinical studies in healthy human volunteers and patients, usually building up to the pivotal clinical trials submitted to the FDA to get drug approval.

Payment for monographs are $50–$75 per hour, which take 80–100 hours for the shorter page range and 150–200 hours for the longer page range, including two rounds of revisions.

Regulatory medical writing involves producing clinical documentation required by national regulatory agencies such as the FDA when assessing the safety and efficacy of drugs. This allows the regulatory agencies to get their drugs and devices approved so that they can start marketing their product. The clinical documentation covers the entire process of drug and device development. The various components of clinical documentation include:

- **Investigator's brochure.** This provides information on everything known about the drug. It is a basic document required in a clinical trial, together with the clinical trial protocol. Investigator's brochures need periodic updating. The brochure should include a title page, confidentiality statement, table of contents, summary, introduction, properties, formulation, nonclinical studies, effects in humans, and summary of data and guidance for the investigator.

- **Clinical study protocols.** This is required to ensure that the clinical trial is conducted properly and efficiently. A drug is subjected to four phases of clinical trials before it is approved and marketed. The clinical study protocol document should include a synopsis (one page), objectives, study designs and methods, inclusion and exclusion criteria, variables measured, analysis methods, materials and legal aspects, study duration, study center, budget, financial resources, and bibliographic references.

- **Clinical study reports.** These provide information gathered from clinical trials. These reports are based on the outcome of the different phases of the clinical trials. The reports should include title page, synopsis, table of contents, list of abbreviations and definition of terms, ethics, investigator and study administrative structure, introduction, study objectives, investigational plan, study patients, efficacy evaluation, safety evaluation, discussion and overall conclusion, tables, figures and graphs, reference list, and appendices.

Regulatory medical writing is a team effort and can be more demanding than educational medical writing. It involves writing in association with diverse professionals like medical professionals, clinical research associates, and statisticians. All these professionals provide data on various aspects of the clinical trials. The regulatory medical writer has to assimilate them and produce a document that meets guidelines. Bigger companies have many in-house medical writers. But smaller companies outsource regulatory medical writing to contract research organizations and freelance writers.

The two important aspects of regulatory medical writing are attention to detail and conciseness of presentation. Since regulatory documents can be lengthy, sticking to the guidelines and making the document concise is very essential. The job may involve handling statistical data. Though knowledge of statistics is beneficial, it is not essential.

What It Takes

A number of colleges offer degree programs in medical writing, including the University of the Sciences in Philadelphia and the University of Chicago Graham School of General Studies.

Medical writing is a specialty in which credentials are valued, although they are more important to employers hiring staff medical writers than to clients hiring freelance medical writers. A certificate or degree in medical writing is a useful credential. Many medical writers have undergraduate or graduate degrees in biology, biochemistry, and a few are PhDs or MDs.

Getting Started

The AMWA publishes a job market pink sheet for members listing a large number of full-time positions as well as some freelance projects. The job listings do not list salary or fees being offered.

Sometimes medical professionals approach seasoned writers to write medical articles for them. The reason could be a busy schedule or an inability to write convincing, clear, and interesting health content. Many of the articles that appear in scientific journals under the bylines of prominent academics are actually written by ghostwriters hired by drug companies. But they tend to keep this fact hidden. A report presented at a medical journal conference found that just 10 percent of articles on studies sponsored by the drug industry that appeared in top medical journals disclosed help from a medical writer.

Additional Resources

Guidebook to Better Medical Writing by Robert Iles (Iles Publications, 2003).

CHAPTER 52

Menus

Overview

You are shopping downtown and are thinking about going to a restaurant for lunch, but you have never been there before or read any reviews. What do you do? Well, most of us check out the menu. If the menu looks inviting, we will try it. There are several printing services out there for restaurants, but few offer experienced copywriters to write the menu itself. As menus are a form of advertising, restaurants, particularly the upscale variety, pay writers to take care of the text for a menu.

What It Pays

This is a new arena for someone who wants it. You have to experiment with prices to see what the market will bear. If you are one of the few writers offering this service, you will be in demand and in a position to charge higher fees.

Nuts and Bolts

Here are guidelines for writing copy for menus:

- An accurate and attractive description of the dishes invites customers to try them. Other information about the dish is sometimes posted, for example, how spicy is it is, how many calories, etc.

- Prices are listed clearly next to the dish description.

- Layout and graphics are important. You will likely work with a printing service or graphics design specialist to put together the presentation.

- Many restaurants do not think of quoting a rave review and putting it right on the menu. But it's an important form of advertising. If a newspaper or dining service gives the restaurant a high rating, customers should know about it.

- Have the restaurant ask loyal customers to write a testimonial.

- Offer interesting food facts. If an uncommon food or spice is offered on the menu, give a little background on it. Most people like to read and order, so don't write a news column. Just a sentence or two to raise an eyebrow. Sometimes curiosity and the desire to try something new sparks a decision.

- Also consider cultural points of interest. Did-you-know kinds of information enhance the dining experience.

What You Will Write

In addition to the standard menu, there are dessert and wine cards, or sometimes there are other inserts in the menu. According to Quantified Marketing (www.quantifiedmarketing.com), the following are common mistakes in menu crafting:

- print size is too small or too ornate
- menu size is too big
- missing translations for a non-English dish
- antiquated presentation
- lacking daily or weekly special inserts
- entrées don't look like their photos
- generic clip art
- mismatch of the type of restaurant and menu style

What It Takes

If you enjoy dining, especially fine dining, this is a job for you. You need a discriminating palate, descriptive vocabulary, and a desire to research food, both by interviewing chefs and looking up needed information. Good people skills are a must. A background in photography and graphics is helpful but not necessary.

Getting Started

1. Eat at restaurants (and you thought this job was hard).
2. Study menus carefully. How would you improve them?
3. Research food and restaurant-related topics.
4. Build a portfolio of samples to show clients.
5. Approach restaurant owners and printers specializing in menus, either by person or phone, and offer your services. Show them your portfolio.
6. Set up a website to advertise your services.

Additional Resources

The Menu Maker's Guide to Restaurant Menu Design by Jane Walter-Ogurek (Graphic Xpress, 2001).

CHAPTER 53

Newspapers

Overview

Many people have argued that television and the Internet have made news-papers an outmoded, inefficient means of delivering news. With online news services, you get news instantly, as it happens. Given the easy access of news and information online, why do newspapers still survive? Editor Tom Hagy says, "If people are massaging and manipulating and shaving the Web down to a point to which they get what they are interested in, and only what they are interested in, how will they learn anything beyond their current interests?"

A recent Roper poll shows that 69 percent of Americans prefer to get their news from television versus only 37 percent from newspapers. In 1980, 62.2 million newspapers were sold each day. By 1995 that figure had dropped to 59.3 million—a decline of 4.8 percent in fifteen years. During the same period, the number of daily newspapers in the United States dropped from 1,743 to 1,548—a decline of 11 percent.

In the United States, the First Amendment to the Constitution established a unique role for American journalism—to become an unofficial watchdog of the government. The best journalists take the responsibility that comes with the right to a free press very much to heart. That responsibility requires reporting accurately and reliably, with the purpose of informing the populace. A noble calling, to be sure.

But the future of print journalism is uncertain. We live in an era of "Citizen Journalism," where readers are more likely to turn to a blogger or website for their news than to a newspaper or news magazine. Magazine and news-paper publishers are seeing declines in both circulation and ad revenues. Some publishers are folding their print editions and continuing to publish online only. Traditional newspapers and magazines that hope to survive are beefing up their websites, and in many cases the revenue from and impor-tance of their digital publishing is overshadowing the print publication that was their origin—a sad trend for those of us who love to write and read the printed word.

What It Pays

Daily newspapers pay better salaries than weekly town papers. As a rule, the larger the circulation, the better the pay. In the directories listed at the end of this chapter, you will find the names and addresses of thousands of daily newspapers.

Most journalists start with smaller dailies, then move to bigger papers. Often their ultimate goal is a job with the *Boston Globe, New York Times, Washington Post, USA Today,* or *Wall Street Journal.* These newspapers have the largest circulations and pay the highest salaries. Of course, the top ten or twenty papers can hire a limited number of reporters and editors. So only a small fraction of reporters ever get to write for the *Times* or *Journal.*

Most reporters enjoy decent salaries, interesting work, and rewarding careers at small- and midsize papers. Staff journalists earn somewhat more than the average full-time freelance writer, but less than staff writers and communications managers in corporate positions.

The average journalist's salary in the United States is about $32,000 a year, but the range is wide. Many small-town reporters, even with several years of experience, earn salaries in the upper teens or low twenties. Reporters for major daily newspapers can make $40,000–$70,000 a year or more. Some syndicated columnists, financial journalists, big-name sportswriters, and other top reporters have incomes in the six figures. Newspaper reporters, especially those at "name" papers, can supplement their income writing magazine articles or books.

Nuts and Bolts

It is difficult—not impossible, but difficult—to get a job in journalism without having majored in the subject at college. Therefore, if you are interested in becoming a reporter, this should be your major course of study at school. You do not have to major in journalism as an undergraduate. In fact, many journalists who cover a specific topic major in that topic. Many computer journalists, for instance, either have degrees in computer science or have worked as programmers. Having an undergraduate degree in subject X can give you in edge in landing a job in journalism covering subject X. However, if your undergraduate degree is in subject X, you probably want to consider a master's degree in journalism.

What will you learn in journalism school? "I teach storytelling in the main," says Craig Wolff, an associate professor at the Columbia School of Journalism. "When all else washes away—new media, round the clock news—that is what will persist as the most vital, sought-after skill a journalist can have.

As a species, we have always been interested in the story, the narrative, the piece-by-piece assembling of how something came to be. This is a native instinct that will be sought and treasured."

Adds writer Barry Sheinkopf, "We want, as readers, not to be persuaded by a sensible and well-modulated argument, but to be overcome by an irresistible force. We want to be absorbed by the tale, rendered speechless, carried away."

The other requirement is that you were active in your high school and college newspapers. This is how you generate published writing samples—known in the business as "clips" or "clippings"—to show editors who might hire you.

"Clarity and accuracy and depth of knowledge and research are indispensable skills," says Wolff. "In these times, with so many competing voices, the ones that can be consistently and reliably on the mark are the ones who will be trusted. People who practice the craft in this way are the ones who will endure, as models for the craft, and in the marketplace as well."

The reason it's hard to get a job without credentials is that the field is so competitive. So many young people want to be reporters and editors that there are many more applicants than there are jobs. Those who have the education and the experience have the advantage. There are exceptions. Expertise in a specific field may substitute for experience in journalism, if the specialty is in demand. For instance, one writer was asked to be a financial reporter, even though his previous job experience was in real estate, because he had written a book on the subject. The book demonstrated both his expertise in the subject and his writing ability, but his experience is the exception, not the rule.

What You'll Write

The newspaper business is deadline driven. As a newspaper reporter, you learn to write and edit quickly. Daily newspapers need fresh stories every day. So newspaper writers work on incredibly tight deadlines. Reporters for small newspapers cover local town council meetings, high school sports, obituaries, and crime reports. The size of the staff usually means you're an all-purpose reporter. This is a great opportunity to learn the trade and can be more interesting for someone who prefers to write on a variety of subjects.

On larger newspapers, reporters generally specialize on a beat. Like the cop who walks a beat and gets to know the neighborhood, a beat reporter gets to know all the necessary background and contacts for covering a specific subject area. Some of the usual beats are police, courts, education, business, entertainment, or sports.

Although newspapers do publish feature stories, most of what is in newspapers has a news slant. You must be aware of what is going on within your beat, whether it's the city council, the city police desk, or the world. If current events do not fascinate you, and you are not already an avid newspaper reader, you might be better off doing another type of writing.

What It Takes

There are two ways to learn about writing for newspapers. The first is in school, either by taking journalism courses or by working on your school paper, or both. High school journalism courses are valuable and can teach you a lot, but a bachelor's degree in journalism is a good idea if you want to pursue this as a career. Another option, if you have a bachelor's degree in another field, is to go to graduate school in journalism.

The second way to learn about journalism is to write articles for practice. Perhaps you have a club or company newsletter. Ask the editor if you can contribute some articles. Small weekly community shoppers occasionally take articles from town residents. Many weekly and some daily papers also accept freelance article submissions. Pay is minimal, often $50 or less per article. One local columnist, when on vacation, is able to get temporary replacements to write her parenting column at no charge—seeing their bylines in the newspaper is payment enough.

The best way to freelance for newspapers is to send query letters, as with magazines. Look at the kinds of articles the newspaper publishes. Study the organization and writing style. Then come up with your own ideas that you think will fit in with the newspaper's format. You can present your ideas to the editor first in the form of a query letter or telephone call, or you can take a chance and write the article to submit on spec—on the speculation that the editor will like it enough to publish it.

Getting Started

One way to start is as a part-time reporter for your town's weekly newspaper, also called a penny saver or shopper. These newspapers pay little or nothing for unsolicited articles, but they are real newspapers, and the experience and the published clip will help establish your credentials as a journalist. Although the pay is close to minimum wage and the standards aren't high, do a good job and you can build your skill and amass a portfolio of clips that could lead to a higher-paying staff job or freelance gig with a better paper.

Many big-city newspaper reporters and editors began their careers on the staffs of weekly newspapers. While many move on to careers on larger newspapers, others stay to advance in editorial positions. They like the small-town flavor and the focus on local news and issues.

Additional Resources

American Society of Journalists and Authors: www.asja.org.

Newsletter and Electronic Publishers Association: 800-356-9302.

CHAPTER 54

Novels

Overview

For decades, countless writers have dreamed of writing the Great American Novel, and while they pursued that dream, they used the other writing opportunities in this book to pay the bills. You are not too old, and it is never too late; Raymond Chandler, author of the Philip Marlowe novels, was fifty-one when he published his first novel, *The Long Goodbye*.

What It Pays

According to literary agent Bob Diforio, the average advance for a first novel from an unknown author is less than $10,000. Of course there are exceptions to the rule, and some unknowns have received advances as high as a million dollars for their first novel.

This advance is paid against the royalties the book earns once it is published. Before you receive a royalty check, you need to earn out your advance. Many books don't earn out their advance, so there's a good chance that the only money you earn on your novel, unless it becomes a bestseller, will be the advance.

The royalty rate is based on a percentage of book sales. A percentage of the retail sales price is a gross royalty, and a percentage of the wholesale price or net revenue is called a net royalty. All else being equal, you make more money from a gross royalty than a net royalty. An average royalty for novels published as mass-market and trade paperbacks is 8 percent. For a hardcover novel, it can range from 10–12 percent or more based on the number of books sold.

Most mass-market paperback novels are eighty-thousand words. That's a manuscript of about four-hundred double-spaced pages. But different publishers and different genres have varying length requirements. Your publisher will specify a required word length in your contract.

Nuts and Bolts

Given the choice, most novelists would rather sell their novel to a publisher rather than self-publish it. Their goal is to publish with one of the big houses such as Bantam, Ballantine, St. Martin's, HarperCollins, Avon Books, and Pocket Books, to name a few. You stand to get a bigger advantage at the major publishing houses, and your novel has a better chance of making more money.

However, if you can't sell your manuscript to one of the big New York publishers, there are lots of small presses who might take a chance on you, pay you a modest advance, and publish your first novel. And many notable authors have started out with small presses. Charles Frasier first sold his book *Cold Mountain* to Atlantic Monthly Press; it was later picked up by Knopf. *Watership Down* by Richard Adams was first published by Rex Collins Ltd. and has remained in print ever since. Tom Clancy sold his first novel, *The Hunt for Red October*, to the Naval Institute Press, where it had a first print run of fourteen thousand copies (and went on to sell more than 465,000 copies).

What You'll Write

Selling a novel starts with paying attention to what kind of novel you are writing. Says mystery author Lori Avocato, "Write what you like to read, learn about, and write about, because you will be living in that fictional world for as long as it takes to get to The End."

"I whole-heartedly agree with this," says novelist Lisa Monodello. "Editors know when authors don't have their hearts in a book. To make your novel as compelling as possible, it must be something you are passionate about writing. If not, it shows in the words you choose and the way the story unfolds."

A beginner's mistake is to write what is hot in the market, simply because it *is* hot and you think it will sell, even if you don't particularly like that kind of book. It almost always fails. For instance, if everyone suddenly started reading stories about aliens invading earth, but you hate those and love reading romance novels, then you should write a romance novel, not a science fiction book.

What It Takes

The bad news is that, for your first novel, you will probably have to write the entire novel—or even several novels—on speculation (that means without a contract) before you write one good enough for a publisher to buy. Stephen King wrote three unpublished novels before he finally sold his fourth book, *Carrie*. Publishers usually need to read the entire novel, at least from a first-time novelist, before making an offer. Once you are better established, you may work with an editor who requires only a synopsis or novel outline to make an offer on your next book.

You increase your chances of selling your novel by finding a literary agent to represent you. A lot of authors find agents through word of mouth or by meeting them at a writers conference. The best way to get an agent is by referral from another writer, preferably one of the agent's clients.

Getting Started

It's highly likely that you won't sell your first novel, and that you will receive many rejection letters for the novel you *do* eventually sell before you find a publisher who says yes. In some instances, the rejection letter may reject the novel as you have written it but give you some suggestions for making it better. The editor will typically end her rejection letter with, "If after reviewing my comments you make the necessary changes to the book, I'd be happy to have another look at it."

When an editor invites you to resubmit after making changes, it does not guarantee an offer of a contract. It does mean that the editor is seriously considering it as a possible manuscript to publish. But there is no promise. You have to decide whether you agree with those changes and, more importantly, if you are willing to invest the time in making them. If you are, do it quickly and get that manuscript back to the editor. Many authors have gone on to sell their novels to publishers after making requested revisions.

Additional Resources

1,000 Literary Agents: 1000literaryagents.com.
Horror Writers Association: www.horror.org.
International Thriller Writers: www.thrillerwriters.org.
Romance Writers of America: www.rwanational.org.
Science Fiction and Fantasy Writers of America: www.sfwa.org.
Western Writers of America: www.westernwriters.org.

CHAPTER 55

Outdoor Writing

Overview

Writing about hunting, shooting, fishing, nature, and the outdoors is an active genre; the Outdoor Writers Association of America has more than thirteen-hundred members. Writing for the outdoors covers a large range of subjects, including hiking and mountain climbing, outdoor photography, bird-watching, hunting and fishing, paintball wars, skiing, boating, and plenty more. You can also write about the latest clothing to wear while outdoors, the latest gadgets, or even review the newest wireless headset to wear while in the park.

Writing about the outdoors, such as hiking through national parks and mountains, is usually more esoteric—about experiencing the wonders of nature and animals that live in the wild. Humans become the intruders, observers of a whole other world that survives just fine without us or, perhaps, in spite of us.

What It Pays

Payment for articles on nature and the outdoors ranges from abysmal to not bad. At the low end are the local fishing and hunting magazines published in many states, which may not pay for contributions. Writing an article for a national outdoor magazine typically pays in the hundreds of dollars per article. *Field & Stream*, which bills itself as the world's leading outdoor magazine, pays from $100 to several thousand dollars per article, according to the quality of the work, experience of the author, and difficulty of obtaining the story. Manny Luftes, a prominent fishing writer, has made a handsome income self-publishing a series of "how to enjoy fishing" books. Perhaps your articles can find a second life as a book or on the Web.

Nuts and Bolts

You need some background on the topic you write about. Read books and watch videos on your intended subject. Interview participants, trainers, and coaches. If possible, go hunting and fishing with an expert, or hike and camp in the outdoors area you're writing about.

If writing about hunting and fishing, make sure you know your current state laws regarding hunting and fishing and obtaining licenses. Contact your state hunters education division to find out what classes are being offered (usually free) and when they will be held and where. If you are already a professional in this field, you might write about laws and regulations and what they mean to those in the field and how they are enforced.

What You'll Write

You might write feature articles or guidebooks that give concentrated information about the outdoor event. You may also write features about others involved in the event, especially if they are celebrities and known experts in the field. If there are unique tools and equipment, write about those and how they work or assist the user in the field.

There is a chance you might be asked to write a video script if you are already familiar with what the publisher or producer is trying to accomplish. There may also be advertising promotions that go to prospective marketers such as TV and radio stations, local and national publications, and websites.

What It Takes

You must have all your facts correct about the outdoor activity or competition you are covering. Many professionals (and those who aren't!) know plenty about this area and will catch you if you misrepresent something in your story.

Getting Started

If you are already knowledgeable in a certain area, compile lists of publications you would like to submit queries to. If you only have limited knowledge about the topic you'd like to write about, then spend some time first gathering information, doing interviews with local participants and trainers, and involving yourself in some manner.

Additional Resources

Writing Naturally: A Down-to-Earth Guide to Nature Writing by David Petersen (Johnson Books, 2001).

About.com has information on writing about the outdoors at www.about freelancewriting.com/articles/writingspecialties/outdoors.htm.

Outdoor Writers Association of America (www.owaa.org) is an association of writers dedicated to sharing the outdoors experience on many levels. Their monthly publication is *Outdoors Unlimited*.

CHAPTER 56

Playwriting

Overview

Many movie stars who came from stage acting will tell you that they enjoyed those days on the stage with the audience being so close up and personal to their work. Acting in plays, dancing on stage, playing a musical instrument while in front of a live audience is not so much about applause at the end (hopefully there is some) but the sense that the audience has joined you in your journey through a character's drama. It's about sharing the emotion, the vision, or the pain of a convoluted mind gone haywire.

Writing plays takes a level of writing perhaps not used in any other writing genre. You, as the writer, must write not only to guide the actor toward what it is you wish to depict, but also for any future reader to be able to grasp who and what you are portraying.

Playwriting covers many genres such as drama (murder, intrigue, suspense), children's stories, young adult, comedy, and even musicals. After all, the singers don't sing all the way through, like in opera, so there are going to be a number of speaking moments. You, however, will not be writing the songs unless you have a talent for that sort of thing.

Playwriting is one of the great venues of expressing mankind's angst with the world around him. Performing live in front of an audience is also the best way to know an audience's reaction to the artistic work as a whole, as the response is immediate. It's either applause or silence. Yet there is nothing more satisfying to the actor than to feel the audience has moved right along with him during a story event and that the portrayal of emotions was felt by everyone that watched the show.

What It Pays

Playwriting is notoriously low paying, at least for those just breaking into this field. The more published work you have under your belt, the more you will be able to ask in payment. In the beginning, however, you will need to pitch your play to different producers and directors and get yourself known in the field. You may have to accept payment from ticket receipts if your client is a small summer theater company that has a tiny budget, but to get accepted for production is a big step in the right direction.

Based on what type of play you write, such as comedy or drama, you can consider talking with other play writers, theater agents representing writers in your genre, and calling local theater companies to find out how to submit your plays and what the general rates are for each potential client.

If you become successful in your field, there are always bigger opportunities to build on your original first step. Your play could be rewritten as a movie script or even a television series. This gives you great residuals especially if your work becomes very successful.

Nuts and Bolts

If you are just starting out with writing plays, you may first want to spend time developing your plot and your characters in some sort of outline development. Over time you will find what works for you in story line and character progression.

You must be able to tie up loose ends in events such as when a murder happens in the first act and it is finally resolved in the third act. What happens between those two points must filter in from all points to meet with the final resolution. If any of these branches of information filtering in does not reach the final resolution point, then it is left floating off to one side and the reader will wonder what happened over there and how it related to the whole.

So definitely, you need the skills of consistency, depicting drama, linear progression in development, and the ability to create characters with definite features and foibles.

What You'll Write

You will write the actual play in its proper manuscript format and any subsidiary notes and explanations. The play in written format, according to "Playwriting 101.com" online is as follows:

- Play's title and author's name and contact information
- Cast page which lists all the characters and a brief description of their place in the story
- If a musical, the musical number page listing of all the songs and dances in each act along with which character sings it
- The act and scene number at the beginning of each section along with the script showing who's speaking, and any accompanying stage directions

- At Rise description, which shows where and when the scene is taking place as the curtain goes up, and some brief historical background

- Transition notes which let you know where you are going within a play's timeline as you fade out from one scene into the next

You will also write a synopsis of the play for presentation to a potential backer, grants and scholarship applications, online and direct mail promotions, and any other promotional campaigns you will need to do to gain notice.

If you are applying for grants and scholarships, then you will be writing all the application documents as well. If you have never done one of those before, be sure you get knowledgeable assistance for the first time you are making your application.

What It Takes

You must have a good sense of organization as you are writing in a timeline of events that have to flow from beginning to end. There cannot be any lost threads, at least not without an appropriate tie off that can easily be picked up later on.

In addition, you will be planning ahead with your story plot, which means that you may need to set up a future event somewhere earlier in the play. Sometimes you can write that in as you are creating that scene. Otherwise, it means you must go back and rewrite an earlier scene in order to prepare for a later event. Continuity will be crucial here.

The script speech must reflect the character's persona and be easily understood as well as sounding natural. Most of us never use words that are overly complicated unless we are talking technical terms with a fellow co-worker. Therefore, it is wise to never deviate from easy and simple language.

Getting Started

Start out by going to the library and getting a list of famous plays and begin reading these. You will want to pay attention to how the writer developed the play, where scenes began and left off, how main events were resolved, and how characters developed over the span of the play.

You can also rent movies made from plays or, better yet, actually go to a few and see how it all works.

Start writing once you have your story idea in place and keep writing. Even if you think what you are writing is not going so well, the idea is to keep going until you need to take a break. Then go back and reread what you have written. You may need to rewrite certain parts, but giving yourself time to step away from it and then going back to read it will be valuable time to you in showing how you think through plots.

Additional Resources

The Elements of Playwriting by Louis Catron (Waveland Pr Inc, 2001).

Writing Your First Play by Roger Hall (Focal Press, 1998).

The Art and Craft of Playwriting by Jeffrey Hatcher (Story Press, 2000).

Naked Playwriting: The Art, The Craft, and The Life Laid Bare by William Missouri Downs and Robing Russin (Silman-James Press, 2005).

The Playwright's Guidebook: An Insightful Primer on the Art of Dramatic Writing by Stuart Spencer (Faber & Faber, 2002).

American Association of Community Theatre (AACT): www.aact.org.

The Children's Theatre Foundation of America (CTF): www.childrens theatrefoundation.org.

Colorado Theatre Guild has links to theatre organizations around the country: www.coloradotheatreguild.org.

Drama Education Teacher Associations (DETA) links to other information: www.drama-education.com.

Educational Theatre Association (EDTA): www.edta.org.

Playwriting 101 Online: www.playwriting101.com.

Theater and Performing Arts Resources links to other information sites: www.tamu-commerce.edu/library/perart.htm.

CHAPTER 57

Poetry

Overview

Getting your first poem published doesn't have to be the daunting, remote notion that beginning poets envision. In fact, the process can be fun, and with more chance of success than you might think, providing you build a bridge that shortens the journey—a way to cut across the mass of information in print and online.

What It Pays

With rare exception, there is almost no money in poetry today, as Americans by and large have abandoned the reading of poetry and lost all appreciation for it. You may get $5–$25 for your poem from a literary magazine, or they may just offer to pay you in contributors' copies of the magazine. Just about the only way to get paid well for poetry is to write and perform it as rap and hope that your act catches on.

Nuts and Bolts

Most poets subscribe to a number of poetry journals, magazines, and market guides, but you can narrow it down by choosing just the finest few. When it comes to changing trends, submission sources and deadlines, and availability of grants and awards, *Poets & Writers* magazine, *The International Directory of Little Magazines & Small Presses*, and *Poet's Market* top the list.

Poets & Writers is one most poets would not do without. It covers news and trends and offers in-depth features, submission calendars for contests, grants, and awards, and much more (www.pw.org). All issues are well worth archiving for later reference.

The International Directory of Little Magazines & Small Presses, called the Bible of the business by *The Wall Street Journal*, is an annual guide that lists more than four-thousand book and magazine publishers with editorial information on both. Entries are indexed alphabetically, regionally, and by subject. You can read it at the library. Although it comes highly recommended, the purchase price is a bit steep (around $38). The *Directory* also includes publishers of fiction, nonfiction, reviews, artwork, long poems, news items, and more. It is published by Dustbooks (www.dustbooks.com).

Poet's Market, an annual Writer's Digest Books guide, is another marketing tool considered indispensable. You'll find submission sources for poets of all skill levels. It includes more than eighteen hundred listings for poetry publishing opportunities and how-to-submit instructions specific to each publication. The guide is comprehensive, easy to use, and woven throughout are many helpful articles and interviews with poets and editors. It runs $30. Both *Poets & Writers* magazine and *Poet's Market* can be found at just about any bookstore, and of course at your local library.

What You'll Write

You may have scribbled your poems on scraps of paper or jotted down ideas in a personal journal. If you're serious about writing poems and sharing them with an eye toward publication, the time has come to type them up. Create folders, either on your computer or in hard copy form.

The first folder is for all ideas in development. Veronica Yates calls this file folder the "greenhouse"—for seeds of what's to come. She says, "The title is significant to me because it means I'm cultivating the soil, nurturing seeds into seedlings, not just a folder sitting idle on my computer desktop."

Concentrate on those ideas that have the power to move you. Then make a separate file for each poem idea and give it a working title. Even though you may have the smallest kernel of an idea, or in some cases, the bare inkling of a simile or metaphor, make files for those as well. It's important to start organizing what soon will become your body of work.

Make the greenhouse folder easily accessible, so you can add to it promptly as you plant new seedlings. You can keep the folder on your computer desktop so that when an idea strikes, you can set up a file right away, before the idea slips away. There's no telling how many fine ideas for poems are lost to competing daily distractions. Then, create a second folder for poems you are working on; include new poems that have graduated from the greenhouse file, as well as older poems in revision or those nearly ready to submit.

While not all will reach maturity, planting them in your greenhouse folder allows you to review them often. Even a short review can be inspiring. New thoughts evolve and you may feel so impassioned that you'll want to rush a poem to completion. That's great—keep writing but resist the temptation to submit your poem right away. Give your poem at least a day or two between revisions. Poems require time to gestate, usually weeks, possibly months or years. Some require much more tinkering than others, but you'll soon enough discover which ones are worthy of further development.

After weeks of working on a poem, you may find yourself asking similar questions. If so, it's a fairly safe bet *that* poem won't make the cut and the idea is best abandoned. Some poets consider this blasphemy; they discard nothing, their files full of would-be, might-be, could-be poems. "Personally, I'm not interested in saving what doesn't work in the hope of an elusive 'someday' when a questionable idea might miraculously show merit," says Yates. "Even in my greenhouse folder, I keep only ideas worthy of nurturing—nothing half-hearted or lukewarm stays there long. Also, if I'm not excited about an idea, it's doubtful I can convince a future reader of its worthiness. Life is short enough; my time is better spent working on poems that stand a chance of publication *now*."

What It Takes

It has been said many times by many people that the essence of writing is rewriting, and nowhere is this truer than in poetry. Most published poets go through multiple revisions, sometimes hundreds, before getting to the final draft. I don't find this knowledge inspiring; nonetheless it's true. Poet Donald Hall wrote that he revised one of his poems six-hundred times. Ultimately, there is no magic number. How many revisions and how much time depends on you. Either the poem will be as good as you can make it and ready for submission, or you will abandon it. If it's the latter, most likely there were clues: the verve and interest you once had began to wane, or you stopped looking forward to working on it.

There's nothing wrong with admitting an idea you had for a poem no longer works or lacks the substance you'd hoped it would contain. Hundreds of ideas for poems float by us every day; the ones that stick in your consciousness are the ones to pay attention to.

Getting Started

Where do poems come from? Anywhere. In the mystery of a fleeting moment, a poem beckons: you pass a stranger on the street who reminds you of someone you haven't thought about in years, the smell of a wood-burning fire evokes childhood memories or a home you once lived in, a midnight thunderstorm catapults you out of the deepest sleep, a blue jay drums for seeds in a rain gutter. It could be any split-second happening. It could be now.

When the senses are engaged, consider it the best of signs: a poem is *inviting you* to write it. These are triggers—desires met and unmet, memories rekindled, all interlaced, influencing how you view the world today. Watch for them.

Whether or not you take action, heed the tapping, is up to you. Many poets keep a pocket notebook handy, even if they only have time to jot down a few words or a couple sentences. But you don't have to wait for the unforeseen. You can start *now*, using whatever time you have to devote to poetry.

You already have what you need to move forward: you have a poem, or at least the essential core of one. One technique for developing the core of a poem, used by William Yeats among others, is to write it out in prose first—just a paragraph or two that contains all your thoughts, feelings, and images about the subject of your poem. Then, underline only the important sentences, those most meaningful to you. You'll be astonished at how many irrelevant phrases you cut. Next, highlight any words that relate to the five senses: sight, hearing, touch, taste, and smell.

This preliminary exercise narrows the focus, eliminates nonessentials, and helps you examine your emotions and sensations more deeply. The crafting of a poem is like exploring an exciting new relationship. You're getting to know your poem and you're learning a bit more about yourself in the process.

Additional Resources

"Writing Poetry" website: www.poetry-online.org.

Poetry Magic: www.poetrymagic.com/uk.

Academy of American Poets: www.poets.org.

CHAPTER 58

PowerPoint Presentations

Overview

In the old days, orators stood at the platform and captivated crowds using nothing more than the power of their voice. But not all of them did. The scientist Michael Faraday, who gave lectures explaining science to the general public, demonstrated each principle with an experiment he performed as he spoke.

"Visuals help you keep your prospects' attention from wandering and reinforce what you're saying," writes Bruce J. Bloom of Bruce J. Bloom Advertising. "Research has shown again and again that any point is far more likely to be remembered if it is heard and seen."

One of the biggest mistakes made by people giving speeches that use multimedia props is that they simply regurgitate the information that is on each slide. Does the speaker not realize that the audience is fully capable of reading what is on the screen? Maybe not.

The most successful speeches use visual aids not for show, but as a springboard to get the core message across and illustrate the supporting points. This is the concrete portion of the speech. The facts, figures, and charts on the screen reinforce and illuminate the message that is being spoken.

You have no doubt heard the expression about one picture being worth a thousand words. Well, in a speech, your time is limited. So visuals can convey extra information you don't have time to fully present. With the ability to show concepts and facts that support and expand the core message of the speech, you don't have to waste time covering that in your speech.

The use of multimedia is to emphasize, illuminate, and illustrate the message the speaker wants to deliver or its supporting facts. Your visuals hold the supporting material for the core message including statistics, examples, credibility, charts, graphs, and pictures.

A number of presentation systems are available for presenting your visuals to your audience. Chief among these is PowerPoint. Despite the tendency of speakers to misuse or overuse PowerPoint, and the proliferation of boring presentations it has spawned, PowerPoint has become the de facto standard for presentation visuals.

What It Pays

Your fee depends on what services you offer. Are you writing a speech or designing PowerPoint slides? I have hired PowerPoint designers to create PowerPoint slides for my presentations. But I gave them the text and rough drawings for each slide; they did not actually write anything. For this service, you can charge $50–$100 an hour. If you are writing a speech, the fee is much higher. Speech writers receive $2,000–$3,000 or more for a twenty-minute speech. That fee may include PowerPoint slides, or you can add 25 percent to the base fee to provide a PowerPoint presentation to go along with your text.

Nuts and Bolts

SAP is a quick, handy formula speakers, writers, and other content providers can use when preparing to deliver presentations. It stands for subject, audience, and purpose.

- **Subject.** The topic on which you speak. Define it as clearly, specifically, and narrowly as possible (e.g., "safe handling of compressed gas cylinders" instead of "plant safety").

- **Audience.** Who you will be speaking to, including the demographics, education, background, and interest (or lack of interest) in your topic as discussed earlier in this chapter.

- **Purpose.** The objective of the presentation—what you or the meeting planner want to have happen as a result of the attendees hearing your talk.

"Purpose" surprises some presenters when I bring it up. Amazingly, they never think about their talk having a purpose. "I was asked to summarize the improvements done to machine #3 in our custom extrusion operation," one engineer told me. "There is no 'purpose.' I just have to present the information."

But people in his company are busy. If there is no purpose to getting the information, why bother to have a meeting about it? Or why not just put it in a memo or post on the company intranet? Clearly, there is some reason management wants the engineer and his audience to assemble in a room while they hear his report in person. Without defining the purpose through SAP analysis, the objective is unlikely to be accomplished—and both the time spent preparing and delivering the talk, and the time spent listening to the talk, will have been wasted.

Before I write a presentation, I ask my client to tell me his objective for the talk. What are the specific objectives for the speech? What skills should the attendees gain, what changes in attitude should take place, what actions do you want the audience to take as a result of attending your session?

This is not a trivial or theoretical consideration for the speaker: it is the crux of the entire speech. With the Internet today, information on just about any topic is easily obtained with a Google search. The reasons to have experts give lectures and speeches and training programs are to accomplish change and improvement: help the attendees do their jobs better, live happier lives, increase their productivity, improve quality, or give better customer service. A live training session by an expert speaker or facilitator can accomplish these objectives in ways printed, online, or broadcast content often cannot.

What You'll Write

For the beginning speaker, one sensible approach is to first write out the full speech word for word. Then, from that full text, prepare your PowerPoint slides along with a set of speaker notes. Bring both with you to the podium. If you are feeling confident and competent, speak from your notes. If your confidence wanes, or you want to make sure to deliver a segment of your speech exactly as you wrote it, switch to the full script.

Writing for the printed page and writing for speech are different. Speeches allow for the use of body language, voice tone, and facial expressions and can be interpreted along with the words that are being spoken. Written text doesn't have these additional components and lacks the ability to convey emotion and emphasis the way speaking does.

The average rate of standard speech in the United States is 100–150 words per minute. This is the range for typical conversation from slow talkers to fast talkers, so when you write your speeches, you may want to figure on a rate of about 120 words per minute (including brief pauses for effect, laughter, or applause).

In every speech, there is a core message to be conveyed. You need to stick with this core message and build your talk around it for your presentation to be memorable and effective. What is your core message? What message do you want to get across to the listener? Tailor the speech to achieve that goal.

If you are writing a speech to be delivered by someone else, often the speaker will have trouble eloquently explaining what that message should be, and this is where you step in to help. Ask questions about the message. Ask the speaker to provide the idea of the message in one sentence. Offer suggestions to refine and clarify the message.

Speakers are not limited to voice, words, tone, and gestures. Most amateur speakers fail to take advantage of interactive and three-dimensional media or to appeal to all five senses in their talks. Enhancements and aides need not be elaborate. Years ago, I taught a seminar on telephone selling. My prop was a plastic toy phone I took from my kids who were then preschoolers. When you hit a button on the phone, it rang loudly. During the workshop, I would have members of the audience practice cold calling, with me playing the prospect. When they dialed, I'd hit the ring tone, and then bring the phone to my ear. It enhanced the effectiveness of the exercise, making it seem more real, and also got a laugh the first time I used it during the session.

Keep the audience interested from start to finish. A series of audio, visual, and even oral devices can be used. Silence, for example, is a speaking technique. If your audience is noisy and won't settle down or stop talking, stand at the front of the stage, staring out into the crowd, and remain totally silent. They will quickly notice you, shut up, and take a seat.

Tailor your information to keep the audience interested in finding out about the message your speaker has to deliver. You don't need to get cute with the information you are trying to provide people. Unless you are writing a presentation to be delivered at an astrophysics or engineering conference, then you probably don't need to get overly technical. You can usually craft a complicated message by using basic examples the average person understands. That's a big part of successful speeches.

Tell stories in the speeches you write and give. By this I don't mean in the literal sense of a short story or fable, but personal or relevant anecdotes. A story should have a beginning, middle, and an end. People like stories—and if you can involve people in the overall story, then you are going to have a successful speech.

As for length, you can suggest standard times from past speeches you have written. The length of a speech can vary between two to three minutes for a wedding speech, or it can be twenty to thirty minutes in the case of a corporate speech at a conference or other event. A training seminar can be a day or longer.

Speechwriter Brian Jenner said, "I am surprised by the number of people that want to speak for ten or fifteen minutes." He uses the example of the lyrics of songs—usually only three to four minutes—to illustrate how quickly you can impart a message, create emotion, and leave an impact on people. Ultimately, you will be guided in length by three things: the information that needs to be covered, the time you have allotted to speak, and your ability to convey your message in a succinct, to-the-point fashion.

What It Takes

Here are a few tips for creating winning PowerPoint presentations for your clients:

1. Simplify the slides and use key phrases and necessary information.

2. Use contrasting colors between the background and the text. Overly dark backgrounds, when you print the presentation, will be difficult to read and will also waste a lot of ink.

3. Make good use of white space so that the text is easily readable and viewer can separate each point.

4. A good rule of thumb is one slide per minute of presentation in a steady linear progression. Constantly flipping from slide to slide can be a bit of a distraction, especially for people who cannot read the slide as fast as others. If you need to refer to a slide more than once, insert it each time it comes up in your talk. Don't worry about the repetition. It's better than flipping back and forth, which is a distraction.

5. Consistency matters. Don't vary the design of each slide by using various colors and fonts. Stick with a simple and clean presentation. Don't go color, font, and picture wild, importing images and graphics simply because they're there and you can.

6. Avoid the overwhelming temptation to use special-effect transitions that PowerPoint provides. These can limit the impact of the overall speech and presentation. You may be taken with the novelty of such techniques, but they are usually nothing more than window dressing. Audiences usually interpret overdesigned and overproduced audiovisual presentation as a way of compensating for poor content or a lousy talk.

7. Make sure you know how to go backward and forward on the presentation when required. If questions arise, it should be easy to go between the slides for further discussion.

8. Don't speak to the slides, speak to the audience. Look at the audience, not the projection screen or your laptop. Don't read from the slides word for word either. You have the PowerPoint presentation for the audience, not for you to dictate from. A quick glance for cues to further the presentation is just fine.

9. Avoid excessive punctuation, and refrain from using all caps when producing slides. If you want emphasis, emphasize in your speech, rather than on the screen. You may occasionally use large type or other graphic devices for emphasis, but do so sparingly. Overuse of any such technique reduces its effectiveness.

10. View the presentation ahead of time from various points in the room. You want attendees from all angles and distances to clearly see the message on the presentation.

11. Use the information on PowerPoint to reinforce what you are saying. Here is an example: the core message of your speech is to show employees of a corporation the effect of day-to-day changes they have made in their operations. On the PowerPoint, a slide comes up that shows a graph illustrating a sharp increase in profit over last year. You say: "We have increased electronic communication between departments, we have reduced costs by buying in bulk, we have increased productivity through bonuses, and you can clearly see the effect it has had on our corporation's bottom line. You should be commended on your efforts." The PowerPoint slide shows a bar chart or graph indicating how each of these variables has increased or decreased as you have said. This reinforces the message with the employees.

12. Avoid using cute pictures, clever visuals, or beautifully designed slides that detract from the overall message. You don't need pictures of flowers, fast cars, and smiling, happy people—unless it deals with the subject matter. Sometimes people putting the slides together use pictures that have little or nothing to do with the core message. They want to break up the text and provide visual eye candy for the audience. They are just there to be...cute.

Run through the speech several times with the slides. Timing is essential when you are coordinating an audiovisual presentation with a speech. The audience may remember the foul up more than the message. Avoid this at all costs.

Getting Started

Creating PowerPoint presentations for corporate clients, professional speakers, and others requires two skills: the ability to write a speech and the ability to design slides in PowerPoint. You also have to decide whether you are a freelance corporate communications writer who offers PowerPoint as one of many services or a specialist in PowerPoint presentations.

Lots of businesspeople today, especially technical professionals and middle managers, are quite proficient in PowerPoint. So why do they need you? One reason is that they are too busy to devote the many hours needed to create a great presentation. Off-loading that task to a freelance specialist frees these managers and professionals to focus on core business tasks.

Additional Resources

Persuasive Presentations for Business by Robert Bly (Entrepreneur Press, 2008).
Knockout Presentations by Diane DiResta (Chandler House, 1998).
Boost Your Presentation I.Q. by Marilyn Pincus (McGraw-Hill, 2006).

View from the Back: 101 Tips for Event Promoters Who Want to Dramatically Increase Back-of-the-Room Sales by Bret Ridgeway (Morgan James Publishing, 2007).

Making Successful Presentations by Terry C. Smith (Wiley, 1991).

How to Give a Damn Good Speech by Philip Theibert (Castle Books, 2005).

Say It with Presentations: How to Design and Deliver Successful Presentations by Gene Zelazny (McGraw-Hill, 2000).

CHAPTER 59

Public Relations

Overview

Ever since the days of P. T. Barnum, publicity, also known as "public relations," has had a seedy connotation. Public relations (PR) people can be derogatorily called "flacks" and have been portrayed in countless books and films as fawning, exploitative, and insensitive. The field of PR is not for applause seekers. The best PR is invisible, and the best PR people stay behind the scenes.

PR is a detail-oriented, high-pressure career. It is known as a thankless profession. If you don't produce results, you're fired; if you do produce results, you don't always get full credit. Now, the good news: PR is growing rapidly, and there are numerous opportunities to find entry-level positions. The field is exciting because you are dealing with the media as well as the public. There's often an opportunity to travel, earn a respectable salary, and use your mind in a variety of ways.

What It Pays

There are about 120,000 people in the PR field, one-quarter of them women. One-half of all people in PR work in New York City, Washington D.C., Chicago, and Los Angeles.

College graduates beginning in PR start at $20,000–$30,000 a year. The salary for experienced PR people can be $50,000–$85,000 or more a year. Salaries are highest in the Northeast and lowest in the South.

PR can also be a lucrative gig for freelance writers. Companies and PR firms often hire writers to ghostwrite articles for company executives, scientists, and engineers. A 1,500-word ghostwritten article for a trade journal can pay $1,250–$2,000 or more. For a 2,500-word article, you can charge $2,000–$3,000.

Nuts and Bolts

Those entering the field of PR have never had such a wide variety of opportunities. Many veer toward consumer public relations, where they publicize products and services used by consumers. Less known, but equally important, are trade and industrial public relations, which involves publicity aimed at business people, including store owners, doctors, and distributors.

The rapidly expanding health field offers public relations opportunities in hospitals, pharmaceutical companies, and medical associations. Another growth area, according to one vice president of PR for a major corporation, is human resources planning, which used to be employee communications. Public policy planning, also a growing area, requires some type of government experience. There are also emerging PR opportunities in the fields of ecology, finance, economic education, and government regulation.

In addition to these choices, the person entering PR must decide whether to work in a corporate communications office or in a PR agency. PR professionals can prosper within an agency, or they can make a home for themselves in nonprofit organizations, hospitals, or foundations, as well as governmental public interest groups (e.g., Common Cause), corporations, and trade associations. A bright newcomer with top writing and presentation skills can succeed in any of these areas.

What You'll Write

Your first break may be your first job or it may be your first client. It will give you the opportunity to discover whether or not you are cut out for the field.

In all probability, your first job will involve what is commonly referred to as "grunt work": answering letters, answering telephones, writing copy for mundane products or services, or simply compiling media lists. You may find yourself in press or consumer relations, political campaigning, fund-raising, or employee recruitment. Whatever you're doing, take good mental notes.

If you are at a small PR agency, your break may come when you land your first substantial client. Suddenly, instead of writing the occasional release or fiddling with mailing lists, you'll be involved with such things as arranging press parties, placing feature articles, designing a direct mail campaign, and working with designers and illustrators in creating brochures, logos, letterheads, and envelopes. This is your chance to fly. You'll see how much responsibility you can handle and how well you can do a number of tasks.

A neighborhood gourmet store gave one small two-person agency the opportunity to get actively involved with the New York City food press. Their job was to launch a new $1 million gourmet store on the Upper East Side.

The assignment called for a wide range of skills, and the two young men did everything from naming the store to organizing the opening-day press party. They both gained twenty pounds as they sampled the food so that they could write about it with conviction!

They wrote a three-page press release and a fact sheet describing some of the food that would be featured. Later on, they designed and implemented a direct mail program that offered the store's catering services to food managers at New York's top corporations.

This account gave these young PR men a variety of clips and other samples of their work that they parlayed into more food accounts. They could point to the stories they had placed in the *New York Times*, *Daily News*, and the *Post*. They even managed to get the *Wall Street Journal* to mention the store on page one. Because the owner gave the public relations specialists full rein, they were able to create a logo, cover letters, brochures, and flyers that were well-produced in addition to being well-written. Most importantly, they created a rapport with the cream of the New York food press, which became a salable commodity when they pitched their services to other food accounts.

Clients require you to stretch yourself as a writer. The challenge is to make a press release so interesting and inviting that an editor will use it as the basis of a story. When you've placed a story, you've made everyone happy: yourself, the editor, and your client. You've also gained a "clip"—a press clipping—that you can use to demonstrate to other clients or employers that you have a track record.

What It Takes

In their book *Public Relations Writing*, Doug Newsom and Bob Barrel note, "Good public relations requires communication skills, expertise in dealing with news media, and a knowledge of mass communication, the dynamics of public opinion, and the principles of persuasion."

As a PR writer, you must become a media junkie. By understanding the media, you can learn how to best shape your communications. If you know that a particular magazine has a three-month lead time, you can immediately determine whether a story that's hot is even worth sending over. Perhaps that item should go to a daily newspaper.

A respect for meeting deadlines can also help you determine which media may be right for which press releases. By dealing with journalists, and by taking courses in journalism, you'll soon become accustomed to seeing your stories as an editor sees them. You'll know how a release should look, and you'll learn to phrase it to rivet the editor's attention. When dealing with television, you'll automatically think of your client's story in visual terms.

Getting Started

PR skills and abilities can be acquired through a blend of college studies and real-world experience. Taking college-level courses in PR is important, but so is a general liberal arts background. Get a course or two in nonfiction writing under your belt and then major in a discipline such as economics, psychology, nutrition, or computer sciences. A degree in journalism is helpful, but only if it doesn't preclude your taking other enriching courses in a variety of fields. College is a place to learn how to think. Later, you can apply these skills to PR through an internship program or on your first job in the field.

To do well in public relations takes an assertive, outgoing person. It takes a knowledge of business and a knowledge of important issues. It also takes reliability and loyalty. Don't worry about not understanding all the minutiae of printing or design. You'll have your whole career to pick up the thousands of details you'll need to round out your PR education.

Additional Resources

Public Relations Writing by Doug Newsom and Bob Barrell (Wadsworth Publishing, 2001).

Public Relations Kit for Dummies by Eric Yaverbaum and Robert Bly (IDG, 2000).

All-in-One PR Directory lists more than 22,000 PR outlets in nine different fields.

Bacon's Publicity Checker is classified by subject or industry.

Burrelle Annuals provides excellent local references.

Cable TV Publicity Outlets Nationwide lists more than 660 contacts.

The Encyclopedia of Associations is a comprehensive and definitive listing of 13,300 trade associations, professional societies, labor unions, fraternal and patriotic organizations, and other voluntary member groups.

O'Dwyer's Directory of Corporate Communications is an annual guide to 2,400 hundred companies and 300 trade associations that are PR intensive.

Radio Contacts is an annual directory on radio programming with 2,500 major market station listings.

Television Contacts is an annual directory on national, syndicated, and local program guest, product, and informational requirements.

The TV News Handbook tells who to contact, what they're looking for, and how to slant stories to the decision makers.

TV Publicity Outlets Nationwide covers 2,500 TV program contacts.

CHAPTER 60

Procedure Writing

Overview

If you are a strict observer of guidelines, rules, and regulations, and are incredibly organized, then procedure writing is possibly for you. It requires great detail and step-by-step, structured information. Procedure writing can include operating procedures, employee handbooks, safety guides, rules and regulations guides, software manuals, and government procedures on filling out forms and filing documents (your tax return, for instance). The list is endless, but for whatever project you take on, ask for previous versions if available, then work on making your edition even better.

What It Pays

Payment depends on your industry knowledge of the area you're writing for, as well as the client's budget. Most businesses have a set publication fee, but don't hesitate to negotiate if you are an expert in the client's field. If you write manuals on a regular basis, then consider a total project fee if you know you can whip the book out fast. Otherwise, stick with an hourly fee until you know how fast you can accurately write. Don't shortchange your client or your readers. Procedure writing is a subset of technical writing, and the pay scales are the same; see chapter 75 on Technical Writing for more information on hourly and project rates for freelance technical writers.

Nuts and Bolts

Detail is essential; you are required to verify each level of what you write. Try to start with a previous edition, and go through each section to find out if any changes were made. Most likely you will have a main contact at the client's office who you work with.

Procedure documents essentially cover what rules are actually in place and the conditions necessary to accommodate those rules. Procedure documents should be easy to understand by the target audience and should provide directions on where to go, what to do, or who to see—or how to fill out documents to meet certain standards.

What You'll Write

You write the main document, which is usually a heavily outlined work with multilevel paths of information branching out from specific points or bullets. Depending on the subject matter, you may also write supporting documents. For instance, if you are a lawyer defending a client in a court case, there are a series of procedural documents you must file, such as motions for discoveries and depositions, in order to push your case toward a trial. The process of discovery and deposition also require their own procedural document to maintain a series of legal steps toward a final goal.

If you are writing a human resource procedure guide for employees, then the document might also include job descriptions, procedures for conducting job interviews, methods and guidelines for promotions and for terminations, dress codes, attendance codes, and any other job particulars that require structure and adherence to a code of conduct.

If you are writing a software manual, testing the steps in the process, just like a recipe, are essential to success. Start by stating the accomplished goal when the process has been followed correctly. Then write each step out so that even the most technically challenged person can understand what to do.

What It Takes

This type of writing requires detail, formal outlining of steps and processes, verification of facts, and a talent for writing in a linear fashion without dropping any threads. Study different types of procedure documents and look at the different ways of outlining information. Break up text with graphics where possible and also use white space so that it doesn't become tedious reading the material. Stay away from elaborate words when simple ones also work.

Getting Started

The companies most likely to hire writers to document new procedures and update written procedures that may have changed over time are manufacturers and service firms complying with ISO 9000 and related quality control standards. Their compliance with ISO 9000 is a big selling point when they are bidding on new contracts, and ISO requires clear and up-to-date written documentation on all manufacturing procedures to maintain compliance. Check your local yellow pages and business directories like Thomas Publishing online for manufacturers in your state. Most of any size either are ISO compliant or want to be. Even many that are not ISO certified document procedures to assure customers of quality control. Find several local companies and offer to do a job for them. Start out small so that you can learn without stress.

Additional Resources

Writing Effective Policies and Procedures: A Step-by-Step Resource for Clear Communication by Nancy Campbell (AMACOM, 1998).

Effective Writing for the Quality Professional: Creating Useful Letters, Reports, and Procedures by Jane Campanizzi (ASQ Quality Press, 2005).

How to Write Policies, Procedures & Task Outlines by Larry Peabody (Writing Services, 2006).

7 Steps to Better Written Policies and Procedures by Stephen Page (Process Improvement Publishing, 2001).

Best Practices in Policies and Procedures by Stephen Page (Process Improvement Publishing, 2007).

Procedure Writing: Principles and Practices by Douglas Wieringa, Christopher Moore, and Valerie Barnes (Battelle Press, 1998).

CHAPTER 61

Professional Speaking

Overview

Many people make a great deal of money as professional speakers. Before writing and presenting any speech, know who your audience will be, what the goal of the speech is (e.g., information or call to action), and how to keep the audience engaged from beginning to end. Know why your audience is coming to hear you speak and base all the points or highlights of your speech as relevant to what they want to hear or know about. In speechwriting, major points are more fully developed so that the audience will remember details of what they heard, as they do not get a chance to rewind or review the speech again like they would an article or book.

You can also focus on writing speeches rather than giving them. The CEO of a large corporation who does not have time to write his own speech or does not have the talent to organize one might hire you to write the speech for him. This would require gathering all related materials and documents as well as interviewing the client and his associates in depth.

The same is true for many politicians who may prefer to hire a professional speechwriter to help them present their issues effectively but don't have the time to organize or research the background materials needed. Aside from interviewing the client directly, you may also be working closely with the client's public relations or marketing group and interviewing key members for more details.

What It Pays

Writing speeches, according to the *2006 Writer's Market*, can pay $167 per hour or $2,700–$10,000 per project, depending on the subject and who is delivering the speech. A government official's speech could bring in $4,500 for a twenty-minute speech or $650 for a politician's fifteen-minute speech. Pricing for a speech depends ultimately on the objective of the speech and the importance of the person delivering it and what kind of media exposure the speech will receive.

Nuts and Bolts

If you are giving the speech, you must have some expertise in the subject matter in order to connect with your audience. If you are writing the speech for someone else, be sure to interview the person and research the topic in more detail. It is important to have research and interviewing skills to gather all the information you need to write an effective and developed speech.

If you want to give speeches, join a local club where you can practice giving speeches so that you can develop your presentation and delivery skills.

What You'll Write

There are five rules for selecting the topic of your speech, according to Jeff Scott Cook in his book *The Elements of Speechwriting and Public Speaking*.

1. Choose a topic that suits the occasion.

2. Choose a topic that you can credibly address.

3. Choose a fresh topic, or a fresh perspective.

4. Choose a topic you care about.

5. Choose a topic you can handle in the time allowed for the speech.

There are also five types of speeches for attaining five communication goals, Cook says, and they are speeches to stimulate, speeches to inform, speeches to persuade, speeches to activate, and speeches to entertain.

In beginning your speech, you want to get the listener's attention immediately and then present the reason why they should listen to the rest of the speech. Establish your expertise on the subject and make a connection with the audience by showing that you care about their needs and are going to provide the answers and information they want to hear.

The body of your speech provides the crux of the subject, whether it be a problem or issue, and its background history. Then the speech moves into how the problem can be solved. The closing provides a call to action, such as donating money to the organization or taking an action that provides the result outlined in the speech.

What It Takes

The speechwriter needs an easy-to-understand and fluent style of writing that translates to the spoken word. Keeping words simple and concise also presents the message of the speech more clearly to a larger portion of the audience, no matter what the audience background.

If you are an expert in certain areas like engineering or scientific research, then you'll have a higher chance of being hired to write speeches in those areas, as you already understand the processes and intricacies of the subject matter.

Getting Started

Opportunities for writing speeches include the political arena, corporate management, and other local associations. You may also assist in writing any presentation pieces such as PowerPoint slides, drawings, and audiovideo scripts.

Join your local chamber of commerce and network with other businesses and their leaders. Check your local business newspaper that focuses strictly on who's doing what in the local business area and also put an ad in the paper outlining your services. Search online for speechwriter clubs or visit the Toastmasters website at www.toastmasters.org to search for the closest meeting. Call your junior colleges or extended education departments of local universities to see if they offer speechwriting classes.

Additional Resources

Persuasive Presentations for Business by Robert Bly (Entrepreneur Press, 2008).

How to Show You Know What You're Talking About! The Speaker's Guide to Illustrative Anecdotes by D. Jamison Cain (Lulu.com, 2006).

Writing Great Speeches: Professional Techniques You Can Use by Alan Perlman (Allyn & Bacon, 1997).

The Elements of Speechwriting and Public Speaking by Jeff Scott Cook (MacMillan, 1989).

Speak and Grow Rich by Dottie Walters and Lily Walters (Prentice Hall, 1997).

Freelance jobs for speechwriters: www.ifreelance.com/Freelance-Jobs/Speech-Writing-Freelance-Jobs.

Speech Tips: www.speechtips.com.

Proposal Writing

Overview

"Proposals are considered one of the highest forms of persuasive writing," says Dr. G. J. Christensen of California State Northridge's Business School. Entrepreneurs and consultants, vendors, and those who sells a product"have to tell and sell the prospective client on the people to do the work, the kind of money requested, the special skills they bring, and the plans and timetables for completing the work."

One thing to understand about business proposals is that they often operate on a system introduced by the U.S. government. The government often needs work done. Either a road needs built or information needs gathered or new technology needs to be implemented in a fighter jet. So vendors (private companies) are given the opportunity to bid on a given project that the U.S. government requests. The vendor with the best proposal wins the project.

To execute the process of choosing the best vendor in the most efficient manner, the government issues what is called a request for proposal (RFP). In this document the government specifies how the bids are to be submitted, under what conditions, in what format, in what order, and specific data required in the bidding process (costs of specific parts, for example). An RFP is a form, of sorts, drawn up for a given project that asks for certain data from the vendor, to be turned in by a specific date.

The government is the initiator of the whole RFP system. But the RFP process—on either the formal or much more casual side of the spectrum, and everywhere in between—has become the standard model for all business proposal writing.

If your client does not hand you an RFP, you need to make one. You must know what your customer needs to even write a proposal. You need to understand the details of your client's wishes to win the job. Get a reputation for winning over clients with your writing, and you will carve a handsome niche for yourself in business proposal writing.

What It Pays

Simplyhired.com lists a business proposal writer's annual salary at $55,000 a year, while proposal managers make $75,000 a year. Freelance writers offering business proposal writing can charge up to $4,000 per proposal, depending upon the scope of the project.

Consider raising your fees if your proposals are typically the ones chosen in a given bidding contest. Or consider writing a bonus into the contract should your proposal win out over the other offers. You want to market yourself as someone who does not just write proposals, but as the writer who wins contracts!

Nuts and Bolts

Captureplanning.com, a valuable resource providing tutorials and tips for business writing, insists that other than the RFP, there is no solid template for business proposals. Each client is the model for the proposal written. This site offers the following advice for business proposals:

- **Who.** Who will do the work, who will manage the work, who does the customer call if there is a problem, who is responsible for what?

- **What.** What needs to be done/delivered, what will be required to do it, what can the customer expect, what it will cost?

- **Where.** Where will the work be done, where will it be delivered?

- **How.** How will the work be done, how will it be deployed, how will it be managed, how will you achieve quality assurance and customer satisfaction, how will risks be mitigated, how long will it take, how will the work benefit the customer?

- **When.** When will you start, when will key milestones be scheduled, when will the project be complete, when is payment due?

- **Why.** Why have you chosen the approaches and alternatives you have selected, why should the customer select you?

What does your client really want, ultimately? The answer to that question will highlight every point and subpoint of your proposal.

What You Will Write

Patrick Riley, entrepreneur and author of *The One-Page Proposal*, claims that brevity is the key to business success. In your proposal, you must cover the fundamental wants of your client, but keep your message brief and readable. Some proposals demand more detail than others, though. It is important to weigh the necessity of each bit of information with your client's time.

It is important that your proposal be clear. June Campbell, a business writer, says that every business proposal is read by people with a wide variety of backgrounds, from all walks of life. A good business proposal assumes very little about the reader's knowledge. It should be free of jargon and abbreviations that are too industry specific, especially in technical matters. A good proofreader for your proposal would be someone who has no background in the industry at all.

Some business deals are discussed, but not decided upon, over lunch or some other meeting. A verbal offer goes out, but the client is undecided. A good business proposal can be a follow-up letter, sent after the conversation, with added details and features.

What It Takes

Good listening skills, empathy, and clarity in writing are key elements to good business proposal writing. For clients requiring specific details in the proposal, for example, the U.S. government, a meticulous and thorough covering of the offer is critical. Don't miss the deadline. The ability to research the needs of your client and the materials necessary to meet your client's goals is an important quality to have if you want to write business proposals.

If you enjoy sports, you will probably do well with business proposals because it is a very competitive practice. If you can consistently outperform the other teams, you will be a winner at this game.

Getting Started

1. Read business proposals from various industries. Could you write one of these? How would you improve upon them? How could you make yours more competitive?

2. Read a number of RFPs, starting with the government, then find some examples in business. How would you use these as a guide to craft a competitive proposal?

3. Offer to write unsolicited business proposals for free to develop a portfolio. Apprentice with someone who has experience. Keep score on proposals that win.

4. Give workshops on writing effective business proposals. A lot of businesses attempt to do this kind of writing in-house, and they need a little guidance. Pass out your card as the local expert. Some attendees may just hire you.

5. Write letters to companies touting your experience, offering to show them writing samples and your portfolio. Explain clearly why your writing is better than their in-house setup, and goes beyond the competition.

Additional Resources

The Elements of Business Writing by Robert Bly (Longman, 1992).

How to Write a Proposal That's Accepted Every Time by Alan Weiss (Kennedy Information, 2003).

Tips for Writing a Business Proposal: www.4hb.com/0350tipwritebizproposal. html.

What a private sector company can learn from government proposals: www. captureplanning.com/articles/12548.cfm.

A training site for proposal writing (tutorials, templates, resources): www. captureplanning.com/index.cfm.

CHAPTER 63

Public Seminars

Overview

Holding a public seminar or workshop is a great way to build recognition and sell your products. You also will be seen as an expert in your field, especially if you write books and get them published. Aside from training the public in your field of expertise, seminars and workshops are also great places to sell your associated books and media, along with a whole course or series of courses.

You might spend a day doing a free preliminary seminar to promote a wealth-building, two-day workshop you will be giving in the next two weeks. During the free seminar, you offer little tidbits of information that grab the audience's attention and persuade them to come back for the intensified training workshop that costs $300 and takes two days.

What It Pays

If a paying seminar is for the public, fees will be lower than for a company-paid seminar. A two-day seminar can run about $300 per person. So if you have fifty people attending, your fee would be $15,000 minus site rental and other seminar costs, such as direct mail campaigns and refreshments.

Nuts and Bolts

You should be an expert in the field you wish to give a seminar in, and it helps if you have degrees, teach at a college, and possibly have written and published books in your niche. If inexperienced at giving seminars, consider offering preliminary sessions either with a business or some other organization like a church or a club. Build yourself up to larger groups over time, until you can rent large hotel conference halls or convention centers. Everything is dependent on your niche and your target market as to how large you grow your base of clients.

What You'll Write

Develop your seminar first by outlining your whole process on paper, with all your highlights in bullet points. If you are at first uncomfortable with ad-lib speaking from just bullet points, then develop your speech on paper in an easy-to-read manner so that you can find your information at a glance if you need it while you're teaching.

You need to grab your audience with your introduction, so careful thought must go into this part and how it will also hit on the rest of your seminar points. Each section should be developed to convey the highlighted point in the outline.

What you write for the seminar is dependent on your seminar theme. If you were giving a writing seminar, then you might also write extended pieces like exercises that the audience will do after each section. For instance, after a sales letter theory section, you may have the audience use exercises you've written to create their own sales letters, based on their businesses. Give attendees feedback on their work. Doing so goes a long way in making contact with your audience and having the members feel you are truly interested in them, not just their money.

The conclusion should be a summary of all that went before with a call to action at the end. This is also a perfect time to point out that you are giving a repeat seminar in two months and audience members can refer friends to that seminar and earn a referral fee (or win one of your books or receive a free one-hour consultation from you).

Once your seminar is defined, decide how you want to market the seminar, whether by direct mail or an email campaign. You write all the marketing pieces, any additional seminar documents, and you may also consider doing a survey after the seminar with an incentive offer.

What It Takes

Having skills in organization, development, and presentation are important in doing seminars. Start with small seminars and presentations and work your way up. Previous teaching experience is also very helpful, as you already have a sense of how to help your seminar attendees so that they can learn how to do what you taught them.

Getting Started

Find workshops or seminars that train you how to train others or how to give your own seminars. Read books on seminar development. Attend seminars to see how others do the training and find a method that feels comfortable for you that you saw as being successful with the audience.

Be sure that all written documents handed out during the seminar are written in a clear and concise manner and can be referred to long after the seminar has ended.

Depending on your niche, offer seminars for small local clubs in your area who would be interested in your subject matter. Check with groups you are currently involved with, such as your church, and see if they would like to have a seminar. In the beginning, you may be doing some of these for free just so you can gain experience in your presentation and interaction skills.

Additional Resources

Getting Started in Speaking, Training, or Seminar Consulting by Robert W. Bly (Wiley, 2000).

Start Your Own Seminar Production Business (Entrepreneur Press, 2003).

Marketing and Promoting Your Own Seminars and Workshops by Fred Gleek (Gleek, 2003).

How to Run Seminars & Workshops by Robert Jolles (Wiley, 2005).

How to Make It Big in the Seminar Business by Paul Karasik (McGraw-Hill, 2004).

How to Develop and Promote Successful Seminars and Workshops by Howard Shenson (Wiley, 1990).

CHAPTER 64

Radio Commercials

Overview

The difference in writing commercials for radio compared to television is that in radio, there are no pictures to go with the words. Each spoken word must deliver the "picture."

Freelance copywriters have a better chance of breaking into writing radio commercials than TV commercials, though radio commercials do not pay as well.

Some TV commercials translate well to radio because the words convey the message without the pictures. Radio commercial messages must be direct, with no doubt about who the company is and why they are advertising. It has to be that way in radio.

What It Pays

Radio commercials and public service announcements (PSAs) can pay about $85 an hour to write or about $600 per running minute, depending on the client, running time allotted, and client's budget. If you already have successful ads under your belt, you can negotiate your terms.

Nuts and Bolts

Writing short concise sentences or phrases that grab attention are paramount to this type of writing. Generally you have thirty to sixty seconds to grab the audience and deliver the message. The opening statement must make a customer take notice and take action to get the results the commercial proposes.

As a radio audience is diverse, your writing should be easy to understand, even by children. While you may be trying to reach a targeted segment of the consumer base, don't use specialized jargon understood only by specialists in the field. Keep it simple and easy for the layman to understand.

What You'll Write

You write the commercial within the time guidelines given by the client. The commercial is usually composed in a line-by-line format, with each character named at the beginning of the spoken section. If you've ever seen a transcription of a tape recording, that is the format that it should be written in. Any sound effects are noted in parentheses.

If the product or service is new, the client may have you create supporting literature for marketing purposes.

What It Takes

Listen to the radio for commercials and study how they are set up. Dissect the commercial by time frame, the opening lead, the message, and then the call to action or closing information.

Listen to these and also note your own reaction. Did you find it funny or did you think you wanted to run right out and buy the product because it would solve a problem you were having? Sometimes, like TV commercials, radio commercials can be funny, cute, or memorable, but no one can identify the company's message, product, or service.

Getting Started

Start with a nonprofit group that could really use your help. This helps you get samples of published or aired work.

Tune into the major stations in your region and note the local advertisers who run spots. Contact the business owner or advertising manager and offer to rewrite or improve a commercial on speculation. Or write some commercials on your own to create a portfolio you can show potential clients. Select what to write about (e.g., lawn services or real estate investments), research it, and write a few sample commercials.

Additional Resources

The Radio & Television Commercial by Albert Book, Norman Cary, Stanley Tannenbaum, and Frank Brady (NTC Business Books, 1996).

Rich and Famous in Thirty Seconds: Inside Secrets to Achieving Financial Success in Television and Radio Commercials by Batt Johnson (Writer's Showcase Press, 2000).

National Association of Broadcasters: www.nab.org.

CHAPTER 65

Reports

Overview

According to Norman Sigband, author of *Effective Report Writing*, the trading of reports allows us to "reach decisions, issue policies, recommend action, and record information." Whether the report you write is for a business, organization, or publication; whether it is an academic exercise, means of communication, or part of a sales pitch, there are elements of report writing that are the same. These are the basics you should know that will propel you forward in writing reports.

What It Pays

Some companies and organizations freelance their report writing, as the in-house employees have too many other responsibilities. "It is not unreasonable for a freelancer to charge a project fee based on $40–$50 an hour," says Linda Alexander of Writers Gazette website. That includes time for research and writing. Become specialized in a niche in report writing and you can make more money, $150 an hour or more.

Nuts and Bolts

Sometimes your report reviews a study, such as the environmental benefits of bamboo. Or your report may cover findings from multiple studies. If your report is financial in nature, it may review data within a company. Or the financial report could be for an investment newsletter, using numbers to prove the prudence in buying a stock. A report could be hundreds of pages long, or it could be a paragraph in a sales letter.

Pay attention to the layout of your report and be considerate of the time of your reader. Jeff Herrington, a freelance writer, notes that a huge mistake is dumping your report text online, not bearing in mind how people use the Web. For online reports, the reader should be able to click on any section in the table of contents, read any aspect of the report, and skip over unwanted reading.

If your report is in hard copy, make it easy for your reader to scan the report and get to the wanted sections. Detailed analysis can go into appendices at the end of your report, which saves the reader time, yet the information is still available for readers who want to scrutinize the data.

Research for your report will take the bulk of your time. You need to find, chart, and sort through data; and you have to present and analyze that data well if you want a convincing report that accomplishes your objectives.

What You Will Write

Formats for reports vary. When a client asks you to write a report, ask whether they have a template or format they want you to follow. And get samples of their other reports. For a scientific or technical report, the following format is fairly standard:

Abstract

A paragraph-long summary of a report. The abstract saves the reader time by summarizing the essential points of the report.

Introduction

State clearly the purpose of your report. Who are your readers? There must be some reason for presenting your data and bringing your findings to light. What problem does your report outline? What information is being communicated? And why is it so needed or why is it important to your reader?

Literature review

A literature review presents other similar studies and the results of those studies. Longer and more formal reports need a literature review. They can propel your argument forward.

Method

How was the data that you are reporting gathered? Who gathered the data and under what circumstances?

Data

What were the results of the study? The actual measurements are often shown in graph form. Subjective commentary can be mentioned in informal reports. However, concrete data is almost always superior when possible. Actual measurements can be graphed, analyzed, and discussed objectively.

Carol A. Vidoli, a NASA scientist at the Lewis Research Center in Cleveland, Ohio, offers the following advice: "Excessive data or data only loosely related to the conclusions will obscure them and confuse your readers. Of course, do not hide contradictory results. When definite contradictions exist, clearly alert your readers to this fact."

Conclusion

A conclusion summarizes the results, the data in the study, and suggests a course of action. What conclusions can we draw from the data? Why is it important? What action should your reader take as a result of reading your report?

References and Appendices

The reference section provides the reader with a list of your sources and suggested reading. The appendix section provides detailed information about your data and analysis.

What It Takes

If you write reports, you probably like research. Some report writing can be very technical and requires either a background in the subject matter or the tenacity to research it. If you write reports, you have excellent written communication skills and can translate data into a meaningful explanation of what that data means in the context of the report. Analyzing data requires a critical eye. If you are trying to convince your reader to buy a certain vitamin supplement, choose studies to support your argument that have good methodology, unbiased researchers (a group proven to be unconnected with the company), and logical conclusions. The more objective the study is, the more convincing your report will be.

An understanding of statistical significance and its application to your subject matter is paramount. Graphing software is a must. Your reader should be able to glance at your clearly labeled graphs and get the gist of the data and findings.

Getting Started

Read as many reports as you can. Who is the reader in each case? What is the purpose of the report and what is the writer trying to accomplish? Which reports could be well written by you?

Be sure you read the reference page and data in these reports. Can you sift through that data as well? How did the writer do in analyzing the data? Was the report objective and organized in its presentation? Could you do a better job?

Take courses in report writing. There are workshops and online classes. People within a company take these to hone their craft. You could take them to jump-start your freelance business.

Network with as many people as you can who write reports on a regular basis, both freelance report writers and individuals within companies who write reports. Join online forums. But don't just sign onto forums; join organizations in the industry of your choosing to get an idea of the report writing needed there. Attend conferences. Ask a lot of questions.

Work for free for a while to build your portfolio. Provide excellent work, build your reputation, and you will do well in a job that analyzes and presents needed information.

Additional Resources

Report Writing Essentials by Lance Parr (Wadsworth, 2000).

Technical Report Writing Today by Daniel Riordan and Steven Pauley (Houghton Mifflin, 2004).

Tips on effective report writing: custom-writing.org/blog/writing-tips/17.html.

An example of a subscription newsletter that connects writers in the workplace and provides tips and articles for writing documents: www.apexawards.com.

A seminar on financial report writing: www.writingandspeaking.com/financial-report-writing.php.

CHAPTER 66

Résumés

Overview

Writing résumés for those out of work and looking for new jobs can be very rewarding, especially if the résumé you created is instrumental in that person getting in the door for the interview. You can run a business solely on writing résumés for out-of-work clients and college graduates who are looking for their first job.

What It Pays

When running your own résumé business, you can charge whatever the target market can bear. Consider the job they are trying to get, what it takes to get the interview, and how developed you need to make the résumé to fit the requirements. In the beginning, start with a low fee but high enough to compensate your time, perhaps $100 per résumé. If you advertise in the college market, you need to set your fees lower. If you are charging a higher amount for one student than another, be prepared to explain why. Be consistent in your fees. For professional workers, you can charge more. About $200 per résumé would be a reasonable beginning fee.

Nuts and Bolts

A successful résumé has key points pertinent to the job requirements, is easy to read and spot information, and relates to the criteria needed to perform the job. That also means that maybe more than one résumé should be written, based on the different skills the client can provide to varying companies. While one job may require research skills, another job may need someone who is more of a direct marketing specialist and great copywriter. The submitted résumé should strongly reflect the special skills needed for that job. Anything less than that will not result in an interview.

Practice writing your own résumé; have a friend review it to see what they think and whether they are impressed with what they see. Study résumé writing books. There are also some workshops you can take to learn how to write attention-grabbing résumés.

What You'll Write

You write the résumé itself, plus you can write the cover letter for an extra fee. Revisions of the résumé, geared to another type of job, also commands an additional fee.

What It Takes

You should have a website and general office machines like a computer and printer. Decide if you prefer to meet people at your home or at a more public place like a coffee shop or bookstore. If you have a laptop, that would be an ideal method of recording or obtaining information right on the spot, as well as accessing the Internet.

You must finish your projects in a timely manner, as jobs are on the line and your clients want to interview as soon as possible. Timing is crucial for most job searchers.

Getting Started

Create a business plan that details where you advertise your services, and follow it religiously. Success is in continuous marketing even when business is going well. When your business gets rolling faster and you feel fairly confident, you can think about raising your rates to new prospects.

Additional Resources

Résumés That Knock 'Em Dead (Adams Media, 2006).

The Elements of Résumé Style by Scott Bennett (AMACOM, 2005).

Résumé Magic by Susan Britton Whitcomb (JIST Works, 2006).

The Résumé.com Guide to Writing Unbeatable Résumés by Warren Simons and Rose Curtis (McGraw-Hill, 2004).

The Only Résumé and Cover Letter Book You'll Ever Need by Richard Wallace (Adams Media, 2008).

More résumé writing information: www.accent-resume-writing.com.

More free tips on writing résumés: careerplanning.about.com/od/resumewriting/Resume_Writing.htm.

Free online résumé tips: www.free-resume-tips.com/10tips.html.

Rockport Institute (www.rockportinstitute.com/resumes.html) has good information on writing résumés.

CHAPTER 67

Romance

Overview

More than half of paperback fiction sales are romance titles, generating $1.2 billion in annual revenue. Compare that with detective fiction at only 28 percent and science fiction at 7 percent, and you'll see that romance gives you the greatest chance for success and a big income.

What It Pays

A first-time author writing for Harlequin might receive a $3,500 advance, while the average advance for an experienced romance novelist with a track record is $5,000–$7,000 for a category book (a novel marketed as a romance). Literary agent Bob Diforio says the advance for a novel from a first-time unknown romance author can be as low as $2,000.

Royalties on romance novels are 4–6 percent. Print runs are usually twenty-thousand books. Marilyn Campbell, a romance novelist, says, "The first book I sold, a light romantic comedy called *Daydreams*, took me three weeks to write. A Harlequin-type publisher called Meteor Books bought it for $4,000 in 1991. Within a year, I was contracted for eight more books."

Nuts and Bolts

You submit a query (a letter requesting consideration of your work) to the editors at a publishing house. Before you even start writing your novel, think about that query. When you are chewing on your pencil, do not think about a story that is dreamy to you. Ask instead what an editor will think is dreamy. What will sell? You have to sell the editor first.

The only place to sell the editor is in the query letter. You hook the editor by writing a vignette that is about a paragraph long in the query letter. The hook is an advertisement for your book that tantalizes your curious reader into a sale, revealing enough to pique interest, without giving it away. Think of the blurb on the back of a book that gets a casual browser to buy it. Consider writing dozens of hooks first before even commencing your novel.

If the editor likes your idea, she may contact you and ask for a partial, or the first three chapters of your manuscript. Or an editor may request your entire manuscript. Your manuscript should have 1-inch margins on all sides. This should keep your words, double-spaced, at two-hundred and fifty per page. You should have twenty-five lines per page. Use a standard font like Courier or Times. This is standard formatting for submissions.

Some editors may require you to work through an agent. Self-publishing is also an option.

What You Will Write

Why does a reader invest money and time in a romance novel? The answer to that question is what brings her back to the shelf, time and time again, getting you paid and published, repeatedly.

A romance novel, in a word, is an escape. She could escape into science fiction or mystery, sure. But the demand for romance books should tell you that a romantic book, well…it's a different kind of escape. Whether the reader is addicted to romance novels or just wants something enjoyable to read on the plane, the desire is the same. She wants to step out of her ho-hum existence for a while. She wants to identify with the heroine in the story, travel to a distant place, and sometimes a different time, and, of course, meet up with a new and exciting romantic interest.

Think about the selling and marketing aspects of your novel as you sit down to write it. Think about your editor, too, and not just your reader.

- **Setting.** Instead of overused settings, think of an original setting that other novelists have not chosen or would not even imagine. The more remote, the better.

- **Character development.** Your reader needs to identify with your characters, especially the heroine. She will follow them into the fantasy if they are genuine but unique and interesting.

- **Conflict.** What is it in romance? According to the romance novelist Patricia Delacroix, conflict in the romantic novel "is some compelling reason, or reasons, for the hero and heroine to not be together." Create conflict in the relationship on many levels to write a page turner.

- **Dénouement.** This is the unraveling of the story. From a marketing standpoint, consider a soft landing. By that I mean, think about your reader. She picked up the book to escape the mundane life, and the climax of the story is over. Consider gently returning her to that life. Only fill it with richness and meaning. If your characters were rolling in money early in the book, remove it; they still have each other. If they went on an exotic trip to Southeast Asia, return them to a wide spot in the road in Oklahoma. Make the predictability and the routine of life desirable, and full of its own blessings and surprises. Bring joy into the lives of your characters, away from thrills.

Return your reader, after an exciting and adventurous ride, to her own living room, with sunlight pouring through the window. Give her the inspiration to call a family member and express love or appreciation. Bring her back to embracing what she has. In this way, you not only provide escape for your reader, but you nurture her in her own life as well. And ultimately, that is what she wants. If you do, she will continue to look for you on the bookstore shelves again and again.

A soft landing, the style of Nora Roberts and others, is not the only way to craft a book so that it fills the needs of your reader. But it is an example. Anticipate the needs of your reader and address those needs in your writing. A good novel does not simply excite. It inspires.

What It Takes

A romantic heart, an engaging writing style, a creative and dramatic imagination, and a soul with empathy are all qualities of a good romance author.

It is a myth that romance must be written by a woman. Some of the greatest love stories are penned by men. *Love Story* by Eric Siegel is one example, as well as *The Notebook* by Nicholas Sparks.

Research is important. It's hard to escape if the facts don't seem quite right. An atlas is also good to have on hand. And be patient: many successful novelists submitted work that was not accepted the first time.

Getting Started

Read a lot of romance novels. Which ones are your favorites and why? Which novels were bestsellers for their time and why? Keep up with the latest trends. "Keep abreast of which houses are acquiring what," advises romance novelist Marcia King Gamble. "Read as much as you can of the genre. Look for new lines that are opening up as they may be receptive to new writers. Be prepared to do what you need to do to market your book."

Read like a marketer. Write the hooks first. What will sell? Use your favorite hooks to craft your novels. Join writers groups and network. Meet agents and publishers at writers conferences. Send agents and publishers your query letters with hooks. Ask them if they would like to read more.

Additional Resources

For agent searches: www.agentresearch.com.
Harlequin has helpful how-to advice on their site: www.eharlequin.com.

Networking, newsletter, and more for romance writers: romancenovels. bellaonline.com/Site.asp.

Romance Writers of America has a membership site: www.rwanational.org.

Tips for aspiring romance writers: www.writerswrite.com/journal/feb05/ delacroix.html.

CHAPTER 68

Science Fiction

Overview

Writing science-fiction stories is a whole other world, literally. Most stories in this genre are set in a world that bears little resemblance to our everyday life. Story background may consist of futuristic settings on other worlds or a technologically developed society on this planet. Characters can range from unusual animal types, other planet societies, or even humans who have developed special skills, a biological evolution of sorts. In science-fiction stories, science and technology are key to the genre.

Be aware that science-fiction writing is not fantasy writing. The difference between the two is in subject matter, although traditional plot lines certainly have a place in both. Fantasy writing deals more with the mystical. *Lord of the Rings* is an excellent example of fantasy with worlds inhabited by elves, goblins, orcs, hobbits, dwarves, and magicians. Science fiction, however, deals with more modernistic settings, worlds, characters—anything that could seem relative to a future direction in our lifestyle.

What It Pays

Check the current *Writer's Market* for the latest fees for magazines and book publishers. An example is *Analog Science Fiction & Fact*, which buys forty to sixty manuscripts per year. Publishers usually pay 4 cents per word for novels, 5–6 cents per word for novelettes, and 6–8 cents per word for shorts. *Asimov's Science Fiction* magazine pays 5–8 cents per word for stories running 750–15,000 words.

Nuts and Bolts

Whichever way the story line may go, what will be very important is consistency in story elements such as scenery, wardrobe, societal history, types of weapons, vehicles, special abilities, and the plot—which must incorporate all those elements.

Like on the set of a movie, you need a continuity director and that means thinking out your story with all the background notes and off-shoot stories about characters that explain why someone does what he does. The off-shoot story does not necessarily get put into the main story but there may be references made to it as part of a character's behavior pattern.

Development of details is essential for unusual characters and plots. You may find that you have to develop the story behind the story, which outlines a science-fiction lifestyle and historical events of a nonexistent world. A good example of building a story behind the story is the *Star Wars* series, especially as done on film.

What You'll Write

You write the story line, character development, world features, maps, and anything else that requires reference or support while creating your story. You then write the story using your reference notes, and even then you may find you have to keep updating your reference notes as events unfold in your story.

What It Takes

Story building requires imagination and close attention to detail. You also need to research certain aspects of science and technology. For instance, if you give biological references to a virus that may wipe out the world, you may need to study virus strains and how they behave in testing situations. Writing about a strange world and characters that do not exist does not mean that you can completely disregard science and technology in our own daily lives. While stories of this nature are fictitious, when there are tie-ins to real life, accuracy is essential.

Getting Started

Read different science-fiction authors to see how they treat their subject matter. Take note of stories that interest you, and study how the author develops characters, plots, and backgrounds. You learn more by studying what you wish to emulate.

Additional Resources

How to Write Science Fiction & Fantasy by Orson Scott Card (Writer's Digest Books, 2001).

The Science of Science Fiction Writing by James Gunn (Scarecrow Press, 2000).

Writing Science Fiction & Fantasy by Crawford Kilian (Self Counsel Press, 2007).

Science Fiction and Fantasy Writers of America offers many resources on their site for free: www.sfwa.org.

www.writesf.com.

CHAPTER 69

Self-Help

Overview

The self-help industry is huge; self-improvement, in all of its forms, is an $8.56 billion business, with 3,500–4,000 new self-help titles published in 2003 alone. Self-help subject matter can range from recovering from a break-up to practicing alternative medicine. As with home repair, there is always an inherent danger in doing things by yourself if you do not get an expert's opinion or assistance from a professional. That said, there is a certain amount of pride in putting yourself back together and telling yourself or your friends, "I did this by myself."

The personal self-help genre has become very big in the past few years, especially with the video and book called *The Secret*. If you choose to write in this area, be sure you have a market that wants your product and be sure that you can offer something special—something outside the box—to your potential customers.

What It Pays

The market you approach determines what you will get paid. Check the latest *Writer's Market*, which lists all the publications and publishing houses that use self-help material.

Impact Publishers, a small press company specializing in the personal self-help field, pays 10 percent royalties on net receipts and, on occasion, will pay an advance, according to *2008 Writer's Market*. Book publisher Focal Press, an imprint of Elsevier, publishes more in the educational field and pays 10–12 percent royalty on net receipts with a possible small advance.

For the most part, sending a query letter first to any publication is the smartest way to go and will allow you to negotiate your fees a bit better if selected for review from the slush pile.

Nuts and Bolts

Writing self-help requires that you be recognized as an expert on the specific topic you are writing about. Having a talent for outlining steps and procedures in a logical sequence is essential for imparting information to the reader, but remember to keep the writing interesting and easy to read.

Personality is at least as important as process; the reader needs to have faith in you before they will subscribe to your methods. Outlining your piece in advance is a good idea so that you don't lose sight of a section's objective, a common mistake in this genre.

What You'll Write

You will write the main piece, be it a book or a magazine story. If a book, you may also write the direct mail package that lists major points of interest considered to be information that grabs the readers and tempts them to make the purchase right away so that they can learn more.

If selling on a website, you will write the landing page and the ordering page plus any email packages and promotions that will be sent out to your client list or to someone else's client list. Use easy to read writing and if you use any religious terms, be sure you have clarified what they represent by some sort of description when you first use them.

What It Takes

Writing a self-help book or article requires focus and self-confidence from beginning to end. It is somewhat like project management, where you outline, through a flowchart, what comes first, then second, third, fourth, and so on, all the way to the end. You can never lose sight of the final goal because your audience expects to see results.

The conclusion in this type of writing is critical. Whether the goal is quitting smoking, strengthening a marriage, managing stress, or finding a new purpose in life, the reader needs to be left with a sense of accomplishment. By indulging in your wisdom, they've been given a second chance at life, if only in a small way.

Getting Started

Think of normal-life areas that you are proficient in, perhaps even considered a pro—dating, time management, handling major change—and decide what it is that readers would really want to know from you. As a professional or experienced person in your field, show your readers you can help them achieve their dreams or desires. Start practicing by writing self-help articles that won't be quite so grueling as doing a whole book. Visit a major bookstore and check out their self-help section; research who these people are and how they write. Talk to your neighbors and local support groups to get a feel for the needs people have in their lives, then set out to address those needs in your writing.

Additional Resources

Your Perfect Write: The Manual for Self-Help Writers by Robert E. Alberti (Impact Publishers, 1985).

Writing Successful Self-Help and How-To Books by Jean Marie Stine (Wiley, 1997).

Writing 101: www.write101.com/writing-self-help-books.htm.

CHAPTER 70

Short Stories

Overview

Writing short stories is like telling about a moment in time, an event that occurs fast and hard, striking a nerve. There is no time to dillydally, so the writer must get right to the point of the story. A short story generally deals with one event and maybe two to three characters, or even only one.

A good story has you glued to the page as you read faster and faster, because that is what the pace demands. Say more in less time about people and events, and catch the reader in your web immediately.

To a degree, the skills for writing a short story are the same as for a novel, yet everything happens faster in a much shorter amount of time. There is the event, then a climax, conflict and tension, and a final resolution to the problem.

What It Pays

The best source on short-story pay is the latest edition of *Novel & Short Story Writer's Market.* You can find the publications that pay for your stories, and note those that just offer a byline. Some magazines may pay only $25 for a 1,000-word story, while other publications will pay more, about $250 for a 1,000-word story.

Nuts and Bolts

Read as many short stories as you can. Learn by example how to create the structure of a short story and character development. Read many different writers to find your voice as a writer. You will uncover the genre you want to write in, such as horror stories (read Edgar Allen Poe).

Give yourself some scenarios to practice writing short stories in a concise manner. Get with a group of writers who can critique your work and also encourage you when you need it. Outline what you will write about and figure out if it is the character or the plot that drives the story.

Carry around a small notebook to jot down notes and ideas.

What You'll Write

You write the short story, usually 1,000–2,000 words. Some authors prefer "quiet" stories where the character or drama builds up gradually. But it's usually better to dive into the middle rather than start at the beginning, or at least start with a scene with action, drama, or suspense, as in the short story "The Rubber Band Man":

> **It was raining steadily from a gray sky with indistinct clouds when I first noticed the rubber bands. I should have taken action at the start, of course. Now, it is too late: I am locked away, my career over, my life ruined—and everyone on the planet is doomed.**

Harlan Ellison says, "An otherwise excellent story can find itself being stuffed back into the SASE and being dropkicked into the mail chute because it had a slow, an obscure, a confusing, or redundant opening section."

What It Takes

You need to keep a thread going in your stories and properly develop events and characters. For short stories, writing concisely and getting to the point quickly is essential to the success of your work. You also need discipline to sit down and write for several hours every day without distractions.

Researching your story subject is very important. For example, if you write about a murder mystery, but you get parts of police investigation wrong, or mess up facts about DNA testing, your readers will be disappointed and not bother to read anything else written by you.

Getting Started

Keep a list of ideas regarding stories you want to write. If you let the idea slide, you most likely will forget about it or lose the enthusiasm you felt when you first thought of the idea. Get a list together of publications and editors to contact regarding your stories. You do not write query letters for short stories, as you do with articles. Instead, you send the complete story to the magazine's fiction editor. The story should be printed double spaced on white paper. Do not staple your manuscript. Use a paper clip or a pocket folder to hold the pages. Mail your story manuscript flat in a 9 x 12 inch envelope.

In the pre-computer days, you had to enclose a return 9 x 12 inch postage-paid envelope to get your story back. But if you have your story on your hard drive, why do you need it back? You only want an answer from the editor.

Type the words "DISPOSABLE MANUSCRIPT" in the upper left corner of the first page of the story. This tells the editor you don't need the manuscript back. Enclose a postage-paid self-addressed stamped #10 envelope the editor can use to send his acceptance or rejection letter.

Always keep stories in circulation. When one comes back rejected, send it out to the next magazine. Keep track of story submissions on a spreadsheet so that you don't accidentally mail multiple stories to one editor at the same time, or send the same story simultaneously to two different magazine editors—a definite no-no.

Additional Resources

The Art of the Short Story by Dana Gioia and R. S. Gwynn (Longman, 2005).
Creating Short Fiction by Damon Knight (St. Martin's, 1997).
Extraordinary Short Story Writing by Steven Otfinoski (Franklin Watts, 2006).
Fiction Factor: www.fictionfactor.com.

CHAPTER 71

Specification Writing

Overview

A *specification* is a statement of needs to be satisfied by the procurement of external resources; manufacturers, software companies, and other businesses hire spec writers to create precise definitions of their requirements for products and services to be purchased.

Whenever parties come together in business, engineering, and construction, there must be an agreement detailing the specific items, chosen by consensus for a project. This write-up is called a specification.

Let's say a U.S. state government wants to build a bridge. The government has a list of specifications needed for that bridge. It has to be so wide and so long, and each of the materials used has to meet a certain quality standard.

Then when the government reviews its plans with the engineers who bid for the contract, one of those engineering firms might come forward in the bid and say, "Material X in your plans is not adequate. We cannot endorse that particular material because in our experience, material X is flimsy; our firm has standards also. You, state government, if you go with us, need to choose material Y instead because it is better and it meets our standards."

Typically, you find specification writers in construction projects. They are in all branches of engineering—from chemical processing to electrical power plants to civil engineering projects to software. Specification writers are in government as well. The specification process does not enforce the implementations of the plans chosen; it only presents them in a document for referral.

What It Pays

Specifications writers, also called spec writers, typically make $40,000–$70,000 per year. Freelance your work, and your services can make you as much as $200,000 per year. As an example, architects are required to complete more and more work in less and less time than they were twenty years ago. Architects themselves have less time to familiarize themselves with the catalogs and manuals needed for construction spec writing. Hiring freelance spec writers saves time, especially in cases where an architectural firm cannot afford to hire a full-time spec writer.

Advancing as a spec writer happens quickly, depending upon your certification and years of experience. Sometimes a senior spec writer is considered to have four or more years of experience.

Nuts and Bolts

A spec writer serves as a guide to a given project. A writer can specify certain products or services. He or she frequently meets with manufacturers who would like their products chosen for projects.

As a spec writer, it is important to understand the needs of your customer as well as manufacturers and service providers. Ultimately, though, your customer (client or employer) needs to be able to choose from an objective variety of options for the project. From a cost and quality perspective, your role is to outline options meeting your company's or your client's objectives, and at the same time to secure the requirements of everyone on the project.

Paul T. Kosakowski notes that there are, at least in construction specification, five main things that specification requirements should include.

1. performance
2. code compliance
3. aesthetics (appearance)
4. budget
5. product reliability

Sometimes requirements falling out of these obligations ultimately serve someone other than the writer's client. Narrowing your client's options to meet the need of a manufacturer is not good spec writing.

What You Will Write

You write the document or manual for specification for a given project. These written works can be anywhere from eight pages to hundreds of pages.

A specification may include:

• persons or groups of people responsible for the specification
• purpose of the specification
• terminology and definitions
• testing methodology
• material requirements/tolerances

- certification requirements

- performance requirements, including administrative (who is to do what when)

- safety and environmental requirements

- local, national, and international codes

- quality consensus

- persons or groups responsible for enforcement of specification

- requirements of completion and inspection

What It Takes

Do you have a background in construction, architecture, manufacturing, or engineering? A mechanical mind? Do you have good communication skills? Then you are a natural for specifications writing.

You are the glue holding an entire project together. Good diplomatic and organizational skills are part of the all-in-a day's work for spec writers. Organizational skills, tenacity, patience, solid team-player skills, and strong writing are all ingredients for solid spec writing.

Some spec writers have a degree in architecture, construction, or engineering and then take up specification writing. Some acquire work experience in one or more of these industries and then pursue spec writing.

Many spec writers receive certification through an instructor-led or online course. In software, the engineers typically write the specs, but too often produce sloppy work that ends up costing companies thousands of dollars. Quality spec writers are needed in this industry.

Knowledge of Word, Excel, and Adobe Acrobat is recommended, as well as other software specific to your industry. Familiarize yourself with the most recent and advanced software.

Getting Started

1. **Look at a sample spec.** Find a specifications manual or document in an industry that interests you and look it over. Does it look like something you could write?

2. **Build your technical writing skills.** Get as much general technical writing experience as possible in either a branch of engineering or manufacturing, construction, architecture, or software—or the government. Familiarize yourself with various documents, writing protocol, and industry materials. Write clear and concise documents for these industries.

3. **Get certified.** Take an online certification class for specification or sign up to attend a four-day workshop to complete certification. As an example, each test

for construction certification lasts four hours and requires a 75 percent score or better to pass:

CDT: Certified Document Technology
CCS: Certified Construction Specifier
CCCA: Certified Construction Contract Administrator

4. Get a portfolio. Consider apprenticing under a spec writer for a low fee to gain experience and then add your assigned projects to your résumé.

5. Get hired. Approach businesses in your chosen industry, and offer your services for their ongoing projects. Pass out your card in trade meetings and advertise your services in trade magazines and on membership websites.

Additional Resources

Writing Engineering Specifications by Paul Fitchet (Taylor & Francis, 2002).

Construction Specifications Writing by Harold J. Rosen and John Regener (Wiley, 2004).

Discussion forum for experienced specwriters: www.4specs.com.

Construction Specifications Institute: www.csinet.org.

National Institute of Governmental Purchasing, online training course: www.nigp.org/educate/OnlineTrainSpecs.htm.

For specification writers in independent practice: www.scrip.com.

Writing software requirements specifications: www.techwr-l.com/techwhirl/magazine/writing/softwarerequirementspecs.html.

CHAPTER 72

Sports Writing

Overview

More than $16 billion is spent annually on attending sporting events, and both freelance and staff writers are needed to cover almost every sport imaginable. But the sports writing industry is a really hard business to break into, and has become increasingly so over the past several years. You have to work extremely hard to make a name for yourself and for people to give you opportunities. It may not be financially what you are looking for in the beginning, but you could make a lot of money writing for several different companies at the same time.

The sports writing industry is going through some tough times. And it will continue to be this way going forward, with most reporting jobs going online. Many newspapers and magazines go years without hiring a sports writer, because they cannot afford to pay the writer. But once you get into the industry, you may be set for a long time.

What It Pays

The pay range depends on who hires you. You could get offered free jobs through the Internet, but many websites offer writers payment, anywhere from $25–$85 per assignment, depending on experience.

Magazines offer anywhere between $300 to several thousand dollars per assignment, depending on length and other factors. The bigger the magazine is, the more money you could potentially make per assignment. There are several magazines that pay $6,000–$10,000 per assignment.

Nuts and Bolts

The basics that each sports writer needs to learn are who, what, when, where, why, and how. This is very important and usually featured in each article. In using the five Ws, you are using the news style of writing, and this is the way for you to get the full story on what you are writing about. Articles usually start with a lead introducing your topic. You always start with the most important thing you are writing about. The lead has to stand out to get people to read your work. It also has to establish why you are writing the article.

Your following paragraphs pertain to the lead, with the least important information at the end of the article.

What You'll Write

Start by covering mainly high school. You may be asked to write several features each week on different players from the games that you cover. During this time, you'll build contacts in the field. Building contacts throughout the high school, college, and pro landscape will assist you with getting quotes for your work.

After several years of covering high school sports, you can move up. You could be assigned to be a beat writer for a college sports team. Typically, you'll have to cover college sports five to ten years before being assigned to cover a professional sports team.

What It Takes

There are a few people in sports writing who do not have a college education, but they know how to write. To be considered for a full-time position, you need to go to college. You should major in English, creative writing, communications, or journalism. These majors teach you the fundamentals on how to write about different things. Obviously, you shouldn't be a sports writer unless you like sports. You don't have to have played the game, but you should at least be a fan, follow teams in the league, and understand the finer points of the rules and regulations.

Getting Started

Search for freelance opportunities online. There are always people looking for freelance writers to cover different competitions. All you have to do is search for your interests and then contact the people regarding opportunities. (Try visiting journalismjobs.com and sportsjournalists.com.) You may be asked to write for free when applying for some online jobs, but there are a lot of paid writing jobs, too. To be considered for a position, be ready to show at least three writing samples.

Additional Resources

Sports Writing: a Beginner's Guide by Steve Craig (Discover Writing Press, 2002).

CHAPTER 73

Syndicated Columnist

Overview

Having written a number of columns over the years—almost all for business magazines and trade journals—I can tell you that writing a column is absolutely a blast. Columns give you more freedom than almost any other nonfiction format except personal essays. You can write about subjects that engage your intellect or your passion, do it in an extremely personal voice, and give your opinions to thousands of readers. The main restriction is word length and making sure each article stays within the theme or subject the column covers.

On the downside, getting a column published—whether in one major daily newspaper or syndicated—is highly competitive. For example, about twenty-five hundred column ideas are submitted to King Features every year, and of these, less than 1 percent are selected annually.

There is a lot for a columnist to write about, and editors are looking for fresh material all the time. As you hone your writing skills and seek to be published at all—somewhere, anywhere—you will be ready to market yourself to the news syndicates.

A news syndication company sells editorial to hundreds of papers all over the United States and in other countries as well. So if the syndicate buys your column, all of those newspapers will be buying your column, too. Not only could you make money doing what you like to do anyway—writing about something important, funny, touching, or useful—you can actually make some serious money doing it.

"I began my career writing for a small community paper in my neighborhood," says Sarah Smiley, a syndicated columnist. "To look back on those first published clips is quite entertaining! But how can I be ashamed? The work I did at *The Julington Creek Plantation Press* became a springboard for my now nationally syndicated column, 'Shore Duty.'"

Quite often, syndicated columnists become instant experts, so they are famous fast. They can write books that sell instantly. Their websites are well visited. They make guest appearances on TV shows.

Even if you don't make it big time, there are other places to write columns that will pay you for your work, like websites. Those spots are also good for showcasing your work, fattening your portfolio, and preparing you for larger venues.

What It Pays

According to Suzette Stranding, author of *The Art of Column Writing* (Marion Street Press, 2008), freelancers are paid anywhere from $5 to $300 per column with a median fee of $50 per column. Salaried columnists can earn $20,000 to $154,000 a year.

Moira Anderson Allen says that online column payment varies from $20–$300 for a column. Most of these sites just want electronic rights to your columns, which means you can publish elsewhere in print.

Nuts and Bolts

When applying for a column at a specific newspaper, Sarah Smiley advises you bypass the department editor, at least initially, and contact the managing editor. This is the person who makes financial decisions for the paper. It eliminates the red tape, and you will get a yes or no. She also advises that you meet deadlines and tighten your writing (make light work for the editors).

Newspaper syndicates sell columns to editors of other papers. CM, managing editor of United Media, a syndication company, offers this advice:

> **Writers will often tell us that their friends love what they write and say they should be syndicated. Our customers are newspaper editors. We have to know why newspaper editors will want to buy a specific column. Look at the things the news syndicates currently offer. Speak to a need that isn't being addressed.**

You eventually submit three to six column samples to a syndication company. A column's standard length is 500–600 words. In the same envelope, mail a query letter, clips of other relevant work that you have published, and other supporting material that might demonstrate to the editors that your writing is in demand.

All syndications have formatting requirements for submission. Check each company's site to find these requirements. A list of syndication companies is provided in the resources section below.

Jodie Lynn, a syndicated columnist, says this about circulation: "Different syndicates do different things. Some sell the column at different prices for different newspapers. Some sell individual columns and some put columns into a series. They evaluate what has worked best the previous years before making a decision on a column. The problem is that they don't know as much as they think they do and are not willing to take a chance on unusual ideas or topics. You have to sell them on the idea and encourage them to move forward, even if you work for free for a while."

In the meantime, as you try to get syndication companies to notice you, continue to do a lot of writing. Publish your work as much as possible so that you can get as much exposure as you can.

What You Will Write

Ideally, your readers should be addicted to you. Remember that you have to sell editors, not just your friends, on fresh and original material. They have to be convinced that your content is of value to your readers.

There are five main categories for columns. Try to figure out where you might make your mark:

- **How-to information.** These columns require some background and expertise. If you have proven expertise in a given area and want to share that experience with others, your column could be of value to readers, especially if it something new and different.

- **Advice.** This one is not easy to break into, as there are only so many advice slots available in a paper, and they are usually occupied. Having credentials is important. Your writing should also establish empathy with your readers.

- **Op-ed.** This is an abbreviation for opinion-editorial. If you are passionate about a subject that is somewhat controversial, and prefer only one side of an argument, op-ed is for you. It is important to give the editor a reason for you to be heard. Identify the people for whom you speak. Convince the editor that you are not alone in your sentiments.

- **Review.** The broader the publication is in its overall content, the more likely you will find a niche in a review column. People like to hear others' opinions about products and services before they buy into them. Items that could be reviewed in a publication include books, music, plays, restaurants, travel destinations, hotels, local parks or attractions, and museums.

  Reviews are a good way to break in because credentials are not required. And sometimes there is room for the review of something new.

- **Humor.** This is one of the hardest categories to penetrate because there are only a few humor slots available, and they are already occupied. Also, because humor is so subjective, you will really have to sell your editors. If you have talent that crushes your competition, go for it.

There are other categories, like "slice of life," a lifestyle musings column—these can be fresh, but they have to be engaging week after week or they won't be read.

What It Takes

An engaging writing style, credentials (sometimes, depending on what you write), patience, persistence, and a general enjoyment in communicating your ideas are the basic ingredients for writing columns. Meet assignments on deadline.

Getting Started

- Read columns in newspapers and online. Do you like what you read?

- Take a journalism class or workshop from someone with published experience in the area of your interest.

- Write. And write a lot, on a variety of topics. In which subject matter are you stellar? Into which category does your writing fall?

- Join writers groups and attend workshops. Get your work critiqued from someone inside the news industry.

- Get publishing experience, even if at a small paper or online site. Commercial websites need columnists, too. Write blogs or articles.

Additional Resources

Creators Syndicate: www.copleynews.com.

DBR Media: www.dbrmedia.com.

How one writer became a syndicated columnist: www.justaboutwrite.com/writing/27689.php.

King Features: www.kingfeatures.com.

Deciding what to charge for your syndicated column: www.market2editors.com/page12a.html.

Washington Post Writers Group: www.postwritersgroup.com.

A site dedicated to syndicated writers: www.syndicatedwriters.com.

The Tribune Media Services: www.tms.tribune.com.

Universal Press Syndicate: www.uexpress.com.

United Media: www.unitedfeatures.com.

Finding syndication success, from *Writer's Digest* magazine: www.writersdigest.com/article/finding-syndication-success.

CHAPTER 74

Tabloids

Overview

Supermarket tabloids revolve around celebrity gossip, miracle diets, and shocking crimes. But for years supermarket tabloids have been viewed with disdain. Due to their notorious reputation, they are rarely seen as a reliable source of information. Nevertheless, tabloids continue to draw readers through catchy headlines, high-interest stories, and clear, succinct writing.

As fascinating as tabloid writing may be, it's not a market for every writer. Only an experienced writer will be able to meet the heavy demands of the tabloid. Even so, if you are willing to put in a little effort and believe you have talent as a writer, tabloids might be your niche.

What It Pays

One of the more lucrative newspaper writing opportunities, supermarket tabloids pay for everything from story tips (articles mailed or phoned in by stringers) to full-length articles. A letter to the editor can reward its writer with as much as $50. Also, tabloids pay about $150 just for a tip about a possible story. An editor at the *National Enquirer* says that the tabloid spends $16 million a year buying articles and photos, noting: "We don't make up any stories; I mean nothing. We can make up stories a lot cheaper than that, I have to tell you." Freelance writers can make $500–$2,000 per story. This is based upon the importance the tabloid places on the story, whether or not pictures are included, and the freshness of the content.

Nuts and Bolts

Though some people subscribe to a particular tabloid, most sales come from one-time, individual purchases. As a result, tabloids must fight week after week to grab the attention of possible readers. Tabloids are constantly on the lookout for something new and surprising to boost their sales.

Fifty percent or more of supermarket tabloid articles are written by freelancers. After coming up with a story idea, the freelancer contacts the supermarket tabloid with a pitch. This might be something unique, or it could be a different angle to an already reported story. (The pitch should include the source of information.) The writer's idea is reviewed by several people. If the information is deemed newsworthy, the editor returns to the writer with an offer.

High-end stories, referred to as a "T" or top page, will pay more than a "D," or down-page story. Once your idea has been approved by the editor, you are paid for your information, or you are assigned to personally cover the story. Of course freelancers are paid more for stories they write. However, they must be prepared to write and rewrite until the editor is satisfied with the article.

What You'll Write

Be prepared to write multiple leads. The more leads you submit to an editor, the better the chances of landing a story. It is the responsibility of the free-lancer to provide the tabloid with possible materials, and not the other way around. Remember, you won't be writing anything for the tabloids unless you come up with the idea.

Leads come from a variety of sources. Celebrity gossip holds the highest attraction for readers. Even so, tabloids also include medical breakthroughs, new beauty products, scandals, murder cases, and anything else that will draw in at least 50 percent of the tabloid's readers.

Stories can be broken down into three basic parts: the lead, the back up, and the conclusion. Stories are generally short and to the point. Details should be given quickly, and superfluous writing left out all together.

What It Takes

The supermarket tabloid writer should have a background in English com-position, journalism, or similar freelance writing experience. Tabloid articles include stories, quotes, and other facts. A writer must know the basics of informative writing to produce solid articles.

But understanding the journalistic side of writing is not enough. Tabloids also depend on strong, informative headlines, compact details, and sensa-tional writing. The writer must keep the attention of their readers. Some knowledge of writing copy will add to the effectiveness of your article.

In addition to being a good writer, freelancers should be investigative. Al-ways have a camera ready and learn to dig for the information you want. The article you write, contrary to past practices, must be factual. Tabloids will not accept your article unless you have a source to back up your information.

Finding sources—such as friends, family, even hairdressers—who are willing to talk will improve your chances of getting a story picked up by the tabloids. Many tabloid freelance writers keep a list of sources on hand, eagerly waiting for whatever tidbits they might pick up.

Getting Started

With a good story, breaking into tabloid writing should not be difficult. Once you have proven yourself to be an effective, informative writer, tabloids will undoubtedly begin relying on you for weekly articles. So, to get started, follow these steps:

1. **Research ideas.** If you don't live and work around celebrities, finding stories might be a challenge. Read other periodicals. Not all stories have to be new. Just find a different angle on an existing story. Also, don't limit yourself to celebrity gossip. Consider other topics such as medicine, government scandals, or new technologies.

2. **Research the tabloids.** Make sure your articles fit the tabloid. Pick up copies of the tabloids in the supermarket, and browse through them. Tabloids stick to recurring themes on each of their pages. Be aware of how your information can add to the tabloid's dynamics.

3. **Write several leads.** The more ideas you generate, the higher the chance of making a sell. If you are presenting old news, make sure you've looked for something no one else has considered.

4. **Contact the tabloid.** Once your leads are written, send a query. Queries do not have to be long. The tabloid is only looking at your story ideas. A few sentences for each idea are sufficient for accomplishing this goal. Be sure to include your contact information and a self-addressed, stamped envelope. Occasionally, tabloids accept phone calls in place of the query. Tabloids frequently change their submission contact information. Finding a directory that accurately lists this information is difficult. Your best chance is to contact the tabloid directly.

5. **Write the article.** Follow the techniques of writing effective copy. Then, write an exciting, interesting, informative article. Be prepared for rewrites because they will happen.

6. **Pick a niche.** Once you have established yourself in the eyes of the tabloid editors, you will want to find an area of specialization. Being an expert gives you more opportunities, leads, and sources to contact.

If you have a flair for the sensational and intend to make a profitable living as a freelance writer, give supermarket tabloids a try. You might just be reading your own article as you wait in the checkout line at the grocery store.

Additional Resources

What we can learn from tabloids: www.asne.org/index.cfm?ID=2424.

Tabloid tips to better writing: www.writersdigest.com/articles/tabloidtips. asp.

CHAPTER 75

Technical Writing

Overview

The Society for Technical Communication (STC) defines technical writing as "the process of gathering information from experts and presenting it to an audience in a clear, easily understandable form."

In our book *The Elements of Technical Writing*, Gary Blake and I define technical writing this way: "Technical writing is defined by its subject matter. It is writing that deals with topics of a technical nature. By *technical* we mean anything having to do with the specialized areas of science and technology." Regardless of whose definition you use, technical writing conveys precise information to a particular audience for a specific purpose. Basically, it explains things clearly.

Sometimes technical writing talks about simple subjects, like how to operate a coffee maker, a DVD or CD player, or an alarm-clock radio. Other times, your technical writing tells users how to access voicemail systems, program cell phones, or how to operate blood-testing instruments. At its most complex, technical writing explains a telecommunications switch, or how to configure a wide area network for geographically distant business offices.

What It Pays

Specific knowledge in technical niches like science and biomedicine typically pay the highest hourly rate for freelance technical writing. Hourly rates are $50–$100 or more per hour, with $75 per hour as the average for writers having five years of experience.

Proposal writers for grants, government contracts, requests for proposals, and private proposals make the second highest hourly rates, about $60–$90 per hour.

Software technical writers who produce materials such as user guides, online help, systems documentation, IT network manuals, and process documentation make the third highest hourly rates, about $50–$80 per hour.

Hardware technical writers who produce documentation like installation, maintenance, and operations manuals earn the fourth highest hourly rates, about $50–$75 per hour.

Nuts and Bolts

Technical writing spans many diverse areas. And those areas are growing and expanding every year with increasingly widespread use of the Internet. Many organizations and individuals find it faster, easier, and more cost-effective to access help texts, manuals, troubleshooting guides, and other materials online. Print materials are expensive to produce because of rising paper costs, and hard copies are also expensive to mail or to purchase. They also take up valuable storage space when compared to online technical documentation. Thus, migrating from hard copy technical documentation to online documentation makes sense from the perspective of convenience, ease in updating, cost-effectiveness, and availability.

Whether you decide to write online technical materials, print materials, or both, write in areas that interest you. You'll enjoy writing about subjects that interest you. Here are a few broad technical fields to get you thinking about which areas you'll target for your freelance writing assignments.

- aerospace
- computer hardware and software
- chemistry
- robotics
- automotive
- electronics
- telecommunications hardware and software
- biotechnology
- all types of engineering
- financial institutions
- retail pricing and register systems
- medical technologies and instrumentation
- geology
- construction
- consumer goods

What You'll Write

The types of technical documents you write vary as much as potential clients and industries. Let's look briefly at a few of the typical projects.

- **Application programming interface (API) guides.** Explain how one software package works with another (i.e., Microsoft Word and QuickBooks). Says Josh Walker, an analyst at Forrester Research in Cambridge, Massachusetts, "Building a [software] application with no APIs is basically like building a house with no doors. The API...is how you open the windows and doors of computing so that different software can exchange information and work together."

- **Hardware repair and maintenance procedures.** Detail how to maintain proper operation or fix a problem with hardware (i.e., changing toner, replacing vehicle operation parts, or replacing parts in a copier). Most industries require this type of documentation, whether in hard copy or online formats (i.e., Ford Motor Company, Xerox, Dell, IBM, and Exxon Mobil).

- **Release notes.** Announce the specific improvements or enhancements in computer software, (i.e., Adobe Acrobat Reader 8.1 from version 8.0). This technical communication lets the general population know an update is ready for downloading, and specifies the improvements in the software. The software programmers are the prime source for content, and they are usually the ones preparing the releases. If you contract inside an organization for a period of time, you are likely to write release notes. However, this project type is *not* likely for freelancers working outside the client organization, because of the close contact required between writer and programmer.

What It Takes

According to the STC, there is a growing trend for technical writers who are (a) experienced in subject matter or (b) proficient in using the authoring tools in which the technical documentation is created.

Authoring tools are defined as specific writing systems and software packages, like Adobe InDesign, Visio, or RoboHelp, which the client expects you to use when writing the technical documentation. The authoring tools provide consistency in the way technical documentation looks and works online. Authoring tools also offer a wide range of sophisticated functionalities that make documentation user-friendly.

If you like learning and using authoring tools, build your expertise in a variety of systems to set yourself apart from other technical writers. Then target your freelance search toward clients who place high value on the ability to use authoring tools.

Or, if you apply for freelance jobs that require design, composition, and Internet functionality in addition to writing the copy, you need the equipment, requested authoring tool expertise, and graphic design skills to complete the project yourself. Otherwise, you'll need your own team to call on for the additional project elements.

Do you understand the topic well enough to explain it to others? If you can, you're probably qualified to write the project. On the other hand, say the content contains extremely specialized or complicated technologies like those in some areas of telecommunications, defense, science, and medical arenas. These highly technical projects may or may not require you to have specific expertise in the topic. If your client provides a subject matter expert (SME) to work with you, maybe you only need to comprehend the information so that you can write about it. Other times, there may be no SME and scarce development notes. In this case, the client might prefer a writer having expertise and/or experience in the subject matter.

Getting Started

When technical companies—or nontechnical companies needing technical services—have projects, they often go to technical contracting agencies to source the work. These agencies hire freelancers for the client projects. The agency keeps a database of freelancers on file. When a client company requests someone for a technical project, the agency matches the needed skill set against its database of freelancers, and calls the freelancers to award the project. The agency will pay the freelancer a lower amount of money for the project than they bill the client company, in order to make a profit.

Talk to and list with as many as of these agencies as you can find (several are listed in the resources section). It's impossible to list with too many agencies; you never know how often they'll call for an assignment that fits your profile. If you receive simultaneous project offers, then choose your favorite. It's better to have a choice than not enough work. Worry about how to handle unavailability issues once you're established enough that it's a problem.

A word about schmoozing with these agencies: you can just submit your application online and wait for a call. However, a better way is to submit your application and call to talk live. Let the agency representative know that you've submitted an application. Begin building a personal relationship. Ask questions to learn what's hot in the marketplace for obtaining assignments. Target your studies and skill building in those areas. Maintaining contact and a personal relationship with a live person at these agencies will likely increase the number of calls and assignments that you receive—provided you perform well for the agency clients.

Additional Resources

Collabis: www.collabis.com.

Computer Xperts: www.computerxperts.com.

Dayton T. Brown, Inc.: www.dtb-infopros.com.

Info Pros: www.infopros.com.

ProSpring Staffing: www.prospringstaffing.com.

Society for Technical Communication: www.stc.org.

Tech Writers: www.techwriters.com.

Writing assistance: www.writingassist.com.

CHAPTER 76

Telemarketing Scripts

Overview

When a company needs to generate more business, they may hire a tele-marketing company to dial up new prospects via cold calls, which can work wonders, even though many consumers hate telemarketing calls.

In 2002, telemarketing generated sales of more than $100 billion. Experienced telemarketers can conduct direct sales, surveys, or prequalify potential consumers for an upcoming product rollout. The writer, whether hired by the telemarketing service or the client, provides the script that produces the results needed, as well as training materials for the telemarketers who make the calls, so that the product or service is clearly understood by the caller as well as the prospect.

While a telemarketing script is often a direct marketing sales tool, scripted surveys are also commonly used to gather information about what current customers have experienced with a product or service they bought from the company. Telemarketing scripts can also assist in keeping contact with current customers and upselling new ancillary products.

What It Pays

A five- to ten-minute script runs $1,000–$3,000. That includes consultations with the client as well as the telemarketing group on script delivery and objection handling (the script usually includes a list of likely objections and a prewritten answer to each).

If the results are not satisfactory after the first 10 percent of calls are made, the client may ask for a rewrite. Be clear in your agreement whether your project fee includes such a rewrite and if so, how many. Also check to see the number of contacts associated with the campaign, as that can also determine the possible return on sales and value of the campaign.

Nuts and Bolts

If you are an expert in your client's product or service field, you know what questions to ask to get the results the client wants. Otherwise, ask the client to provide several previous campaign scripts on the subject matter. If none are available, get copies of all current marketing promotions and product information before you even go into your first detailed consultation with the client. Study them and write down any questions you have about the product. Ask for contacts within the client's company and interview them for more detailed information on the product or service.

Ask to visit the client's customer service and sales departments, and ask to sit and listen in on the calls. These calls can help you learn what prospects and customers care about and respond to.

What You'll Write

A typical sales script always starts with the greeting to the customer, a reference to how the caller got the customer's contact information (usually from an opt-in list), and why the telemarketer is calling. This leads into the pitch about how the product or service can enhance the prospect's life or workplace based on previous qualifying questions. The telemarketer then closes the sale.

You may also write a summary or detailed background information piece for the telemarketers so that they understand what they will be talking about with the customer and how to proceed based on the varied answers a prospect might give. Depending on the client and type of marketing call, you may also write the information-gathering forms used to collect answers that can be used for product analysis.

What It Takes

It helps if you have a customer service, sales, or market research survey development background, as building an interactive script is crucial to the success of the project. If you do surveys, then learn all you can about statistics, charts, graphs, and tables. If you can provide the client with presentation analysis reports at the end of the campaign, then you have added value to the client and may be able to increase your fee.

Getting Started

Confused about how to develop a script? A telemarketing script has four major parts: (a) the introduction, (b) the sales pitch, (c) the close, and (d) the objections. In the introduction, the challenge is simply to get the prospect not to hang up—and to listen long enough for you to explain who you are and why you are calling. At that point, you briefly describe your offer and its benefits. In the close, you ask for action, whether it's to buy a product or agree to a risk-free thirty-day home trial. As the writer, you must ask the client what the most common objections are—the reasons why prospects don't buy the product—and craft stock answers to each for the telephone sales rep to use as needed.

Also check out the books listed below. Contact a telemarketing company that is willing to provide you with a successful script and study the structure. One typical structure outline you can use:

1. Present the product or service as the latest and greatest on the market.

2. Show what this product or service promises to do for the client.

3. Tell about other customers' successes with the product or service.

4. Close with a strong and clear offer.

Additional Resources

Stephan Schiffman's Telesales by Stephan Schiffman (Adams Media, 2003).

How to Sell More, in Less Time, with No Rejection by Art Sobczack (Business by Phone, 1995).

This company uses programming to write scripts: 5star-telemarketing.com/telemarketing-scripts.html.

More telemarketing script information: www.allbusiness.com/marketing/direct-marketing-telemarketing/3474083-1.html.

American Teleservices Association is devoted exclusively to four-thousand call center companies, trainers, and suppliers, and provides training programs for members and the public on the latest technological developments and regulatory guidelines: www.ataconnect.org.

See an example of a mortgage telemarketing script: www.leadbull.com/mortgage_telemarketing_scripts.php.

Information on the value of good telemarketing scripts: www.telemarketing tips.info/telemarketing-script.html.

Download a sample chapter from this site to see some of the questions asked: www.telemarketing-scripts.com.

CHAPTER 77

Training and Development

Overview

Do you have a big name in your industry? If you have years of experience in an area that business people want to know about, then turn that knowledge into extra profit by developing training programs and seminars. You can consult with a business to find out what they need, and develop a program that directly assists with their issues, or you can market your programs to businesses and tailor them to provide specific information. For instance, if you are a market research analyst and report writer, you can develop a three-part training program or workshop on how to create effective surveys, gather information and do the analysis, and create the report. A detailed seminar of this nature would run about four to six hours.

What It Pays

For the above defined intensive seminar or workshop, $3,000 per day, plus all expenses paid, would not be unreasonable. Discuss with the client exactly what you provide in the way of training materials and what equipment you require.

Nuts and Bolts

When preparing your training manuals, decide exactly how you are going to show your audience each step, then develop each section accordingly. Don't forget that while you may know this subject inside and out, some of your audience will be seeing this information for the first time. Each step must be a logical progression into the next step, and you should explain why it is done.

What You'll Write

You write all the training and presentation pieces, which includes the course outline, teacher's guide and notes, any PowerPoint and video scripts, and student workbooks and handouts. You also write follow-up materials, such as surveys and requests for testimonials. Any profiles or biographies you include about yourself in the materials should list your education, titles of books you have written, and any awards you have received. This gives you a greater level of respect as an expert in your field.

What It Takes

You should have a degree or work experience in the subject you are teaching. Other requirements include good writing and presentation skills, good interactive people skills, including the ability to deal effectively with indifferent or difficult students, and attention to detail.

It also helps to have software skills when you create your training materials, especially if you teach how to use software to create analysis reports or other technical documents. It is useful to know presentation software such as PowerPoint, but you can also hire someone with those skills. Outsourcing can save you money, freeing up valuable time to work on other parts of your seminar.

Getting Started

Start on your home turf. If you are already connected with a business, look at some training issues you could solve if you developed a program that your fellow employees could take. Talk to the director of your department or the department you want to target, and show how you can benefit the company and employees by providing this service.

Once you've done several seminars or workshops, you will have more confidence about going out and contacting other businesses to see if they need your help. Be mindful that you do not give presentations at a competing company unless you are no longer involved with your current one.

Place ads in publications that service your target market and consider an online exchange of links with non-competing fellow trainers. Also use network sites such as Facebook and LinkedIn to connect with business contacts. Be clear you are there for business networking only.

Additional Resources

Getting Started in Speaking, Training, and Seminar Consulting by Robert Bly (Wiley, 2000).

Training in Organizations by Irwin Goldstein and Kevin Ford (Wadsworth Publishing, 2001).

The Ultimate Training Workshop Handbook by Bruce Klatt (McGraw-Hill, 1999).

American Society for Training and Development (ASTD): www.astd.org.

Bob Pike Group: www.bobpikegroup.com.

CHAPTER 78

Travel Writing

Overview

Travel writing is a fun genre for writers who love to travel. You write about everything around you: hotels, restaurants, the overall experience. When you walk out the hotel door, anything you see can be the subject of your next story. Architecture, museums and exhibitions, local news, a religious holiday parade, and so on can give readers a close view of where you visited.

What It Pays

The biggest perk as a travel writer is having all your expenses paid, whether by the assigning publication or by the hotels and restaurants you visit on an independent trip. If you are traveling solo, you may not get all expenses paid, but airlines and hotels may offer discounted fees that are later reimbursed by the publication, or become a write-off on your business expenses. Check with your tax adviser in advance.

As a travel writer, you could earn $50,000 or more a year. Many publications pay extra for photos. For instance, Canadian publication *Aruba Nights* pays $50 per photo. For a written piece on night life of 250–750 words, *Aruba Nights* will pay $100–$250.

Consider writing pieces for non-travel publications, such as international real estate publications, architectural markets, nature and conservation publications, and landscaping magazines, which could bring in another few thousand dollars or more a year.

Nuts and Bolts

Descriptive writing is key to this genre, as the goal of any travel piece is showing the reader what you saw and experienced. Like any good feature story, the first paragraph should draw the reader right in with a visual picture, and create a desire to read the rest of the story and know how it felt to be there.

As Loriann Hoff Oberlin says in *Writing for Money*, take the reader with you by using action verbs to describe what it's like to ride the roller coaster or skim the waves in a catamaran. At the same time, avoid clichés.

Also give practical information. Let the reader know how they can go to the local fair, where it is, how much the tickets cost, or what it costs to rent a catamaran and for how long.

What You'll Write
You write the article, as well as any sidebars that might list restaurants or websites associated with the trip, and photo captions. Take notes about everything you see and hear in case you need to refer back for extended information. Make sure you have contact numbers for people to call in case you need to conduct follow-up interviews.

What It Takes
On the technical side, take a laptop with wireless capabilities, lots of memory, and a big hard drive. Also consider a good digital camera

If you don't know the language of the country you're visiting, consider lessons before you leave and also take dictionaries so that you can communicate with the locals as best as possible.

Getting Started
Use *Writer's Market* to start a list of travel magazines and websites. Start by sending query letters indicating what kind of story you would like to write for publication.

Additional Resources
The Travel Writer's Handbook by Louise Zobel and Jacqueline Butler (Surrey Books, 2006).

International Food, Wine & Travel Writers Association: www.ifwtwa.org.

North American Travel Journalists Association: www.natja.org.

Society of American Travel Writers: www.satw.org.

www.transitionsabroad.com.

www.travelwriters.com.

Travel writing and resource site: www.writtenroad.com.

CHAPTER 79

T-shirts

Overview
T-shirt design and writing has evolved into an art form and business all its own. The Internet abounds with sophisticated sites where you can design your own logos and pictures and write memorable phrases. Not only that, you can set up shop at these stores, and they will produce what you design, sell it for you, and you receive commission from the sales. You don't do anything else except design and write to your heart's content.

What It Pays
Writing T-shirt slogans and phrases could net you $10 a word when selling to regular catalog outlets. Unless you can get a residual agreement with the company, the payment is a one-time shot. Compare that with reselling your ideas over and over again on the Web, either through your own business or an existing store, and you might decide that designing through an online outlet might be the better way to go over time.

Nuts and Bolts
Word and image association skills are useful. Try taking an image that you like and come up with as many one-word associations as you can to sell the image, idea, product, or service. From there, you can also work on two or three-word phrases based on the one-word list you created.

If you want to write in certain markets, like the Christian and religious niche, read inspirational works and poetry to brainstorm for new materials.

What You'll Write
Writing slogans means writing short concise lines of text. At a glance, you might see four to five words if you consider how you look at a T-shirt someone is wearing. If you use designs, then the writing should also reflect or complement the design idea. You must always consider what market you are targeting, and make sure your work specifically hits on that theme.

If you write for a catalog T-shirt or online shop, you may also be writing the descriptive catalog copy that goes with the T-shirt entry. If you have a chance to get your foot in the door to write T-shirt copy, see if you can write the rest of the catalog for them as well.

What It Takes

Use a computer to create your designs and writing. While you can create your art on paper, scan it into design software when you are done. Having your work in file form also protects you until you sell your rights to a client.

If you create your work on the computer, have plenty of memory and storage capabilities as graphics files can get quite large. Standard programs include Adobe Photoshop, an advanced image software program, and easy-to-use programs like Paint Shop Pro, which offer less functionality.

When you send examples of your work to potential clients, use Adobe Acrobat to convert your document into a PDF file, usable on all computer platforms. Converting your documents to PDF also protects your work from being changed.

Getting Started

If you are full of original ideas, consider marketing your designs to friends on MySpace and other networking communities. Every time you have a newly designed T-shirt, let all your friends know.

Other ways to sell your writing for T-shirts is to check out different catalog companies who create their own T-shirt lines and contact them for what they pay.

You can also take a company's focal point of business (computer companies, airlines, etc.) and create writings and designs, then approach them about becoming their personal T-shirt designer. Consider this a walking advertisement job for these niches and sell that concept when presenting your work.

Additional Resources

Another place to create and sell your ideas: www.cafepress.com.
Design By Humans: www.designbyhumans.com.
Another site for T-shirts: www.shirtcity.com.
A place to create your own T-shirt design and slogan: www.zazzle.com.

CHAPTER 80

TV Commercials

Overview

TV ad scripting is considered a top-line advertising assignment. There are many approaches to writing a TV commercial, and the approach depends on what the client wishes to tell the audience and how to convey that in a memorable but limited amount of time.

Aside from a typical TV commercial, there are also two-minute direct response ads and thirty-minute infomercials, both of which have an immediate call to action with a bonus if you make the purchase within a certain time frame. You either pick up the phone and order with a credit card, or go online.

What It Pays

For a thirty-second spot, a writer could get $950–$1,500, or $2,500–$4,000 for a two-minute direct-response ad, or $8,000–$15,000 for a thirty-minute infomercial.

Nuts and Bolts

Think pictures and storytelling through pictures, and write a script to meet that message. A writer works with the image artist or film production group to convey that message.

What You'll Write

There are twelve types of TV commercials.

1. Demonstrations show how a product is used and can also show a competing product that fails in a side-by-side frame.

2. Testimonials are effective when using well-known personalities who state how this product has changed their lives.

3. Stand-up presenters are actors who deliver a straight-forward message to the camera on the product's benefits.

4. Slice-of-life are sometimes considered a cliché type of ad, showing a situation where a problem is solved by using the product.

5. Lifestyle advertising is a product associated with a certain lifestyle, like beer for the blue-collar segment or a fancy Porsche for the wealthy.

6. Animation sells almost any product without having to use live actors.

7. Jingles use a memorable tune associated with the product, such as McDonald's "You deserve a break today."

8. "Visual as hero" is a short movie-style ad depicting the product in some kind of scenario.

9. Humor becomes a trademark theme to a product, like Wendy's "Where's the beef?" commercials.

10. Continuing characters are ads in a series with the same characters, but different developing scenes.

11. "Reason why" shows the product and a voice-over lists the benefits.

12. Emotion is a memorable moment that has us feeling happy, sad, or patriotic, and we remember the product associated with that emotion.

What It Takes

Study TV commercials. Consider whether you can take an existing commercial and write it better. Enroll in advertising classes and even film courses at a junior college. While there, start building a basic portfolio to show prospective buyers. You can also go to YouTube, search for ads, and watch for continuity and directness.

Getting Started

Build a portfolio of sample scripts you've written, and if you are able to produce a few ads while taking classes for advertising, put them in a portfolio you can show a potential client. Check your local area for advertising agencies to see if they work with freelancers. You can also approach local companies with your ideas. Another good way to build your portfolio is to team up with a video designer in your area and then approach a nonprofit group that needs help raising funds. You may have to create the ad for free, but it will be great material for your portfolio.

Additional Resources

The 100 Best TV Commercials and Why They Worked by Bernice Kaner (Times Books, 2000).

How to Product Effective TV Commercials by Hooper White (McGraw-Hill, 1994).

View sample ads and scripts: www.specbank.com.

CHAPTER 81

Video Games

Overview

If you already write fantasy, science fiction, or scripts, then the gaming industry may just be your ticket. Video games are one of the most popular forms of entertainment. While this may have once been considered a kid's arena, more and more adults are now playing advanced games, even those in their fifties and sixties.

Video games are a great escape from the world. Gaming gives one the feeling of actually being there, being involved in the war or flying the plane or shooting the bad guy. Can't be a hero in real life? Then video games give you the opportunity to experience that.

For older folks, video games can provide a daily dose of mental alertness and concentration that is not found at work anymore. The ability to keep up with characters' actions and making split-second decisions forces a player to stay alert.

Video games can also provide a creative path to a future in a graphics development career. This also includes plenty of opportunities for writers to assist with story development as well as character development. Writers work in conjunction with the graphics department in developing a story line, or several versions of a story line, based on what a player does during a game.

Networking in this industry is important if you want to break into writing scripts and character development. Find out about trade shows and game conventions so that you can attend and show samples of your work.

What It Pays

A staff writer at a well-known video game company can make $35,000–$75,000 a year, based on experience. Articles of 2,000–4,000 words for a video gaming magazine might pay $350–$1,000, depending on the publication. Of course, a bestselling video game could make you rich if you get a cut of royalties from the publisher or market it on your own. Another opportunity is to write video game code books. These are illustrated user manuals that give strategy tips and advice on how to beat a particular game.

Nuts and Bolts

You need a background in video game playing to understand how the setup and plot development happens.

The first step into this genre of writing is to play many games on different platforms (Sony PlayStation, Xbox 360, Nintendo Wii). Even the same game played on different platforms will change somewhat in its development based on the ability to translate actions from one platform to a different company's platform.

What You'll Write

You write the plot development in conjunction with the design group that is building the game. You also build and develop the characters in the game, which can be pretty extensive if writing for a role-playing game (RPG). RPG characters develop not only through the game but also through stages of abilities acquired after battles and other action events.

Guidebook writing happens while you are building the game, and is then finalized when the game is done and testing begins. Playing the game is important in making sure the guide is accurate.

You can also write any game descriptions that appear on packaging, so people know what kind of game experience to expect.

What It Takes

Having a background in scriptwriting for the screen and television is helpful as more top-notch video companies like Microsoft and Ubisoft hire full-time writers to work with their design groups. Experience in character and script development is crucial to getting a good full-time job with one of these companies. Much of what you need to know about script game development is learned on the job, but it helps to have the scripting background and to have experience playing different games.

Getting Started

Playing video games is a given as far as getting started. Study plot and character development while playing to see how it works. Study the guide and explore as much of the game as possible. Take scriptwriting classes at a local college or university. Check out any game development programs in your area.

Make a list of video game companies and their contact information, and apply to each as a freelance scriptwriter to get experience under your belt.

To find out names of game developers, go online to any video game magazine, like *Gamespot* (www.gamespot.com), and check out a review listing that gives game name, genre type, developer, publisher, and the platforms it comes on.

Additional Resources

Game Writing: Narrative Skills for Videogames by Chris Bateman (Charles River Media, 2006).

Game Writing Handbook by Rafael Chandler (Charles River Media, 2007).

The Ultimate Guide to Video Game Writing and Design by Flint Dille and John Platten (Lone Eagle, 2008).

Writing for Video Games: A Scriptwriter's Guide to Interactive Media by Steve Ince (A&C Black, 2007).

International Game Developers Association: www.igda.org.

Entertainment Software Association serves the business and public affairs requirements of video game publishers with the latest news and government interaction on policies and standards: www.theesa.com.

CHAPTER 82

Video Scripts

Overview

Video scripting is used in taped visual presentations running five to eight minutes and usually promotes a product, service, or an organization. The script is written to prompt the viewer to either buy a product or to perhaps donate money to a worthy cause, a call to action.

An organization that helps children adjust to cancer therapy and treatment might show a video where a child sits alone in a corner of his hospital room and looks downcast. A children's helper from the organization comes in and sits down with the child while carrying a small dog. The dog looks up at the child and wags its tail and whines. The child responds with a smile and a gesture to hold the dog in his arms. The helper starts talking gently with the child and the spot voices over with information about the organization and what they do for children in cancer treatment programs at local hospitals. At the end, the ad calls for volunteers to help with these services by calling a phone number and getting on a service list or perhaps donating money to assist in funding for the program. The video short promotes the service as well as the organization that provides the service.

What It Pays

For a short video script of five to eight minutes, a writer can be paid $2,000–$4,000 or, according to the *2006 Writer's Market*, $500 per running minute. Business film scripts can pay $300–$500 per running minute with $75 per hour on development of the script.

Nuts and Bolts

Sales and story writing skills are helpful in knowing how to present a story, then giving an effective call to action. A marketing or journalism background is useful, as is experience gained from working with an ad agency.

You need to know who your audience is, what the final goal of the video is, where and when the video will be shown, and with whom you will be working while creating the script. Having a good sense of production and video techniques and editing capabilities also helps in deciding what can be scripted, illustrated, and developed in the medium.

You work with the video or production team to provide the essential vision of the piece while you write the script. You also write the story development and scene development, including descriptions of what is in the scene such as props, buildings, streets, cars, or anything else that relates directly to the video line.

What You'll Write

You write the action sequence in the left column (or in italics above the spoken script) and the scripting goes in the right column on the page format. This is a progression of action shown as it corresponds with the voice heard on the video, whether it is the actor speaking or a narrator.

You may also write any accompanying documentation for the piece and for funding of the work presentations.

What It Takes

Writers should have good scriptwriting and development skills to put the video content into story format. The writer consults with the film team and presenting company as to their goal for the video's theme. As time is limited in these videos, saying a lot in a short amount of time with the fewest words to convey all the right ideas is crucial.

Getting Started

Start in an area of expertise you are comfortable in. If you have history or background in the medical field, then start out with hospitals, doctors, dentists, and medical instrument suppliers. Starting at the local level may be easier for you to break in and do any research needed for on-the-spot background work.

If you don't have a "reel" (a DVD of productions you have scripted), then find a group that needs help and offer to do the video writing for free if they provide all the other professionals.

Contact national associations and related publications, and advertise your services.

Additional Resources

Documentary Storytelling, Second Edition by Sheila Bernard (Focal Press, 2007).

Writing for Corporate Video by Grant Eustace (Focal Press, 1990).

An Introduction to Writing for Electronic Media by Robert Musburger (Focal Press, 2007).

Writing, Directing and Producing Documentary Films and Videos by Alan Rosenthal (Southern Illinois University Press, 2007).

Spirit Media is a company specializing in videos. Check the portfolio section to see different examples of scripted videos: www.spiritmedia.com.

CHAPTER 83

Websites

Overview

If you are in any kind of business or service, you need a website. When it comes to content, however, what you put on your website related to your product or service could make or break your business.

As website development and promotion progress, with improved search engines and keyword researching, online copywriting becomes more important for grabbing the viewers' attention at first glance. Not only how you write it, but the way it's laid out on the page, with highlights, bullets, or other defined catch points, determines conversion of onlookers and scanners into site members and paying customers.

What It Pays

Depending on the customer and product, you can make $500–$1,000 per web page. If you write a microsite that promotes one product or service, such as e-books, specialized software, and other information products, you use long copy with testimonials and other selling points. Your fee for a microsite starts at $1,000 for beginners and $7,500 at the higher end for those with experience and a proven track record.

Landing pages are sites within a website where multiple products can be sold and, depending on the design complexity, your pay can be $1,000–$7,500. It also depends on the client's budget as to how much you can logically charge to build those pages.

Other ways of pricing your work, according to the *2006 Writer's Market* is $150 per hour, $1.50 per word, or up to $7,000 per project.

Nuts and Bolts

If you are already an experienced copywriter, then much of what you do can translate to the Web. However, one big difference is page setup for highlights and attention grabbers. You may create more overviews with links to other pages or documents if potential customers want more in-depth materials.

Most online readers will not sit and read a copy-intensive piece except in the case of a microsite as mentioned above. But linking from summarized information to downloadable documents are great in terms of grabbing information to be read at a later time, when the reader is off work, for instance.

If you do not have much experience with online website writing, look at successful websites such as eBay and Amazon.com to see how they put their information together and how the websites are laid out in terms of links and information pages. Create a process or organization tree chart, based on effective sites you see.

How do you know it's a good site? If it's an area or specialty that you are in, and you think you want to buy nearly everything on the site, and the links make it easy to make a purchase, then it's a well-written (persuasive), well-arranged site.

What You'll Write

Online website copywriting can encompass a number of areas. Not only can you write the basic web pages, microsites, landing pages, and supporting documentation, but you can also write the email promotions for a call to purchase special products. Letting your client know you can also write brochures, annual reports, and press kits means you can grab that work and put it on the Web, too. In some cases, you need to work with the client's graphic designer or marketing department, just as you would for offline copy.

What It Takes

Journalistic techniques of writing concisely and effectively, using the fewest words possible, are important, as readers will not spend a lot of time at one site. Words must be attention-grabbing and summarize information quickly. Links to related information must be easy to see, and pages must load quickly.

Getting Started

If you do not have copywriting experience under your belt, take a good copywriting course to build elementary skills. Get preliminary samples from your coursework, and offer local clients your services on speculation.

Offer to write a small website for a local client for a small fee first, and if they balk, then offer to do it free. This is an excellent way to begin building a portfolio. Put samples of web pages you have written on your own website (as PDFs). Do not rely on live hyperlinks to client websites as your portfolio, as companies constantly change their sites.

Additional Resources

The Online Copywriter's Handbook by Robert W. Bly (McGraw-Hill, 2003).

Persuasive Online Copywriting by Brian Eisenberg, Jeffrey Eisenberg, and Lisa Davis (Wizard Academy Press, 2002).

Net Words: Creating High-Impact Online Copy by Nick Usborne (McGraw-Hill, 2001).

Web Copy That Sells by Maria Veloso (AMACOM, 2004).

American Writers and Artists Institute offers an Accelerated Program for Six-Figure Copywriting and a Master's Program for Six-Figure Copywriting: www.awaionline.com.

Sign up for the free newsletter and check the article archive at Gary Bencivenga's site: www.bencivengabullets.com.

Monthly Copywriting Genius: www.monthlycopywritinggenius.com/write.

CHAPTER 84

Webinars

Overview

The development of webinars has meant huge savings in money and time for entrepreneurs and companies who've previously spent millions of dollars and out-of-office time flying to meet clients, prospects, or bringing a nationwide sales force to one location for extended training. Now everyone can stay home or at the office, and attend training or a sales presentation anytime, anywhere, with just a computer and high-speed Internet connection.

Webinars are conducted online and allow you to share information online with work colleagues, sales teams, and potential clients. The presenter runs the meeting and, like any classroom or convention site, can draw on a "board" and show slides, whether via PowerPoint or some other program.

Speech communication can be through the webinar online technology or through an add-in phone service also run by the webinar company. Questions can be asked by attendees during the webinar via chat or email.

Tele-seminars are done strictly by telephone using a centralized phone call center that allows hundreds of contacts to dial in using a code number to spend an hour or two listening to speakers. For the most part, there is a moderator and a guest speaker who is interviewed about a new product or service and how people can purchase it.

Tele-seminars can also be training classes, particularly when documents have been sent to the attendees who can review everything while they're on the phone with the teacher.

What It Pays

Payment is based on the fees received from each person who signed up for the webinar or tele-seminar, minus vendor fees for web and phone usage and the operating package you chose from the vendor.

If you charge $59 per person to attend a seminar, and three-hundred people attend, then you gross $17,700. If your audio conference service charges $1,000 for one hour's usage for up to four-hundred contacts, then you make $16,700.

Ideally, for a webinar, you can also promote a product to the group. At the end of the call, you give a call to action for the prospect to purchase a product. Let's say the product sells for $500. If you sell to 10 percent of your attendees, that's thirty orders, resulting in gross product sales of $15,000.

If your product or service is an online information product or extended training class, which requires no purchase of materials or financial production overhead, then you've made a very nice salary for just one hour's worth of work (not counting what it cost to put together the product).

Nuts and Bolts

Teaching skills or previous moderator skills involving presentations in front of audiences are very helpful as your voice will project that confidence to your audience. As it is unlikely that you will be seen on a webinar unless you use a computer video, then the audience will be working off of your voice and how you say things.

If you are showing slides in a presentation, review everything to make sure your grammar is correct. Also post your slides as a PDF on your website and let attendees know where they can download it.

What You'll Write

You'll write an outline of how your webinar or tele-seminar will develop from one given point to the next. You'll then develop each section (usually) in a printed document that is handed out, mailed, or emailed to attendees so that they can follow along and take notes.

Any presentation slide show also requires page headlines and bullet points, along with any graphics and pictures. Another area to write is a preview survey of attendees, which can be distributed to the attendees or accessed on the Web, returned, and analyzed before the event takes place. This allows you to see areas to be addressed for the audience during the session.

You may also want to do a follow-up survey with an incentive thrown in, such as a free CD recording of the audio portion of the session. This allows you to stay in touch with what's important to the audience and can give you opportunities to write other documents for a client.

What It Takes

Personality and voice skills are important in presenting your information. If you have speech issues, go to a voice coach and work with the instructor until your speech delivery sounds professional. Your written materials should be informative and easy to read—no long or run-on sentences. Background in the subject area of the webinar is important if you are the main presenter or the interviewee. If you know others who have given webinars in your subject area, or at least have more experience than you, then spend time with them and find out what to expect.

Getting Started

If you have a product or service that you would like to promote through a webinar or tele-seminar, then start on the Web and check out several different companies for package pricing and their own background experience. Go to my site, www.bly.com, click on vendors, and look under Audio Conference Services and Webinars for some recommended vendors.

Find out what options they have in expanding from a basic package to more advanced features, such as recording the sessions, which you can then use over and over again to generate more cash as future online presentations. You just don't have to be there the next time!

Additional Resources

WebEx Web Meetings for Dummies by Nancy Stevenson (Wiley, 2005).

The Web Conferencing Book by Sue Spielman and Liz Winfeld (AMACOM, 2003).

Webinar Conferencing Services: www.B2B-Exchange.com/Web_Conference.

GoTo Webinar is another advanced provider: www.gotowebinar.com.

WebEx is a multifaceted provider for webinars: www.webex.com.

CHAPTER 85

White Papers

Overview

Go to any large business or corporation website and 95 percent of the time you will find a white paper written on some aspect of a product or service. The white paper is a marketing tool but more on the decision-making side rather than a straight-forward sales pitch—a soft sell instead of a hard sell.

A good white paper has a common structure, starting with an introduction to a problem. The white paper then shows how the company developed a solution to the problem. The product or service is described in a generic manner rather than advertising any names. The story line is more important, along with detailed information about the solutions, whether it be technical or a new process or methodology.

The white paper closes by showing how the solution (product or service by name) specifically answers the problem. The close is a call to action to sign up for the service or product.

What It Pays

Depending on what the white paper addresses, a moderately experienced writer could be paid about $4,000–$7,000 for a ten-page paper. The *2006 Writer's Market* states that $125 per hour would be appropriate. The pay scale is based ultimately on the company's budget and market recognition.

Nuts and Bolts

Use good research, outlining, and interviewing skills in writing these papers. Most papers are more technical and detailed than a standard advertising piece, which tends to be more minimalist in nature. Of course it helps if you have some background to match the company's focus, but general business sense works for the most part.

You need to meet with the company's top-level decision makers and get the following information: define the topic or issue of the paper and who the readers will be, decide on the paper's objective and outline it to that end, and know the deadline for completion of the paper. Then you set up your plan of action via research time, key personnel interviews, and writing time.

In an article in *DM News,* Marc Blumer lists the characters of a good white paper.

- Answers a compelling question for the target prospect
- Provides information or a viewpoint unavailable elsewhere
- Positions the author as a thought leader in his field
- Reinforces the company value proposition
- Generates inquiries from highly qualified prospects

What You'll Write

Your main job is to write the white paper. Word length varies, but 3,000–4,000 words is typical. The client may have you work on other associated pieces, such as a landing page where prospects can download the white paper, and a postcard driving prospects to that URL.

Have the client send you all the background information they have on the topic of the white paper. Research the Internet as well. Go to www. bitpipe.com and print out white papers on your topic published by other companies.

Outline your paper and set up a time line for project completion. Your ten-page paper outline, as detailed in Michael Stelzner's e-book, *Writing White Papers,* will look like this:

- **Problem.** Showing all aspects of the problem, some of which your readers may not have encountered or thought of yet.

- **Solution.** What the company developed to solve the problem, usually discussed generically rather than by product name.

- **Benefits.** Highlights of issues solved as part of the problem overall.

- **The "What to Look For" pitch.** A reader's guide to know what to look for in a company that claims to solve this issue. As Stelzner says, it's an opportunity for the company to shine by showing it can provide that service and accountability to the reader.

- **Specific advantages.** While the white paper has shown up to this point what the benefits are for the solution provided, the reader now finds out about the product or service specifically and how it is advantageous to purchase or sign up with this company. They've already thought everything through, so the reader doesn't have to do anything but make the first move. The company takes care of the rest.

What It Takes

You need knowledge in the area you are writing about; if you don't have that, you should do extended research and interviewing to become acquainted with the industry in question. Knowing your audience tells you how to write the article, particularly in word usage and terminology.

Experience in writing business reports is helpful, especially if you've done market research and analysis. Using pictures, graphs, charts, and tables helps prove your points and breaks up text and page layouts, making it easier to keep the reader's attention. In most cases, the client provides you with documentation containing charts and graphs you can use. You can also find relevant charts and graphs online. Be sure you know how to read these, and if not, have someone from the analysis side show you what each chart represents. Be sure you've not missed a story edge that no one else documented.

Getting Started

Start work with companies in an area that you are knowledgeable about. Contact local companies and let them know you are available for this service. If you have a website, put a sample white paper there where your prospect can take a look at what you can do. Additionally, include a link to an online brochure or even send one in the mail to your contact along with a sales letter and business card. If you don't have samples, look online and study a few, then approach a small company to see if you can do one for a minimal fee.

Additional Resources

The White Paper Marketing Handbook by Robert Bly (Racom, 2006).

Writing White Papers by Michael Stelzner (WhitePaperSource Publishing, 2006).

White Paper Source: www.whitepapersource.com.

CHAPTER 86

Word Processing

Overview

Word processing consists mainly of data entry, transcription from tapes, and typing documents into electronic format, or even processing a company's rebate forms. Jobs of this nature provide a steady income as you build your clientele, and if you can work faster, you make more money.

There are many websites promoting these services that you can sign up with and start working. However, check into each company before joining them, especially if they are charging sign-up fees. Research some of your favorite writers' websites to see whom they recommend. Most groups simply charge a percentage of your fee or else assign you the job, charge a fee to the client (you won't know what that is), then pay you a prearranged amount, like a temp service.

Word processing is not considered a creative line of writing, as you are working with information already set in one format and you will be moving that information into another format. It is a solution for slow times.

What It Pays

Typing documents into electronic format pays about $3 a page. One quick way to work is to scan your documents using a popular scanning software program and scanner. Then review each page for errors in case the software didn't read the information correctly.

If you need to include diagrams, tables, or charts, and you are handy with Microsoft Word's design capabilities, then you can recreate those and lock them into the document. Charge extra for those. If a complicated diagram, charge $5–$10 per diagram.

Medical transcription can be charged by the hour or by the page depending on the tape length. Typing quickly is an asset in this type of business. If you have shorthand skills (almost a lost art now), that will benefit you greatly, as you can go through the tape first and do the documentation by shorthand and type it out afterwards.

Data entry can range from entering people's information into a mailing database or can consist of numbers that go into a spreadsheet. This type of work is fairly monotonous, but money is money when you have to pay living expenses.

Nuts and Bolts

Typing quickly is your greatest asset for this kind of work. If you are not much of a typist, consider practice sessions to get up to speed. If doing medical transcription, you may need to provide your own tape recorder.

Backing up all your work is vital, not only to protect yourself and your clients; you really don't want to retype everything all over again. Once is enough. Purchase discs or flash drives, and back up your work every ten minutes or so. You can also check online backup services or try out Google Documents where you can put all your working documents.

If you can write macros for Word and Excel, and portions of your work are done continuously over and over again, consider building a macro to make life easier for you. This will be important when billing by the project.

What You'll Write

The only writing you might do here is summarizing pieces of work, such as what the medical transcription was about. If you are advertising your services independently, then you would write all your direct mail packages and email sales letters that you send potential clients.

What It Takes

You need a computer with an Internet connection and back-up capabilities. If doing transcription, then you'll need a good recorder.

You do not need a degree for this type of work, but it helps if you have some business background, or in the case of medical transcription, some medical background. Keep a medical dictionary on hand or else know how to access one online. Fast typing with a high level of accuracy and tremendous concentration are important skills.

Getting Started

If you have remained in contact with former employers, give them a call to see if they need help with work. If you have a good reputation with these people, they may be very happy to hire you, leaving others in the office to move on to other projects. When you have worked with these people several times, ask for testimonials that you can use in your business brochures or on your website. Ask for referrals to other prospects your employers know.

Check out large local companies, especially those who deal with many documents and databases. They most likely have ongoing work and could keep you very busy.

Additional Resources

How to Start and Manage a Word Processing Service Business by Jerre Lewis and Leslie Renn (Lewis & Renn, 2004).

How to Start a Home-Based Writing Business by Lucy Parker (Globe Pequot, 1997).

Techno R&B, for learning about word processing and legal secretary work: www.technorbinfo.com.

The Association of Executive and Administrative Professionals: www.theaeap.com.

CHAPTER 87

Writing for the Government

Overview
Writing for the government is not as daunting as it might seem at first glance. There is the initial process of applying to work with a government agency, which may require that you submit a proposal and bid to win the job contract. As there are so many different agencies, it is best to contact those you are interested in working with and find out the precise application procedure to ensure success.

If you have never worked with a government agency before, you might prefer to join or register with a company that connects contractors and government agencies needing help. These groups can also give you some idea of what projects pay, but know that when working with these groups, they take a percentage if they help you hook up with a project.

The U.S. government is the world's biggest customer for contract workers, and there is always plenty of work. Getting your foot in the door will be the hardest part. Once you have acquired experience working with two or three agencies, your chances of winning contracts goes up.

What It Pays
As mentioned above, this field pays by the bid, but if you are working with a group that can help you, you can get a basic idea of what projects usually run. If you win a contract to write materials on a consistent basis, this can be very lucrative. Newsletters and weekly or monthly periodicals are always in demand, whether it be a matter of keeping the general public informed about new services or keeping employees informed of events in the agency.

Nuts and Bolts
Clear, concise writing skills are very important here, and depending on what type of writing project it is, your tone of voice is important to delivery. Acquire previous samples of work from the agency, and find out what they liked and didn't like about those samples.

In the case of government documents that help readers accomplish certain objectives, like filing for unemployment, be sure your document is clear, in a step-by-step format. Accuracy is very important.

Use the second-person "you," as this gives the reader the feeling the document was written directly for him to help solve his problem. Avoid using advanced technical wording when simple words can say the same thing more easily.

Use informative headers so that the reader can scan the information to find the sections he needs to read, rather than wading through a whole document to find it. Questions the reader might have make excellent headers. Keep your information visually appealing in its layout even while following a template design. Use short sentences, indented paragraphs, bullets, anything that helps reading flow. Think of questions and answers your readers may ask while reading the document and present those either throughout the document or at the end of the related section.

What You'll Write

You write the outline, main document, and any summaries that might be needed, like on a website landing page. You may also write the email the government entity might send out to people who have requested such information. There may be other accompanying documents, such as brochures. There is also the chance that if you are a website writer, you can write the information page this document is linked with.

Other documents you can write include annual reports, direct mail packages, agency profiles, white papers, case studies, pamphlets, market research reports—almost anything that you would do as a copywriter for a standard large business company.

What It Takes

Having experience in the area you are writing about is very helpful. Get samples of previous versions to see what was done before and find out what was successful and what approach was not successful. If you have limited knowledge in the area you are writing about, be sure to call people associated with the project and request interviews to get the information you need.

Getting Started

Making initial contacts with people who can steer you in the right direction is very important. Call local government agencies about resources to get started. If you know any writers who work with government agencies, call them to see what information they can give you.

Additional Resources

Writing for the Government by Libby Allison and Miriam Williams (Longman, 2008).

Government contracting assistance: aptac-usorg.zcreative.com/new/Govt_Contracting/index.php.

More government writing tips: www.fedmarket.com/articles/government-proposal-writing.shtml.

Government writing information: www.library.unt.edu/govinfo/browse-topics/research-and-writing-tips/government-writing.

ONVIA is site for connecting bidders with government projects: www.onvia.com.

Deborah Kluge has a wealth of information and links about working with the government: www.proposalwriter.com.

Take online courses in working with the government: sba.gov/services/training/onlinecourses/index.html.

Government grant writing information: www.us-government-grants.net.

CHAPTER 88

Young Adult

Overview

When writing for young adults—readers who are nine to nineteen years old—writers may feel a responsibility to write books that promote good behavior, show consequences of bad actions, or preach from the pulpit. Young people, however, want to know how to solve problems, how to get out of bad situations, and how to be popular in their circle of friends.

What It Pays

Most YA novelists receive an advance, then royalties after the advance is earned out. Advances for first YA novels from unknown authors are modest. Delacorte Press pays a $7,500 advance to new authors who win its First Young Adult Novel annual contest. Success depends on a certain amount of circumstance—the right story with the right publisher at the right time in the right market.

YA short stories are also in demand, but don't expect a big paycheck, and that's if you get one at all. Smaller publications reward you by putting your byline with your story, so you are a published author, but not a paid one. Research listings in the annual *Children's Writer's and Illustrator's Market* for the latest payment information.

Nuts and Bolts

Communicating well with young people, reading other YA books, and studying what is important in young adults' lives in the contemporary world help in writing effective stories. Use terminology or slang that is current in their culture. Avoid any writing that is condescending and preachy.

What You'll Write

You write the actual story and, if you find it is the best way for you to work, you create the plot outline, character development, and any notes for future reference. Especially in a complicated plot, keeping notes of what happened and when, who did it and where, is important for consistency within the framework of the plot. The same is also true of characters, their backgrounds, their development within the plot, and actions within the plot and with other characters. Consistency and continuity are essential to any story. You may also write story summaries for marketing purposes as well as any promotional copywriting pieces.

What It Takes

Take classes on writing for the YA market, and read books for young adults. Talk to young people and find out what issues are important to them. If you have young adults in your family, get together to talk about what's important to them. Find out what problems they have with adults, family members, teachers, and other people they are in contact with regularly. The whole point is to relate to them on their level.

Getting Started

Make a list of publications and publishers that focus on subjects you think you can write about, whether historical, romantic, or suspenseful. Set up a database with names and contacts of editors, and create a system to keep track of submissions.

Additional Resources

Writing & Selling the YA Novel by K. L. Going (Writer's Digest Books, 2008).

The Complete Idiot's Guide to Publishing Children's Books by Harold D. Underdown (Alpha, 2004).

Cynthia Leitich Smith's website has information on writing for children and young adults: www.cynthialeitichsmith.com.

Society of Children's Book Writers and Illustrators offers great information on awards and grants to apply for, a calendar of upcoming events nationwide, and listing of regional chapters: www.scbwi.org.

Index

GRAYSLAKE AREA PUBLIC LIBRARY
100 Library Lane
Grayslake, IL 60030

About the Author

Robert Bly has been a professional writer since 1979 and a full-time free-lance writer since 1982. He earns more than $600,000 a year from his writing and is a self-made multimillionaire.

Bob is the author of more than seventy books, including several popular volumes on writing. These include *Careers for Writers* (McGraw-Hill/VGM), *Secrets of a Freelance Writer* (Henry Holt), *The Copywriter's Handbook* (Henry Holt), *The Elements of Technical Writing* (Allyn & Bacon), and *The Elements of Business Writing* (Allyn & Bacon).

McGraw-Hill calls Bob Bly "America's top copywriter." His copywriting clients include AT&T, IBM, Kiplinger, Boardroom, and Swiss Bank. He has published more than one-hundred articles in *Amtrak Express*, *Cosmopolitan*, *Writer's Digest*, and many other publications.

Bob writes monthly columns for *DM News*, the weekly newspaper of the direct marketing industry, and *Early to Rise*, a daily e-newsletter on business success. He publishes a monthly e-zine on writing, copywriting, and marketing with more than fifty-thousand subscribers.

Bob has given lectures on writing, publishing, and freelancing to numerous groups, including American Writers & Artists Inc., National Speakers Association, Learning Annex, Newsletter Publishers Association, and American Society of Journalists and Authors.

Questions and comments may be sent to:

Bob Bly
22 E. Quackenbush Avenue
Dumont, NJ 07628
Phone: 201-385-1220
Fax: 201-385-1138
Email: rwbly@bly.com
Web: www.bly.com